MACROECONOMETRIC SYSTEMS

Also by Challen and Hagger

Modelling the Australian Economy

Unemployment and Inflation: An Introduction to Macroeconomics

Unemployment and Inflation: Questions and Answers

MACROECONOMETRIC SYSTEMS
CONSTRUCTION, VALIDATION AND APPLICATIONS

D. W. CHALLEN and A. J. HAGGER

First published 1983 by
THE MACMILLAN PRESS LTD
London and Basingstoke
Companies and representatives
throughout the world

ISBN 0 333 31084 5 (hard cover)
ISBN 0 333 34850 8 (paper cover)

Typeset in Great Britain by
PHOTO-GRAPHICS
Honiton · Devon

Printed in Hong Kong

To Anne and Rona

CONTENTS

Preface x

List of Abbreviations xiii

Part I Introduction

1 CONCEPTS AND DEFINITIONS 2
- 1.1 The concept of a macroeconometric system 2
- 1.2 Features of KK macroeconometric systems 3
- 1.3 An early KK macroeconometric system 5
- 1.4 Modern KK macroeconometric systems 9
- 1.5 Other systems 10

2 SOLUTION OF LINEAR AND NON-LINEAR SYSTEMS 25
- 2.1 The solution concept 25
- 2.2 Solution of linear systems 25
- 2.3 Solution of non-linear systems 32

Part II Construction of KK Systems

3 SPECIFICATION OF KK SYSTEMS 46
- 3.1 The Keynesian macro-analytical system 46
- 3.2 Disaggregation of aggregate demand 48
- 3.3 Specification of individual equations 50
- 3.4 Endogenisation of G, M_s and W 55
- 3.5 Open-economy relationships 60
- 3.6 Expectational variables 61
- 3.7 General observations 65

4 ESTIMATION METHODS 70
- 4.1 The information content of a system 70
- 4.2 System estimators 80
- 4.3 Single-equation information estimators 81
- 4.4 Limited information relating to the whole-system estimators 85
- 4.5 Full information relating to the whole-system estimators 91

5 FINITE-SAMPLE PROPERTIES OF SYSTEM ESTIMATORS 104
5.1 Analytical results 104
5.2 The Monte Carlo method 108
5.3 Monte Carlo studies of system estimators 117

6 FROM THEORY TO PRACTICE: THE CHOICE OF ESTIMATOR 125
6.1 Handling non-linearity 125
6.2 The undersized sample problem 128
6.3 Other practical issues 132
6.4 The choice of estimator 135

Part III Validation

7 MULTIPLIER ANALYSIS IN KK SYSTEMS 142
7.1 Linear multiplier analysis 142
7.2 Non-linear multiplier analysis 151

8 EVALUATION PROCEDURES 161
8.1 Individual-equation procedures 161
8.2 Whole-system procedures — tracking performance 164
8.3 Whole-system procedures — dynamic properties 172

Part IV Applications

9 FORECASTING 178
9.1 Arithmetical KK forecasting 178
9.2 Forecasting the predetermined variables 179
9.3 Judgemental KK forecasting 184
9.4 How accurate is KK forecasting? 190

10 COUNTER-FACTUAL ANALYSIS 194
10.1 Counter-factual analysis in outline 194
10.2 A US example of conditional forecasting 195
10.3 A US example of causal analysis 199
10.4 An Australian example of analysis of alternative regimes 201
10.5 A criticism of causal analysis 203

11 POLICY EVALUATION 205
11.1 Types of policy evaluation 205
11.2 Evaluation of historical policies: search 205
11.3 Evaluation of historical policies: optimal control 207
11.4 Evaluation of policy rules 214

Part V Conclusion

12 THE FUTURE OF KK SYSTEMS 222
12.1 The evolution of KK systems 222
12.2 Some developments in the field of KK systems 222

Index 228

PREFACE

Our object in writing this book was not to produce yet another textbook on econometrics but rather to remedy a major deficiency which all existing books appear to share. We refer to their highly unsatisfactory treatment of 'systems'.

Our quarrel with the standard textbook treatment of systems is that it has the appearance of being (and, in fact, is) almost totally divorced from what actually goes on in 'the systems world'. This was more or less inevitable in the 1950s and early 1960s when working macroeconometric systems were comparatively rare and when, therefore, there was very little going on in the systems world. It is no longer inevitable (and is certainly undesirable) now that the USA alone has some eight major working systems, the UK and Canada have four and almost every country, large or small, developed or undeveloped, has at least one.

Two examples will help to amplify our statement that the standard textbook treatment of systems is almost totally divorced from what goes on in the systems world. The first relates to estimation.

The standard way of approaching the topic of systems estimation is to show that equation-by-equation estimation of OLS and/or its derivatives – Almon, non-linear least squares, ARMAX and the like – is unacceptable and then to proceed with a very detailed treatment, complete with proofs, of system estimators such as 2SLS, 3SLS and FIML. One or other of these is supposed to constitute the alternative. However, when authors face up to the question of what estimators are actually used in working systems, as at some point they must, they are forced to admit, usually rather lamely and without explanation, that for all practical purposes the estimators most commonly used in working systems are OLS and its derivatives! Why, then, the reader is bound to ask, was so much time spent on the others?

The second example concerns applications. Invariably the discussion which leads up to the chapters on applications of systems is couched in terms of *linear* systems. Thus it is natural that the discussion of applications, when it comes, should focus on the various multipliers that can be calculated from linear systems and on forecasting from linear systems. However, the author is unable to draw on actual econometric studies in which these techniques can be seen in action because effectively they are never used, the reason being that modern macroeconometric systems are invariably non-linear.

In the present book the main focus, right from the beginning, is on practice; it is a book about how modern macroeconometric systems are actually built, which estimation techniques are available in practice, as distinct from in principle, and which are chosen, how systems are assessed in practice and how they actually are, as distinct from how they might be, put to work.

This does not mean that the theoretical material which forms the essential ingredient of the systems chapters of most texts is ignored, only that it is put in what we believe to be its proper place. For example, Chapter 4 presents a comprehensive discussion of available estimators. The emphasis, however, is on how they work and on what we know about them because the ultimate purpose of the discussion is to show (in Chapter 6) that, in practice, most of them, have, for one reason or another, to be ruled out. No proofs are presented, though references to where the proofs can be found are given. Again, the various linear multipliers – impact, delay, intermediate-run and long-run – are discussed in detail, and in a rigorous way, in Chapter 7. As is made clear at the outset of the chapter, however, the reason for discussing these multipliers is not that they are now used but that they provide a natural entry-point to certain evaluation procedures – discussed in Chapter 8 – which *are* in widespread use.

In our opinion, the practical focus we have adopted has two great advantages. One is that it facilitates the introduction of certain important material which does not sit easily in the standard textbook framework and which is, therefore, either omitted altogether or given very brief treatment in the typical text. Examples are the material on the solution of non-linear systems (nowadays all working systems are non-linear) presented in Chapter 2 and the Monte Carlo and other finite-sample material presented in Chapter 5. The second advantage is that it facilitates the discussion of studies in which an estimated system is used to attack some policy or other economic problem of obvious practical significance and so helps to convince the readers that they are being asked to master difficult material because it is useful, and not, as they must feel when working through the typical text, because of its intellectual challenge *per se*.

The book assumes that readers have completed an introductory course in econometrics at the level of such texts as Johnston's *Econometric Methods,* Kmenta's *Elements of Econometrics* or Intriligator's *Econometric Models, Techniques and Applications*. Thus, for example, one should be familiar with the mechanics of OLS estimation, with the 'classical' assumptions under which OLS is the BLUE estimator of a linear stochastic relationship, with concepts such as consistency and efficiency and, in general, with the basic econometric tools and concepts. Some familiarity with elementary macroeconomics is also desirable, though by no means indispensable.

The main use of the book will be in follow-up courses in econometrics, at the third- and fourth-year undergraduate and postgraduate levels. In addition, the book should be suitable for use in advanced courses in macroeconomics and possibly in related courses in such areas as operations research and decision-making. With its emphasis on the practical side of systems it should also be found helpful by practising economists in the civil service and in business.

Many people have made significant contributions to the writing of the book and to these we extend our sincere thanks. We owe a particular debt to Professor D. E. A. Giles of Monash University who read through an earlier draft with great care and made numerous detailed suggestions for improvement. The book is much better than it would have been without his help. Another painstaking reader to whom we are greatly indebted is Dr G. M. Wells of the Victoria University, Wellington. He, too, made many helpful and penetrating comments. We must also express our thanks to two of our colleagues in the University of Tasmania, Mr J. R. Madden and Mr M. L. Kerslake, both of whom scrutinised the manuscript with great care. Finally we owe yet another great debt to Mrs Patricia Combes, who typed the manuscript in her customary impeccable fashion.

University of Tasmania
December 1982

D. W. Challen
A. J. Hagger

LIST OF ABBREVIATIONS

ACF	AutoCorrelation Function
ARMAX	AutoRegressive Moving Average eXogenous
BLUE	Best Linear Unbiased Estimator
CA	Constant-term Adjustment
CO	Cochrane–Orcutt
D-W	Durbin–Watson statistic
FIIV	Full information Iterated Instrumental Variables
FIML	Full Information Maximum Likelihood
FISE	Full Information relating to the whole-System Estimator
FP	Fixed Point
h	Durbin's *h* statistic
IIV	Iterative Instrumental variables
IV	Instrumental Variables
KK	Keynes–Klein
LIIV	Limited information Iterated Instrumental Variables
LIML	Limited Information Maximum Likelihood
LISE	Limited Information relating to the whole-System Estimator
MAE	Mean Absolute Error
MS	Muth–Sargent
MSE	Mean Square Error
NLLS	Non-Linear Least Squares
NL2SLS	Non-Linear Two-Stage Least Squares
NL3SLS	Non-Linear Three-Stage Least Squares
OLS	Ordinary Least Squares
PB	Phillips–Bergstrom
PDL	Polynomial Distributed Lag
RMSE	Root Mean Squared Error
RMSPE	Root Mean Squared Percentage Error
RRF2SLS	Restricted Reduced-Form Two-Stage Least Squares
SIE	Single-equation Information Estimators
2SLS	Two-Stage Least Squares
2SPC	Two-Stage Principal Components
3SLS	Three-Stage Least Squares
WJ	Walras–Johansen
WL	Walras–Leontief

Part I Introduction

1 CONCEPTS AND DEFINITIONS

1.1 The concept of a macroeconometric system

As will become clear shortly, this book is concerned with a particular class of macroeconometric system. The concept of a 'macroeconometric system' is thus fundamental to the entire discussion and must be dealt with at the outset.

The best way to present this concept is to begin with the more general concept of 'an economic system'. An *economic system* may be defined as a set of n mathematical relationships which link $(n + m)$ economic variables, n of which are classified as endogenous (determined by the system) and m as predetermined (determined outside the system). Economic systems can be divided into: (i) macro systems; and (ii) micro systems. A *macro* system is an economic system whose $(n + m)$ variables relate to the economy as a whole or to particular sectors of the economy, e.g. particular geographical regions, particular industries. A *micro system*, on the other hand, is one whose $(n + m)$ variables relate to individual economic agents, e.g. individual firms, individual households. We shall be concerned in this book only with macro systems.

Macro systems can be divided, in turn, into: (i) econometric; and (ii) analytical. A *macroeconometric system* is a macro system whose relationships are numerical. This means: (a) that all relationships have specific mathematical form characterised by various parameters (intercepts, coefficients of variables, exponents of variables, etc.); and (b) that all parameters appear as specific numbers, having been estimated in one way or another from the relevant statistical data. By contrast, a *macroanalytical system* is a macro system whose relationships are non-numerical, either because the mathematical form of some or all relationships remains unspecified or because some or all parameters appear as unspecified, as distinct from actual numbers. In the present book attention is confined to macro*econometric* systems. Examples of books which are concerned exclusively with macroanalytical systems are Gandolfo (1971), Allen (1967) and Turnovsky (1977).

Macroeconometric systems can be divided into several families of which the five most important are here labelled KK (Keynes–Klein), PB (Phillips–Bergstrom), WJ (Walras–Johansen), WL (Walras–Leontief) and

MS (Muth–Sargent). This taxonomy of macroeconometric systems is an extension of that due to Challen and Hagger (1979). (See also Powell, 1980.) The second name in each label is the name of the econometrician who produced the prototype – the father of the family, so to speak. The first name belongs to the theoretical economist who provided the vision – whose special way of looking at the working of the macro economy was taken over by the second-named and used as the framework for his prototype.

1.2 Features of KK macroeconometric systems

Nowadays, macroeconometric systems are in use in virtually every country of the world, market economy and command economy, developed and developing. The variety of contemporary macroeconometric systems is thus immense and it would be impossible to deal satisfactorily with them all in a single book. Faced with the need to be selective, we have decided to concentrate in this book on macroeconometric systems of one type only – those which belong to the KK family. We have chosen KK systems for discussion because they occupy a dominant position in the developed market economies and are used, in relation to these economies, in a host of interesting and important ways.

KK macroeconometric systems have five main distinguishing features. The first is that they assume that the product market always clears economy wide, i.e. that a balance exists at all times between the aggregate desired expenditure on currently produced goods and services and the aggregate supply of such goods and services. Given this assumption the basic problem in building a KK system becomes one of devising a set of relationships which simultaneously determine both the aggregate desired expenditure on, and the aggregate supply of, currently produced goods and services. Typically the demand side is modelled in much greater detail than the supply side, though nowadays the latter tends to be given considerably more emphasis than was formerly the case. The basic strategy in modelling the demand side is to split aggregate desired expenditure into a number of components (sometimes a very large number) and then to formulate a determining relationship for each. Further relationships (sometimes a very large number) are then added, both to explain the variables which have been introduced as explanatory variables in these basic expenditure functions and to provide a feedback to other macro variables of interest – variables such as the unemployment rate and the inflation rate. Typically, however, it is the basic expenditure functions – consumption functions, investment functions, and the like – which form the core of the system and which justify the 'Keynesian' part of the label.

A second important feature of KK macroeconometric systems is that they are formulated in discrete time. By this we mean that, in constructing the system, time is viewed as a succession of time periods (months, quarters, years) rather than as a continuum of time points and that each of the $(n + m)$ variables of the system is defined in relation to a particular time period. In the case of stocks, e.g. the stock of physical capital, the labour force, the money supply, the variable is related to a particular point of time in the relevant period, e.g. the end of the period. On the other hand, in the case of flows the variable is related to the period as a whole. This requires some elaboration. Take the flow *consumption expenditure* as an example. At each instant of time in the period consumption expenditure will be flowing at a particular rate, expressed as a certain number of dollars per annum. Over a particular time period (a particular quarter, say) these continuously varying rates of flow will give rise to a particular volume of consumption expenditure. This aggregate, expressed as a certain number of dollars, is related to the quarter as a whole and typifies the flows which appear in KK macroeconometric systems. Thus the flows of KK systems are analogous to the volume of water, expressed in litres, which collects in a bucket over, say a thirty-second interval when the bucket is put under a tap and the rate of flow of water from the tap, expressed in litres per minute, is varied, second by second, by adjusting the tap.

A third noteworthy feature of KK macroeconometric systems is that they are dynamic. That is, the system implies, through its structure, that today's macroeconomy has grown out of yesterday's and that tomorrow's will, in turn, grow out of today's. This particular feature results from the fact that some of the m predetermined variables (the variables which are determined outside the system and which, so to speak, drive the system) relate to periods prior to the period for which the n endogenous variables are determined. If we refer to the period for which the n endogenous variables are determined as 'this period', we may rephrase the present point by saying that the dynamic character of a KK macroeconometric system derives from the fact that some of its m predetermined variables are 'lagged', i.e. some relate to 'last period', some to 'the period before last', and so on.

Typically the predetermined variables of a KK system are of two types: (i) lagged endogenous variables; (ii) the rest. Those predetermined variables which fall in group (ii) are usually referred to as 'exogenous variables'. Exogenous variables may be either lagged or unlagged. Using this terminology we can say, therefore, that the predetermined variables of a KK macroeconometric system usually comprise lagged endogenous variables and exogenous variables – lagged and unlagged. The unlagged exogenous variables are, of course, variables which relate to 'this period' but which are not among the n variables classified as endogenous.

KK macroeconometric systems are usually non-linear. This is a fourth very important distinguishing feature of these systems. A macroeconometric system is said to be non-linear if *any one* of its n relationships is non-linear. A relationship is non-linear: (a) if the variables which enter the relationship do so non-linearly, e.g. if there is a term of the form $+ \beta(X_1 \cdot X_2)$, where β is a parameter and X_1 and X_2 are variables; (b) if the parameters which enter the relationship do so non-linearly, e.g. if there is a term of the form $+ 1/(1 - \beta) X$, where β is a parameter and X is a variable; (c) if both the variables and parameters which enter the relationship do so non-linearly, e.g. if there is a term of the form $+ \beta_1(X_1/\beta_2 X_2)^{\beta_3}$, where the βs are parameters and X_1 and X_2 are variables.

Finally, KK macroeconometric systems are stochastic. By this we mean that, with certain exceptions, the most important of which are purely definitional relationships, every relationship of the system contains a so-called 'random disturbance'. These random disturbances are viewed as a set of stochastic variables, e.g. as a set of variables covered by some joint probability distribution and are included to allow for non-systematic influences of one sort or another in the relationships. One such influence which is taken care of by the set of random disturbances is 'omitted-variables' error. Take a consumption function as an example. The aim of a relationship of this type is to explain some component of consumption expenditure in terms of a specific set of explanatory variables, including some aggregate income variable. Now this set of explanatory variables will not be exhaustive; it will be no more than a list of the major systematic influences on the consumption-expenditure component in question. One of the functions of the random disturbance which will appear in the relationship is to take care of the 'missing' explanatory variables – those which are not sufficiently important to be included in the $(n + m)$ explicit variables of the system.

As we shall see in Chapter 4, the set of random disturbances plays a key role in the various methods which have been devised for estimating (finding specific numbers for) the parameters of a KK macroeconometric system. All of these estimation procedures are based on a set of assumptions about the joint probability distribution believed to generate the random disturbances of the system – assumptions both about the parameters of this joint probability distribution and about its mathematical form.

1.3 An early KK macroeconometric system

In this section we shall present one of the earliest examples of a KK macroeconometric system – one relating to the US economy developed in the late 1940s by Klein (1950, pp. 84–122) – and use it to illustrate the various points touched on in the previous section.

The Klein system consists of sixteen relationships ($n = 16$) in forty-four variables. Of the forty-four variables, sixteen are classified as endogenous (determined by the system). The endogenous variables are as follows:

I = net investment in private producers' plant and equipment, measured in billions of constant dollars
p = price index of output as a whole
X = output of the private sector of the economy (excluding housing services), measured in billions of constant dollars
K = stock of business fixed capital, measured at the end of the year in billions of constant dollars
H = stock of inventories, measured at the end of the year in billions of constant dollars
W_1 = private wage–salary bill, measured in billions of current dollars
Y = disposable income, measured in billions of constant dollars
C = consumer expenditures, measured in billions of constant dollars
D_1 = gross construction expenditures on owner-occupied, single-family, non-farm residences, measured in billions of constant dollars
r = index of rent
D_2 = gross construction expenditures on rented, non-farm residences, measured in billions of constant dollars
i = average corporate bond yield
v = percentage of non-farm housing units occupied at the end of the year
M_1^D = demand deposits + circulating currency, averaged during the year, measured in billions of current dollars
M_2^D = time deposits, averaged during the year, measured in billions of current dollars
R_1 = non-farm rentals, paid and imputed, measured in billions of current dollars

The sixteen relationships of the system (note that they are numerical, i.e. that the system is, indeed, a macro*econometric* system) are as follows:

$$W_1 = 4.70 + 0.47(pX - E) + 0.12(pX - E)_{-1} + 0.19(t - 1931) + e_1 \quad (1.1)$$

$$I = 5.24 + 0.08\left(\frac{pX - E}{q}\right) + 0.07\left(\frac{pX - E}{q}\right)_{-1} - 0.12K_{-1} + e_2 \quad (1.2)$$

$$H = 1.06 + 4.66p + 0.13(X - \{H - H_{-1}\}) + 0.48H_{-1} + e_3 \quad (1.3)$$

$$C = 9.70 + 0.77Y - 0.01Y(t - 1931) + 0.76(t - 1931) + e_4 \quad (1.4)$$

$$D_1 = -7.49 + 3.14\left(\frac{r}{q_1}\right) + 0.02(Y + Y_{-1} + Y_{-2}) + 0.0039\Delta F + e_5 \quad (1.5)$$

$$D_2 = -1.99 + 2.93r_{-1} + 0.16(q_1)_{-1} - 0.44(q_1)_{-2} + 0.0013(\Delta F)_{-1} - 0.25i + e_6 \quad (1.6)$$

$$v = 181.62 + 0.24Y - 1.05r + 1.57(t - 1931) - 3.88N^S + e_7 \quad (1.7)$$

$$r - r_{-1} = -2.13 + 0.02v_{-1} + 0.0013Y + 0.16\frac{1}{r_{-1}} + e_8 \quad (1.8)$$

$$M_1^D = 9.55 + 0.23p(Y + T) + 0.02p(Y + T)(t - 1931) - 0.95(t - 1931) + e_9 \quad (1.9)$$

$$M_2^D = 14.25 - 1.00i - 0.92i_{-1} + 0.84(M_2^D)_{-1} - 0.26(t - 1931) + e_{10} \quad (1.10)$$

$$i - i_{-1} = 2.00 - 0.17E_R - (1 - 0.63)i_{-1} - 0.0052(t - 1931) + e_{11} \quad (1.11)$$

$$X - X_{-1} = 2.64 - 4.41(e_3)_{-1} + 80.64(p - p_{-1}) + e_{12} \quad (1.12)$$

$$Y + T \equiv I + (H - H_{-1}) + C + D_1 + D_2 + D_3 - D'' + G \quad (1.13)$$

$$X \equiv \frac{p(Y + T) - W_2 - R_1 - R_2}{p} \quad (1.14)$$

$$K - K_{-1} \equiv I \quad (1.15)$$

$$R_1 \equiv 0.278r\left(\frac{vN^S}{100} + \frac{v_{-1}N_{-1}^S}{100}\right)^{1/2} \quad (1.16)$$

The variables which appear in the above relationships but not in the list of endogenous variables presented earlier constitute the predetermined variables of the system. Altogether there are twenty-eight predetermined variables ($m = 28$). They are set out in full in Table 1.1. (Note that the subscript -1 indicates that the variable concerned relates to 'last period', and the subscript -2 indicates that the variable concerned relates to 'the period before last'.)

The above system possesses all of the essential features of a KK macroeconometric system, as listed in the previous section. To begin with, the system has a *solid 'Keynesian' core* consisting of the 'market-clearing' condition (1.13) and the behavioural relationships (1.2)–(1.6), each of

Table 1.1 Predetermined variables of the Klein system

Unlagged exogenous variables	Lagged exogenous variables	Lagged endogenous variables
E = excise taxes, measured in billions of current dollars	$(q_1)_{-1}$	$(pX - E)_{-1}$
$(t\text{–}1931)$ = time in years measured from 1931	$(q_1)_{-2}$	$\left(\frac{pX - E}{q}\right)_{-1}$
q = price index of capital goods	ΔF_{-1}	
q_1 = index of construction costs	N^s_{-1}	
ΔF = thousands of new non-farm families		K_{-1}
N^S = millions of available non-farm housing units at the end of the year		H_{-1}
T = government revenues + corporate savings − transfer payments − government interest payments, all measured in billions of constant dollars		Y_{-1}
E_R = excess reserves, averaged during the year, measured in millions of current dollars		Y_{-2}
D_3 = gross construction expenditures on farm residences, measured in billions of constant dollars		r_{-1}
D'' = depreciation on all residences (farm and non-farm), measured in billions of constant dollars		v_{-1}
G = government expenditures on goods and services + net exports + net investment of non-profit institutions, all measured in billions of constant dollars		i_{-1}
W_2 = government wage–salary bill, measured in billions of current dollars		$(M_2^D)_{-1}$
R_2 = farm rentals, paid and imputed, measured in billions of current dollars		p_{-1}

which determines one of the five endogenous expenditure components of the system. Second, the system is *formulated in discrete time*, as befits a KK system. It is in fact an annual system. For the purposes of the system, time is viewed as a succession of years and each of the forty-four variables of the system relates to a particular year – the stocks (e.g. K) to a point of time in the year and the flows (e.g. C) to the year as a whole. Third, the system is *dynamic* in that its list of variables includes both lagged endogenous and lagged exogenous variables. Again, the system is *non-linear*. Examples of non-linear relationships are (1.1), in which the variables enter non-linearly via the terms $+ 0.47(pX - E)$ and $+ 0.12(pX - E)_{-1}$, and (1.2), in which the variables enter non-linearly, once again, via the terms involving pX, E and q. Finally, the system is *stochastic* in that all of its behavioural relationships, i.e. (1.1)–(1.12), contain an estimate of the random disturbance. In (1.1) this estimate of the random disturbance is denoted by e_1, in (1.2) by e_2, and so on.

The reference in the last sentence of the previous paragraph to 'estimates' of the random disturbances raises an important point which should be dealt with before we proceed. To clarify this point consider a behavioural relationship which expresses Y as a linear function of X. Denote the *true* parameters in the relationship by α_0 and α_1 and *estimates* of these true parameters by $\hat{\alpha}_0$ and $\hat{\alpha}_1$. Then the disturbance is given by:

$$u = Y - (\alpha_0 + \alpha_1 X)$$

i.e. the disturbance is the true non-systematic component of Y. Evidently the disturbance is non-observable since α_0 and α_1 are not known. An *estimate* of the non-observable disturbance denoted by e is given by:

$$e = Y - (\hat{\alpha}_0 + \hat{\alpha}_1 X)$$

That is, an estimate of u can be obtained by replacing the true parameters, α_0 and α_1 by the corresponding estimates, $\hat{\alpha}_0$ and $\hat{\alpha}_1$. It follows from the expression for e that:

$$Y = \hat{\alpha}_0 + \hat{\alpha}_1 X + e$$

By applying this argument to (1.1)–(1.12) we reach the conclusion that the *e*s in the Klein system are to be thought of as estimates of the respective disturbances.

The e (estimated disturbance) term in a numerical behavioural relationship is usually referred to as the *residual*. We shall use this expression throughout the book.

The immediately preceding discussion raises another important point. It is clear from this discussion that any KK system, e.g. the Klein system, has an underlying 'true' counterpart – a system which is identical with the KK system in question except that the parameters have their unknown true values as distinct from their estimated values. On the few occasions on which we shall need to refer to this underlying system we shall describe it as the *true system*.

1.4 Modern KK macroeconometric systems

The illustrative KK system presented in the preceding section can be regarded as a prototype of the latter-day KK systems with which this book is concerned. Today's systems have developed from the prototype in three main directions. In the first place, they are in most cases *post-war, quarterly* systems, whereas the Klein system was a pre-war annual system. Second, whereas the prototype was, so to speak, a 'once-off' model, today's KK systems are *working models* in the sense that they are the subject of continuous team research and of regular updating and they are intended for general and varied use on a regular basis. Finally, today's KK systems are *very much larger* than the prototype. As mentioned earlier, the Klein prototype consists of 16 relationships in 16 endogenous variables. In modern KK systems the corresponding figure is typically not less than 50 and in many cases it runs into hundreds. For example, of the various KK systems which have been constructed for the US economy, the Wharton system has around 80 relationships in 80 endogenous variables (depending on the version), the MPS system has around 170, the Brookings system around 200 and the DRI system around 700. The Canadian KK system, RDX2, has some 250 relationships and endogenous variables and NIF, the best-known KK system of the Australian economy, roughly 250.

Thus, because of their sheer size, modern KK macroeconometric systems are exceedingly difficult to reproduce and to comprehend. On the other hand, we consider it essential that a book which is concerned exclusively with such systems should give the reader some opportunity to actually *see* one. Readers will be most interested in a system which relates to their own country. Accordingly, a good reference is Waelbroeck (1976), which presents the models of project LINK. Here will be found KK systems for Australia, Austria, Belgium, Canada, Finland, France, West Germany, Italy, Japan, the Netherlands, Sweden, the USA, the UK and of regional groupings of some developing countries. In addition Table 1.2 presents information on the sources of several other major KK systems not represented in LINK. Not all of these systems have been published. Where this is the case or where the published source provides insufficient information, it is usually possible to obtain details of the system by writing to the organisation concerned.

1.5 Other systems

As already explained, the only macroeconometric systems to be considered in detail in this book are those which fall in the KK class. In this, the final section of the chapter, we shall try to present a bird's-eye view of the rest of the field, both to improve the balance of the book and also to give the reader some appreciation of the task to be faced should he or she decide to acquire expertise over the entire range of contemporary macroeconometric systems. Since the variety of modern non-KK systems is considerable this introduction to the systems which have been put on one side for the purposes of this book will, of necessity, be both brief and fairly selective and will need to be filled out with the help of the references given at the end of the chapter.

Table 1.2 Major KK systems

Name of system	Country	Organisation(s)	Published source*
Bank of England	UK	Bank of England	Latter (1979)
Brookings	USA	Brookings Institution	Fromm and Klein (1975)
Candide	Canada	Economic Council of Canada	Waslander (1979)
DRI	USA	Data Resources Inc.	Data Resources Inc. (1976) Eckstein, Green and Sinai (1974)
LBS	UK	London Graduate School of Business Studies	Ball, Burns and Warburton (1979) Ball, Boatwright, Burns, Lobban and Miller (1975)
MPS	USA	University of Pennsylvania Federal Reserve Board Massachusetts Institute of Technology Social Science Research Council	Ando (1974)
NIF	Australia	Department of the Treasury Australian Bureau of Statistics	Department of the Treasury (1981)
RBNZ	New Zealand	Reserve Bank of New Zealand	Giles and Morgan (1977) Spencer (1979)
RDX2	Canada	Bank of Canada	Maxwell (1978) Bank of Canada (1976)
Treasury	UK	HM Treasury	HM Treasury (1979) Shepherd, Evans and Riley (1975)
Wharton	USA	Wharton School of Finance and Commerce University of Pennsylvania	Duggal, Klein and McCarthy (1974) McCarthy (1972)

* Wherever possible, at least one easily accessible source has been given. The quoted source does not always provide details of the system specification. In such cases, this information is usually presented in unpublished technical reports, available on request from the organisation concerned.

PB systems

One class of macroeconometric system which has not yet achieved great prominence but which appears likely to do so in the future is the PB class. PB systems have been constructed for the UK economy in recent years by Bergstrom and Wymer (1976) and Knight and Wymer (1976) and for the Australian and New Zealand economies by the Reserve Bank of Australia and Reserve Bank of New Zealand, respectively. The Australian system, known as RBA79, is detailed in Jonson and Trevor (1979), and the New Zealand system, known as the RBNZ Core model, in Spencer (1980). Both RBA79 and the RBNZ Core model are genuine working systems, as defined in the preceding section, in contrast to the British PB system of Bergstrom–Knight–Wymer, which is apparently a once-off system.

PB systems resemble KK systems in two main respects. In the first place, they are demand-orientated in the sense that aggregate desired expenditure is split into various components some or all of which are explained by means of consumption functions, investment functions, and the like. Second, they introduce a variety of non-linearities – typically non-linearities of an even more complex kind than are to be found in KK systems.

On the other hand, there are several important differences between PB macroeconometric systems and the KK systems to be discussed in this book. In the first place, they are formulated in continuous time rather than discrete time. That is, the builder of a PB model views time as a continuum of time points, rather than as a succession of time periods, and relates all variables – flows as well as stocks – to a specific time point. For example, in a PB system we find not only, say, the capital stock at time t among the list of variables but also, say, desired consumption expenditure at time t, the latter being the rate of flow of consumption expenditure (in $ per annum) which characterises time t. Thus all variables are viewed as continuous functions of time and this makes it possible to talk about the time derivatives of the variables.

Second, in a PB system one usually finds a *pair* of relationships associated with each endogenous variable. One of the pair explains the desired (or long-run equilibrium) value of the variable, while the other specifies the process by which the variable adjusts to its long-run value. In most cases the 'adjustment' relationship specifies that the rate at which the variable adjusts to its desired value at time t depends on the discrepancy between the actual and desired values at that time point, i.e. the adjustment process is typically 'partial' in character. Frequently, however, the partial-adjustment process is modified, in that the rate of adjustment of the endogenous variable in question at time t depends not only on the extent to which the variable departs from its desired level at time t, but also on the *level* of some other endogenous variable at time t and/or on the discrepancy between the actual and desired levels of some other endogenous variable at time t.

Take consumption expenditure as an example. The pair of relationships associated with this particular endogenous variable might take the form:

$$C^* = \alpha Y \tag{1.17}$$

$$D \ell n\, C = \beta_1 \ell n \left(\frac{C^*}{C}\right) + \beta_2 \ell n \left(\frac{M^*}{M}\right) \tag{1.18}$$

where C^* and C denote, respectively, the desired consumption expenditure and the actual consumption expenditure at time t, Y is disposable income at time t and M^* and M, respectively, are the desired and actual money stock at time t. D stands for the time derivative of the variable in question and α, β_1 and β_2 for a positive, positive and negative number respectively; 'ℓn' is short-hand for 'log to the base e'.

Relationship (1.17) is quite straightforward. It merely says that the desired level of consumption expenditure at time t is proportional to income at time t.

Relationship (1.18) is slightly more complicated. On the left-hand side we have the *proportional* rate of change of consumption expenditure at time t ($D \ell n\, C = d/dt\, (\ell n\, C) = dC/dt/C$). Turning to the right-hand side we note that $\ell n\, C^*/C$ is (approximately) the proportional excess of desired consumption expenditure over actual consumption expenditure at time t.

This can be seen as follows:

$$\ell n \frac{C^*}{C} = \ell n\, (1 + x)$$

where x is $C^*/C - 1$, i.e. x is the proportional excess of C^* over C. But

$$\ell n\, (1 + x) = x - \frac{x^2}{2} + \frac{x^3}{3} - \frac{x^4}{4} + \ldots$$

Hence $\ell n\, (1 + x) \simeq x$ when x is small, as it is in the present context (let's say it's 0.03). It follows that:

$$\ell n \frac{C^*}{C} \simeq x$$

when x is small. Thus if the second term on the right-hand side is ignored for the moment we see that (1.18) says that the proportional rate of change of consumption expenditure at time t is some positive fraction of the proportional excess of desired over actual consumption expenditure at time t. In other words (1.18) specifies that the adjustment process governing consumption expenditure is of the partial-adjustment type. The second term on the right-hand side serves to modify the partial-adjustment character of the adjustment process. Recalling that β_2 is negative we see that the role of this second right-hand term is to cause the proportional rate of adjustment of consumption expenditure at time t to fall below its 'partial-adjustment' level if the desired money stock exceeds the actual money stock ($\ell n\ M^*/M$ will then be positive) and vice versa.

Finally, PB macroeconometric systems typically contain one or more policy-reaction functions. A policy-reaction function is a relationship which specifies the way in which policy-makers adjust a particular policy instrument in response to developments in the private sector. Take the exchange rate as an example. In a PB system a policy-reaction function for this instrument might take the form:

$$D\ \ell n\ E = \gamma_1\ \ell n\ \frac{R}{R^*} + \gamma_2\ \ell n\ \frac{M}{M^*} \qquad (1.19)$$

where E denotes the exchange rate (expressed as units of domestic currency per unit of foreign currency), R and R^* the actual and desired levels of foreign reserves, respectively, and M and M^* the actual and desired levels of the money stock, respectively; γ_1 stands for a negative number and γ_2 for a positive number. According to (1.19), the policy-maker will adjust the exchange rate at time t if there is a discrepancy between R and R^* and/or between M and M^* at time t. Given $M = M^*$ at time t (i.e. given $\ell n\ M/M^* = 0$), the exchange rate will be revised *upwards* if R is less than R^*, i.e. if the level of foreign reserves is too low; the first term on the right-hand side will then be a product of two negative terms and hence be positive. Furthermore, the rate of adjustment will be higher (in proportional terms), the greater the deficiency of R in relation to R^*. Similarly, given $R = R^*$ at time t, the exchange rate will be revised *downwards* if M exceeds M^*, i.e. if the domestic money stock is too high, the rate of adjustment being greater the greater the excess.

At the outset of this discussion of PB systems reference was made to two working systems of this class – an Australian system known as RBA79 and a New Zealand system known as the RBNZ Core model. Both have interesting and unusual features and deserve some attention before the PB class is put on one side. We begin with RBA79.

In the preceding general discussion of PB systems three major distinguishing features of the PB class were mentioned. RBA79 possesses all three. In the first place, as befits a PB system, RBA79 is formulated in continuous time. Second, it possesses a substantial quota of 'adjustment equations' – equations specifying how the actual level of some variable adjusts towards an equilibrium or desired level. In fact, more than half of the twenty-six equations in RBA79 are of this type. Finally, the RBA79 equation system includes three policy-reaction functions relating, respectively, to the bond rate, the bill rate and the exchange rate. The idea behind this group of equations is that the bond rate, the bill rate and the exchange rate constitute policy instruments which are manipulated by the authorities in a systematic way in response both to discrepancies between the actual and desired values of certain target variables and also to discrepancies between the actual and desired values of the instruments themselves.

Two other notable features of RBA79 warranting mention are: (i) that it imposes a variety of restrictions on the parameters of those equations which, so to speak, pair with the adjustment equations, i.e. the equations which explain the desired levels of the various endogenous variables; and (ii) that it is long run in character. We take these points in turn.

The imposed parameter restrictions in RBA79 comprise both within-equation and across-equation restrictions and take two different forms. In some cases the restriction consists of allotting a certain value to a parameter rather than allowing it to be freely estimated from the sample data. In other cases it consists of imposing a certain relationship on the parameters in a particular equation or in two or more equations, e.g. that they be equal or that they sum to unity.

An example of the first type of restriction is provided by the equation for equilibrium household expenditure which expresses the level desired for this variable as a log-linear function of disposable income and the bond rate. The coefficient of the disposable-income variable in this equation is set in advance of estimation at unity. Thus, in view of the log-linear form of the function, the builders of RBA79 have, in effect, required that the model show constancy of the average propensity to consume, for a given bond rate.

An example of the second type of restriction can be drawn from the equation governing non-bank demand for government securities. The equilibrium level of this variable is made to depend log-linearly on, among other things, the domestic bond rate and the world interest rate. The builders of RBA79 have required that both of these variables have the same coefficient, which amounts to saying that, in this case, they have taken the position that the relevant explanatory variable is the domestic bond rate *relative* to the world interest rate. As a second example, we may point to the fact that the output–labour elasticity is allotted the value 0.7 in advance of estimation throughout the model and the output–capital elasticity the value 0.3. Thus it is required that each of these two parameters has a common value in all equations rather than being freely estimated and, further, that the two common values sum to unity.

Turn now to the second noteworthy feature of RBA79 mentioned above – its long-run character. The distinction between 'short-run' and 'long-run' economy-wide systems is somewhat fuzzy but is useful nevertheless. A 'short-run' system is one which purports to show how the economy responds to a specific exogenous change in the short term, say in the first one to two years following the change. By contrast, a 'long-run' system is one which purports to show the nature of the response in the long term, say in the first five to ten years following the change. To decide whether a system is short or long run we need, then, to look at three things.

The first is the classification of variables into endogenous and exogenous. Some variables, of which the capital stock and population are examples, are by their nature incapable of rapid change and so can be legitimately held fixed (treated as exogenous) when the short-term response of the economy to exogenous change is being considered. Consequently if we find such variables in the *endogenous* list (*not* treated as exogenous) we conclude that the model is intended to throw light on *long*-term responses and we can give it the 'long-run' label.

A second thing to be looked at is the list of parameters. When only short-term responses are at issue all parameters can be treated as constants. Consequently the appearance of some of the parameters as *variables* is a sign that the model is intended to handle long-term responses – that the 'long-run' label is appropriate.

Finally, we should look at the set of parameter restrictions. The appearance of restrictions which are supportable, theoretically and empirically, only as long-run tendencies is a further guide to the intentions of the model-builder and provides further evidence that the model should be called 'long run'.

Viewed in this light, RBA79 is clearly a long-run system. Among its endogenous variables are several which one could legitimately place in the exogenous list if one's time horizon were short, e.g. the exchange rate, stock of business fixed capital, labour supply and real exports of goods and services. Also in some instances factors of proportionality are treated not as constants but as functions of endogenous variables. Finally, certain of the parameter restrictions can be justified only as long-run tendencies – the restriction which imposes constancy on the average propensity to consume is a case in point.

Turn now to the RBNZ Core model. Like RBA79, this model is comparatively small, consisting of some forty relationships. Since it is formulated in discrete rather than continuous time it is not strictly speaking, a fully fledged PB system. Nevertheless its affinities with the PB class would appear to be sufficiently strong to justify our decision to place it under the PB umbrella. In particular, the format of the model is dominated by the 'pair-of-relationships' device mentioned earlier as one of the key characteristics of PB systems. One can also find policy-reaction functions, albeit of a somewhat primitive kind. Finally, there are several instances of the within-equation and across-equations parameter restrictions which were mentioned earlier as a feature of RBA79 – the most noteworthy working system of the PB class.

MS systems

Like PB systems MS systems warrant a brief treatment because they are likely to become more and more important. At the time of writing it would appear that there are no more than two published macroeconometric systems which fall in the MS class. They are the small quarterly system (six relationships only) built for the US economy by Sargent (1976) and the twenty-relationship annual system built by Minford (1980) for the UK economy. Since neither can be regarded as a working system in the sense in which we are using this term it would seem that MS systems are still very much in the prototype phase.

MS systems resemble KK systems in several important respects. In particular, they are discrete-time, dynamic, non-linear and stochastic. The main way in which they differ from KK systems is in their treatment of expectations. In MS systems expectations variables are invariably treated as 'rational', whereas, as we shall see in Chapter 3, this treatment is, for all practical purposes, non-existent in systems of the KK class. A helpful and essentially accurate way of categorizing the two classes is to say that MS systems are systems in which all expectations variables are treated as rational but which are otherwise KK.

When we say that in an MS system all expectations variables are treated as 'rational' we mean that every expectations variable is replaced throughout the system by the appropriate expected value (mathematical expectation) of the variable concerned as determined by the system as a whole on the basis of information available at the time of the formation of the variable.

For an example turn to Sargent's US system. Two of the six relationships of this system contain as an explanatory variable the expectation of the inflation rate for period t formed at the beginning of the previous period, i.e. period $t - 1$ is the formation time in this case. Denote this expectations variable by ${}_{t-1}p^e_t$. What makes Sargent's system an MS system is that ${}_{t-1}p^e_t$ is replaced in both relationships by $E(p_t|Z_{t-1})$, i.e. by the mathematical expectation of the inflation rate for period t as determined by the system as a whole on the basis of information available at the beginning of period $t - 1$, represented by Z_{t-1} – and similarly for all other expectations variables.

Thus in MS systems economic agents are supposed to form their expectation of a particular variable by feeding into the estimated system, which they take to be the 'true' system, information which is available to them at the relevant formation time – in particular, information about the values which will be assumed by the predetermined variables of the system in the period for which the expectation is being formed. They then use the system to work out the expected value of the variable concerned. It is because expectations are formed in this way that they are described as 'rational'.

It should be noted that while the expectations variables which appear in MS systems are commonly of the form ${}_{t-1}X^e_t$, more complex cases are also found. For example, in Minford's system one finds an expectations variable of the form ${}_{t-1}X^e_{t+1}$, i.e. the expectation is formed at the beginning of period $t - 1$ for period $t + 1$. We may therefore say that in general every expectations variable in an MS system is replaced by $E(X_{t+j}|Z_{t-i})$, where i and j are positive integers, $t - i$ and $t + j$ indicating, respectively, the period *in* which, and the period *for* which, the expectation is assumed to be formed.

The builder of an MS system faces one difficult problem of a technical nature which is not faced by the builder of a KK system. In both cases, because of the dynamic, discrete-time nature of the system, estimation cannot proceed until a time series covering a sequence of T past time periods $(1, ..., t, ..., T)$ has been obtained for every variable in the system. (This will become clear in Chapter 4.) In the case of an MS system this means that series have to be found for variables of the form $E(X_{t+j}|Z_{t-i})$. However, as already explained, the value of $E(X_{t+j}|Z_{t-i})$ for any period, period t, is generated in a particular way by the estimated system. Thus the problem builders of MS systems face is that they need series for variables of the form $E(X_{t+j}|Z_{t-i})$ before they can begin estimation but cannot obtain such series until estimation has been carried out. This circularity problem has been the subject of active research in recent years and various possible ways of dealing with it have been suggested. The problem has, however, not yet been fully disposed of and, together with other difficult technical problems into which we shall not enter, is likely to impose a fairly slow rate of development on MS systems in the next few years.

WJ systems

A third prominent class of non-KK macroeconometric systems consists of those which view the macroeconomy as some form of general-equilibrium system. Members of this class have most, though not necessarily all, of the following broad features:

1. They disaggregate the economy into sectors – in particular into industrial sectors.
2. They relate to an equilibrium situation, by which is meant a situation in which the values of all endogenous variables are consistent with the given levels of the predetermined variables throughout the disaggregated economy.
3. They feature relationships which focus on the interrelationships that exist between sectors, e.g. which highlight the fact that the output of one industry is used as an input by many of the others.
4. They also include production and consumption relationships which

allow for substitution among factors in production and among commodities in consumption.

5. They include equilibrium prices and outputs throughout the disaggregated economy in the list of endogenous variables.
6. They impose perfect competition – all firms and consumers are assumed to be price-takers.
7. They view all economic agents as optimisers in some sense.

An important sub-class of general-equilibrium macroeconometric systems are those which derive from the system developed by Johansen (1960) for the Norwegian economy. Such systems form the WJ family. Another important sub-class are WL systems. These will be discussed below.

In the Johansen system the macroeconomy is disaggregated into twenty-three sectors. Twenty-two of these are domestic-production sectors; the remaining sector is a rest-of-the-world sector. Each domestic-production sector produces just one good; this is also available from the rest of the world, i.e. there are 'competitive' imports of each of the twenty-two domestically produced goods.

Of the twenty-two domestic-production sectors only twenty require inputs of labour and capital; the other two merely collect and allocate goods which are produced by other sectors. Each of the 'genuine' domestic-production sectors operates under a Cobb–Douglas production function (with technical progress) as regards capital and labour inputs. Inputs of raw materials drawn from other sectors and from competitive imports bear a fixed proportion to output, as do inputs of raw materials drawn from non-competitive imports. Profits are maximised subject to these production relationships and with all output and input prices treated as parameters. In the case of the two domestic-production sectors which merely collect goods from, and allocate goods to, other sectors, both goods drawn from other sectors and from competitive imports and goods drawn from non-competitive imports are assumed to be proportional to output. Profits are put at zero in each of these two sectors.

Apart from various definitions the other relationships of the system consist of a set of consumption functions – one for each of the nineteen domestically produced goods that find their way into consumption (and for their equivalent competitive imports) and one for non-competitive imports. Each of these expresses total consumption of the good concerned as the product of *per capita* consumption of the good and total population, the former being made some function (specific to each good) of the twenty relevant prices and aggregate income.

The system just outlined is highly non-linear, and for this reason alone is difficult to handle. To derive a manageable system Johansen engages in logarithmic differentiation. By this means he produces a set of linear relationships which link percentage rates of change in the endogenous equilibrium levels of the system with percentage rates of change in the variables which are taken as predetermined. After making a number of substitutions among these relationships, Johansen emerges with a linear system of 86 relationships in 86 endogenous rates of change and 46 predetermined rates of change. The solution of this system can be interpreted as showing the percentage changes in the endogenous equilibrium levels that are implied by any specified set of percentage changes in the predetermined variables from their levels at time t. This interpretation is, of course, subject to the qualification that the exogenous percentage changes in question must be small.

A notable instance of a working WJ system is the general-equilibrium system built for the Australian economy under the IMPACT project – an official study in which several agencies of the Australian government are participating. Details of the original version of this system, known as ORANI, are to be found in Dixon *et al.* (1977); details of a second version known as ORANI 78 can be found in Dixon *et al.* (1982).

Because of its enormous size and also because it is highly non-linear ORANI could not be put to work as it stood. To produce a usable system ORANI's builders proceeded in two distinct stages. First, like Johansen, they applied the technique of logarithmic differentiation to the individual relationships to produce a linear system in percentage rates of change of variables rather than levels. They then tackled the problem of size by substituting certain of the equations in this linear system into others, thereby eliminating an equal number of equations and variables. In its final form the system is a linear system of 392 equations in 3,844 percentage rates of change.

ORANI has one other interesting feature which deserves a mention. In the case of KK and PB macroeconometric systems, the classification of variables into endogenous and predetermined is made by the system-builder himself prior to estimation and the user of the system is given no freedom to switch variables from one category to another. In the case of ORANI, on the other hand, the system-builder allows the user, within very broad limits, to choose as predetermined any 3,452 of the 3,844 percentage rates of change which constitute the variables of the final form of the system; as the first step in any ORANI application users must exercise this freedom in the way which best suits their purpose.

WL systems

Another sub-group of general-equilibrium systems which are even more widely used than WJ systems are input–output systems. To these we have given the label WL. They play an especially important role in macroeconomic planning in developing countries and are also extensively used, particularly at the regional level, in developed countries.

A very simple example of a WL system will now be set out in terms of the following notation:

q_s = output of commodity s in year t
q_r = output of commodity r in year t
f_s = final demand for commodity s in year t
q_{sr} = output of commodity s used as a current input (raw material) in the production of commodity r in year t
a_{sr} = output of commodity s used as a current input in the production of commodity r in year t per unit of output of commodity r.

In terms of this notation, our illustrative WL system is as follows:

$$q_s = \sum_{r=1}^{n} q_{sr} + f_s \quad (s = 1, 2, \ldots, n) \tag{1.20}$$

$$q_{sr} = a_{sr}q_r \quad (r, s = 1, 2, \ldots, n) \tag{1.21}$$

The first of these blocks of n relationships says, for each of the n commodities produced by the economic system, that the entire output of the commodity in any period is used either as a current input, i.e. raw material, in the manufacture of other commodities, or for the purpose of satisfying final demand, while the second block of $(r \times s)$ relationships says that the *total* output of commodity s used in the production of commodity r is the product of the *per unit* usage (a_{sr}) and the output of commodity $r(q_r)$. By substitution from (1.21) to (1.20) the system can be reduced to the following set of n relationships:

$$q_s = \sum_{r=1}^{n} a_{sr}q_r + f_s \quad (s = 1, 2, \ldots, n) \tag{1.22}$$

The endogenous variables of the sytem are the n outputs $(q_1, \ldots, q_n)$ while the nfs are predetermined; a_{sr} stands for an actual number which is either positive or zero.

This set of relationships can be conveniently expressed in matrix form. For this purpose we define the following matrices:

$$\mathbf{q} = \begin{bmatrix} q_1 \\ q_2 \\ \vdots \\ q_n \end{bmatrix} \quad \mathbf{f} = \begin{bmatrix} f_1 \\ f_2 \\ \vdots \\ f_n \end{bmatrix} \quad \mathbf{A} = \begin{bmatrix} a_{11} & \cdots & a_{1r} & \cdots & a_{1n} \\ \vdots & & \vdots & & \vdots \\ a_{s1} & \cdots & a_{sr} & \cdots & a_{sn} \\ \vdots & & \vdots & & \vdots \\ a_{n1} & \cdots & a_{nr} & \cdots & a_{nn} \end{bmatrix}$$

Using these matrices we can write (1.22) as:

$$\mathbf{q} = \mathbf{A}\mathbf{q} + \mathbf{f} \tag{1.23}$$

This gives the following expression for the output vector $\mathbf{q}$:

$$\mathbf{q} = (\mathbf{I} - \mathbf{A})^{-1}\mathbf{f} = \mathbf{B}^{-1}\mathbf{f} \tag{1.24}$$

where $\mathbf{I}$ is the identity matrix and $\mathbf{B} = \mathbf{I} - \mathbf{A}$. From (1.24) it would be possible to determine the amount which each industry would need to produce in some year t (elements of the $\mathbf{q}$ vector) if a specified final bill of goods for that year (elements of the $\mathbf{f}$ vector) were to be met.

Like the WJ systems discussed in the preceding section, the above illustrative WL system is an equilibrium system; it tells us what the values of the endogenous variables (the n outputs) would be if the macroeconomy were to reach a state of rest, relative to a given set of values of the predetermined variables (the n final demands). While most working WL systems have this characteristic, dynamic WL systems are also to be found, Like KK and PB systems, dynamic WL systems portray a macroeconomy which is on the move – which has not yet reached a state of rest relative to a given set of values of the variables which are treated as predetermined.

This concludes our brief review of macroeconometric systems which fall outside the KK class. From now on we shall devote our attention exclusively to KK systems, as defined in sections 1.2, 1.3 and 1.4. Chapter 3 will deal with the specification of KK systems. Chapters 4–6 will be concerned with estimation in such systems, Chapters 7 and 8 with their evaluation and Chapters 9–11 with their uses. Chapter 2 will be devoted to a discussion of certain technical matters which are fundamental to a full understanding of the material presented in Chapters 4–11, and Chapter 12 to a brief discussion of important developments in the field of KK macroeconometric systems.

References and further reading

ALLEN, R.G.D. (1967) *Macro-Economic Theory*, Macmillan, London

ANDO, A. (1974) 'Some Aspects of Stabilization Policies, The Monetarist Controversy, and the MPS Model', *International Economic Review,* vol. 15, pp. 541–71.

BALL, R.J., BOATWRIGHT, B.D., BURNS, T., LOBBAN, P.W.M. and MILLER, G.W. (1975) 'The London Business School Quarterly Econometric Model of the UK Economy', in G.A. Renton (ed.), *Modelling the Economy*, Heinemann, London.

BALL, R.J., BURNS, T. and WARBURTON, P. J. (1979) 'The London Business School Model of the UK Economy: An Exercise in International Monetarism', in P. Ormerod (ed.), *Economic Modelling,* Heinemann, London.

BANK OF CANADA (1976) *The Equations of RDX2 Revised and Estimated to 4Q72,* Bank of Canada Technical Report 5, Ottawa.

BERGSTROM, A.R. (1967) *The Construction and Use of Economic Models,* English Universities Press, London.

Bergstrom, A.R. and Wymer, C.R. (1976) 'A Model of Disequilibrium Neoclassical Growth and its Application to the United Kingdom', in A.R. Bergstrom (ed.), *Statistical Inference in Continuous Time Economic Models,* North-Holland, Amsterdam.

Challen, D.W. and Hagger, A.J. (1979) 'Economy-Wide Modelling with Special Reference to Australia', Paper presented to Eighth Conference of Economists, Melbourne.

Data Resources Inc. (1976) *The Data Resources National Economic Information System,* North-Holland, Amsterdam.

Department of the Treasury (1981) *The NIF–10 Model of the Australian Economy,* Australian Government Publishing Service, Canberra.

Dixon, P.B., Parmenter, B.R., Ryland, G.J. and Sutton, J. (1977) *ORANI: A General Equilibrium Model of the Australian Economy,* Australian Government Publishing Service, Canberra.

Dixon, P.B., Parmenter, B.R., Sutton, J. and Vincent, D.P. (1982), *ORANI: A Multisectoral Model of the Australian Economy,* North-Holland, Amsterdam.

Duggal, V.G., Klein, L.R. and McCarthy, M.D. (1974) 'The Wharton Model Mark III: A Modern *IS–LM* Construct', *International Economic Review,* vol. 15, pp. 572–94.

Eckstein, O., Green, E.W. and Sinai, A. (1974) 'The Data Resources Model: Uses, Structure and Analysis of the US Economy', *International Economic Review,* vol. 15, pp. 595–615.

Fromm, G. and Klein, L.R. (1975) *The Brookings Model: Perspective and Recent Developments,* North-Holland, Amsterdam.

Gandolfo, G. (1971) *Mathematical Methods and Models in Economic Dynamics,* North-Holland, Amsterdam.

Giles, D.E.A. and Morgan, G.H.T. (1977), 'Alternative Estimates of a Large New Zealand Econometric Model', *New Zealand Economic Papers,* vol. 11, pp. 52–67.

HM Treasury (1979) 'Some Problems in the Development of the Treasury Model', in P. Ormerod (ed.), *Economic Modelling*, Heinemann, London.

Johansen, L. (1960) *A Multi-Sectoral Study of Economic Growth,* North-Holland, Amsterdam.

Jonson, P.D. and Trevor, R.G. (1979) *Monetary Rules: A Preliminary Analysis,* Research Discussion Paper 7903, Reserve Bank of Australia, Sydney.

Keynes, J.M. (1936) *The General Theory of Employment, Interest and Money,* Macmillan, London.

Klein, L.R. (1950) *Economic Fluctuations in the United States 1921–1941,* Wiley, New York.

Knight, M.D. and Wymer, C.R. (1976) 'A Monetary Model of an Open Economy With Particular Reference to the United Kingdom', in M. J. Artis and A. R. Nobay (eds), *Essays in Economic Analysis,* Cambridge University Press, Cambridge.

Latter, A.R. (1979) 'Some Issues in Economic Modelling at the Bank of England', in P. Ormerod (ed.), *Economic Modelling,* Heinemann, London.

Leontief, W.W. (1941) *The Structure of the American Economy 1919–1939,* Oxford University Press, New York.

McCarthy, M.D. (1972) *The Wharton Quarterly Econometric Forecasting Model Mark III,* Studies in Quantitative Economics No. 6, University of Pennsylvania.

Maxwell, T. (1978) 'A Primer on RDX2', *Bank of Canada Review*, January, pp. 3–10.

MINFORD, A.P. (1980) 'A Rational Expectations Model of the United Kingdom Under Fixed and Floating Exchange Rates', in K. Brunner and A.H. Meltzer (eds), *On the State of Macro-Economics,* North-Holland, Amsterdam.

MUTH, J.F. (1961) 'Rational Expectations and the Theory of Price Movements', *Econometrica*, vol. 29, pp. 315–35.

PHILLIPS, A.W. (1954) 'Stabilization Policy in a Closed Economy', *Economic Journal,* vol. 64, pp. 290–323.

PHILLIPS, A.W. (1956) 'Some Notes on the Estimation of Time-Forms of Reactions in Interdependent Dynamic Systems', *Economica,* vol. 23, pp. 99–113.

PHILLIPS, A.W. (1957) 'Stabilization Policy and the Time-Forms of Lagged Responses', *Economic Journal*, vol. 67, pp. 265–77.

POWELL, A.A. (1980) 'The Major Streams of Economy-Wide Modelling: Is Rapprochement Possible?', in J. Kmenta and J.B. Ramsey (eds), *Large-Scale Macro-Econometric Models,* North-Holland, Amsterdam.

SARGENT, T.J. (1976) 'A Classical Macroeconometric Model for the United States', *Journal of Political Economy,* vol. 84, pp. 207–37.

SHEPHERD, J.R., EVANS, H.P. and RILEY, C.J. (1975) 'The Treasury Short-Term Forecasting Model', in G. A. Renton (ed), *Modelling the Economy,* Heinemann, London.

SPENCER, G.H. (1979) *The Reserve Bank Econometric Model: A Revised Structure and Some Policy Simulations,* Research Paper 28, Reserve Bank of New Zealand, Wellington.

SPENCER, G.H. (1980) *Experiments with a Core Model of the New Zealand Economy,* Research Paper 29, Reserve Bank of New Zealand, Wellington.

TURNOVSKY, S.J. (1977) *Macroeconomic Analysis and Stabilization Policies,* Cambridge University Press, Cambridge.

WAELBROECK, J.L. (1976) *The Models of Project LINK,* North-Holland, Amsterdam.

WALRAS, L. (1874) *Eléments D'Économie Politique Appliquée [Elements of Pure Economics],* Paris and Lausanne.

WASLANDER, H.E.L. (1979) 'The Dynamic Properties of CANDIDE Model 1.2M', *Canadian Journal of Economics*, vol. 12, pp. 139–50.

2 SOLUTION OF LINEAR AND NON-LINEAR SYSTEMS

2.1 The solution concept

In the previous chapter we defined a macroeconometric system as a set of n numerical relationships linking n endogenous variables and m predetermined variables. Since KK systems are just a special type of macroeconometric system, this definition applies to a KK system. A KK system can thus be viewed as a set of n numerical simultaneous equations in which the n endogenous variables are the 'unknowns' and the m predetermined variables the 'knowns'. Moreover, as with any set of simultaneous equations which has as many equations as unknowns, one can use a KK system, at least in principle, to solve for the unknowns (the n endogenous variables) in terms of the knowns (the m predetermined variables). In other words, with the help of a KK system one can find those values of the n endogenous variables which satisfy the system as a whole for specified values of the m predetermined variables, i.e. for specified values of the lagged endogenous variables and the lagged and unlagged exogenous variables. In this chapter we shall explain the procedures which are commonly used in practice to solve KK systems in this sense. A good understanding of these solution procedures is essential at this stage because in the chapters which follow we shall be dealing with a number of topics relating to the construction, evaluation and use of KK systems in which system solution plays a vital part.

We shall begin by considering the procedures used to solve *linear* systems. Some discussion of the linear case will prove helpful in the rest of the book even though our focus there will be primarily on the large *non*-linear systems which nowadays dominate the field.

2.2 Solution of linear systems

The standard procedure for solving a linear system is to substitute the specified values of the m predetermined variables into the solution expressions which are implied by the system. Before we can explain this procedure we must consider the question of the matrix representation of linear KK systems.

As our starting-point we take the following simple illustrative linear KK system to which we shall refer henceforth as SYSTEM I:

$$C_t = 0.6X_t + 0.2C_{t-1} + e_{1t} \quad (2.1)$$

$$X_t \equiv Y_t - T_t \quad (2.2)$$

$$Y_t \equiv C_t + G_t + I_t \quad (2.3)$$

$$T_t = 0.3Y_t + e_{4t} \quad (2.4)$$

The notation is:

C = real consumption expenditure
G = real government expenditure
I = real investment expenditure
Y = real gross domestic product
X = real disposable income
T = real net tax collections
e_1, e_4 = residuals

The numbers in (2.1)–(2.4) are to be thought of as parameter estimates made by applying one of the estimation techniques to be discussed in Chapter 4 to the appropriate data.

Equations (2.1)–(2.4) are described as the *structural* form of SYSTEM I. This term is used to convey the idea that each of the relationships describes an aspect of the structure of the economy. Equation (2.1) is a consumption function – a relationship which describes the way in which this period's consumption expenditure is determined from this period's disposable income and last period's consumption expenditure. Relationships like equation (2.1) which describe the way in which the behaviour of households or firms enter into the determination of an economic aggregate are called *behavioural relationships*. Equations (2.2) and (2.3) belong to the class of *definitional relationships*. The first defines real disposable income as the difference between real gross domestic product and real net tax collections. The second sets out a simple form of the equality between aggregate output and aggregate demand. The final relationship of SYSTEM I describes an aspect of the institutional structure of the economy and, as such, is a member of the class of *institutional relationships*. It says simply that net tax collections are proportional to real gross domestic product.

Seven variables appear in the system – C_t, X_t, C_{t-1}, Y_t, T_t, G_t and I_t. Of these C_t, X_t, Y_t and T_t are the endogenous variables, while C_{t-1}, I_t and G_t are the predetermined variables ($n = 4$ in this case and $m = 3$). The first of the three predetermined variables is a lagged endogenous variable; the other two are exogenous variables.

It will be seen that there are no lagged exogenous variables in SYSTEM I. Thus if we denote the maximum lag on the lagged endogenous variables of a KK macroeconometric system by p and the maximum lag on the lagged exogenous variables by q, we can say that in SYSTEM I we have the case $p = 1, q = 0$. In working KK systems p will typically be greater than 1 and q will typically be greater than 0.

The question we now consider is how to express SYSTEM I in matrix form. The first step is to rearrange the four equations of the system so that only terms involving endogenous variables appear on the left-hand side. We have:

$$C_t - 0.6X_t = 0.2C_{t-1} + e_{1t} \tag{2.5}$$

$$X_t - Y_t + T_t \equiv 0 \tag{2.6}$$

$$-C_t + Y_t \equiv G_t + I_t \tag{2.7}$$

$$-0.3Y_t + T_t = e_{4t} \tag{2.8}$$

In this form the system can be given matrix representation as follows:

$$\begin{bmatrix} 1 & -0.6 & 0 & 0 \\ 0 & 1 & -1 & 1 \\ -1 & 0 & 1 & 0 \\ 0 & 0 & -0.3 & 1 \end{bmatrix} \begin{bmatrix} C_t \\ X_t \\ Y_t \\ T_t \end{bmatrix} = \begin{bmatrix} 0 & 0 \\ 0 & 0 \\ 1 & 1 \\ 0 & 0 \end{bmatrix} \begin{bmatrix} G_t \\ I_t \end{bmatrix} + \begin{bmatrix} 0.2 & 0 & 0 & 0 \\ 0 & 0 & 0 & 0 \\ 0 & 0 & 0 & 0 \\ 0 & 0 & 0 & 0 \end{bmatrix} \begin{bmatrix} C_{t-1} \\ X_{t-1} \\ Y_{t-1} \\ T_{t-1} \end{bmatrix} + \begin{bmatrix} e_{1t} \\ 0 \\ 0 \\ e_{4t} \end{bmatrix} \tag{2.9}$$

The generalisation of (2.9) is quite straightforward. Any linear KK system which contains n relationships in n endogenous variables and m predetermined variables and in which $p = 1$ and $q = 0$ can be represented in matrix form as follows:

$$\mathbf{Ay_t} = \mathbf{B_0x_t} + \mathbf{C_1y_{t-1}} + \mathbf{e_t} \tag{2.10}$$

where $\mathbf{y_t}$ is the $(n \times 1)$ vector of endogenous variables, $\mathbf{x_t}$ is the $(k \times 1)$ vector of (unlagged) exogenous variables, $\mathbf{y_{t-1}}$ is the $\mathbf{y_t}$ vector lagged one period and $\mathbf{e_t}$ is the $(n \times 1)$ vector of residuals; $\mathbf{A}$, $\mathbf{B_0}$ and $\mathbf{C_1}$ are all numerical matrices of coefficients; $\mathbf{A}$ is the $(n \times n)$ matrix of the coefficients of the endogenous variables, the first row being the coefficients in the first equation, the second row the coefficients in the second equation, and so on; $\mathbf{B_0}$ is the $(n \times k)$ matrix of the numerical coefficients of the k (unlagged) exogenous variables, while $\mathbf{C_1}$ is the $(n \times n)$ matrix of the coefficients of the (one-period) lagged endogenous variables. The entry of intercepts into the structural equations is accommodated by defining a (dummy) exogenous variable which always takes the value unity.

If we denote the number of columns in $\mathbf{C_1}$ which have at least one non-zero element by n_1, we can say that m, the number of predetermined variables in the system, is given by:

$$m = k + n_1 \tag{2.11}$$

The expression (2.10) applies to the case where $p = 1$ and $q = 0$. The generalisation of this expression to cover any values of p and q is also quite straightforward. Any linear KK macroeconometric system consisting of n relationships in n endogenous variables and m predetermined variables can be written in matrix form as follows:

$$\begin{aligned}\mathbf{A}\mathbf{y_t} = \mathbf{B_0}\mathbf{x_t} + \mathbf{B_1}\mathbf{x_{t-1}} + \ldots + \mathbf{B_q}\mathbf{x_{t-q}} + \mathbf{C_1}\mathbf{y_{t-1}} + \mathbf{C_2}\mathbf{y_{t-2}} + \ldots \\ + \mathbf{C_p}\mathbf{y_{t-p}} + \mathbf{e_t}\end{aligned} \tag{2.12}$$

In this expression $\mathbf{A}$, $\mathbf{y_t}$, $\mathbf{B_0}$, $\mathbf{x_t}$, $\mathbf{C_1}$, $\mathbf{y_{t-1}}$ and $\mathbf{e_t}$ are defined as in (2.10); $\mathbf{x_{t-1}}$ is the $\mathbf{x_t}$ vector lagged one period, and so on up to $\mathbf{x_{t-q}}$, which is the $\mathbf{x_t}$ vector lagged $\mathbf{q}$ periods. Similarly $\mathbf{y_{t-2}}$ is the $\mathbf{y_t}$ vector lagged two periods, and so on up to $\mathbf{y_{t-p}}$, which is the $\mathbf{y_t}$ vector lagged p periods. Finally, $\mathbf{B_1}$, ..., $\mathbf{B_q}$ and $\mathbf{C_2}$, ..., $\mathbf{C_p}$ are matrices of numerical coefficients. $\mathbf{B_1}$ is the $(n \times k)$ matrix of coefficients of one-period lagged exogenous variables, and so on up to $\mathbf{B_q}$, which is the $(n \times k)$ matrix of coefficients of q-period lagged exogenous variables, while $\mathbf{C_2}$ is the $(n \times n)$ matrix of coefficents of the two-period lagged endogenous variables, and so on up to $\mathbf{C_p}$, which is the $(n \times n)$ matrix of coefficients of p-period lagged endogenous variables.

Denote the number of columns of $\mathbf{B_0}$, ..., $\mathbf{B_q}$ which have at least one non-zero element by k_0, ..., k_q. Likewise denote the number of columns of $\mathbf{C_1}$, ..., $\mathbf{C_p}$ which have at least one non-zero element by n_1, ..., n_p. Then m, the number of predetermined variables in the system, is given by:

$$m = k_0 + \ldots + k_q + n_1 + \ldots + n_p \tag{2.13}$$

If we multiply (2.12) through by $\mathbf{A}^{-1}$ (we assume that the inverse exists) we obtain:

$$\mathbf{y_t} = \pi_{10}\mathbf{x_t} + \pi_{11}\mathbf{x_{t-1}} + \ldots + \pi_{1q}\mathbf{x_{t-q}} + \pi_{21}\mathbf{y_{t-1}} + \pi_{22}\mathbf{y_{t-2}} + \ldots + \pi_{2p}\mathbf{y_{t-p}} + \mathbf{e'_t} \qquad (2.14)$$

The πs in this expression are given by:

$$\begin{aligned} \pi_{10} &= \mathbf{A}^{-1}\mathbf{B}_0 \\ \vdots \quad & \quad \vdots \\ \pi_{1q} &= \mathbf{A}^{-1}\mathbf{B}_q \\ \pi_{21} &= \mathbf{A}^{-1}\mathbf{C}_1 \\ \vdots \quad & \quad \vdots \\ \pi_{2p} &= \mathbf{A}^{-1}\mathbf{C}_p \end{aligned}$$

The $\mathbf{e'_t}$ vector is given by $\mathbf{A}^{-1}\mathbf{e_t}$, i.e. each of the elements of the $\mathbf{e'_t}$ vector is a linear combination of the elements in the $\mathbf{e_t}$ vector; $\pi_{10}, \ldots, \pi_{1q}$ are $(n \times k)$ matrices of numerical coefficients of order $n \times k$, while $\pi_{21}, \ldots, \pi_{2p}$ are matrices of numerical coefficients of order $n \times n$.

We are now ready to consider the standard procedure for solving a linear system. In (2.14) we have a set of n equations each of which expresses one of the n endogenous variables of the system as a numerical linear combination of the m predetermined variables and the disturbances. To solve a linear KK system for a specified set of values of the m predetermined variables we have merely to substitute these values into the right-hand side of (2.14) together with a specified set of values for the structural-form residuals (the elements of $\mathbf{e_t}$) and hence for the elements of $\mathbf{e'_t}$. Frequently the solution is generated by putting all residuals equal to zero, though, as we shall see later on, this is by no means always the case.

Since the equations in (2.14) enable us to generate the solution of the system for any specified set of values of the predetermined variables, they may appropriately be called the *solution expressions* which are implied by the system. A more common (though less appropriate) name is the *reduced form* of the system. Recall that the system itself (2.10) is referred to as the *structural form*. The elements of the $\mathbf{e'}$ vector are called the *reduced-form residuals* and the elements of the π matrices the *reduced-form coefficients*.

A further distinction which will be put to good use in Chapters 4 and 6 is that between the restricted and unrestricted reduced forms of the system. The essential point here is that the reduced-form coefficients of (2.14) can be derived in two different ways. They can be estimated directly just like the parameters of the structural form. Alternatively they can be derived by substituting the estimates of the structural parameters in the expressions for the π matrices given below (2.14). In the first case (2.14) is referred to as the *unrestricted* reduced form. In the second case it is called the *restricted* reduced form because the numbers which characterise it have been derived by taking into account all the restrictions on the reduced-form coefficients imposed by the structural form.

We shall now illustrate the above discussion by applying it to SYSTEM I. From earlier discussion we know that, for SYSTEM I, (2.12) reduces to:

$$\mathbf{A}\mathbf{y_t} = \mathbf{B_0}\mathbf{x_t} + \mathbf{C_1}\mathbf{y_{t-1}} + \mathbf{e_t} \tag{2.15}$$

where

$$\mathbf{A} = \begin{bmatrix} 1 & -0.6 & 0 & 0 \\ 0 & 1 & -1 & 1 \\ -1 & 0 & 1 & 0 \\ 0 & 0 & -0.3 & 1 \end{bmatrix}$$

$$\mathbf{B_0} = \begin{bmatrix} 0 & 0 \\ 0 & 0 \\ 1 & 1 \\ 0 & 0 \end{bmatrix} \qquad \mathbf{C_1} = \begin{bmatrix} 0.2 & 0 & 0 & 0 \\ 0 & 0 & 0 & 0 \\ 0 & 0 & 0 & 0 \\ 0 & 0 & 0 & 0 \end{bmatrix}$$

$$\mathbf{y_t} = \begin{bmatrix} C_t \\ X_t \\ Y_t \\ T_t \end{bmatrix} \qquad \mathbf{x_t} = \begin{bmatrix} G_t \\ I_t \end{bmatrix}$$

$$\mathbf{y_{t-1}} = \begin{bmatrix} C_{t-1} \\ X_{t-1} \\ Y_{t-1} \\ T_{t-1} \end{bmatrix} \qquad \mathbf{e_t} = \begin{bmatrix} e_{1t} \\ 0 \\ 0 \\ e_{4t} \end{bmatrix}$$

The inverse of the coefficient matrix **A** in this case is:

$$\mathbf{A}^{-1} = \begin{bmatrix} 1.7241 & 1.0345 & 0.7241 & -1.0345 \\ 1.2069 & 1.7241 & 1.2069 & -1.7241 \\ 1.7241 & 1.0345 & 1.7241 & -1.0345 \\ 0.5172 & 0.3103 & 0.5172 & 0.6897 \end{bmatrix}$$

from which it is a simple matter to show that π_{10} and π_{21} are given by:

$$\pi_{10} = \mathbf{A}^{-1}\mathbf{B}_0 = \begin{bmatrix} 0.7241 & 0.7241 \\ 1.2069 & 1.2069 \\ 1.7241 & 1.7241 \\ 0.5172 & 0.5172 \end{bmatrix}$$

$$\pi_{21} = \mathbf{A}^{-1}\mathbf{C}_1 = \begin{bmatrix} 0.3448 & 0 & 0 & 0 \\ 0.2414 & 0 & 0 & 0 \\ 0.3448 & 0 & 0 & 0 \\ 0.1034 & 0 & 0 & 0 \end{bmatrix}$$

Thus the reduced form (set of solution expressions) of SYSTEM I is:

$$\begin{bmatrix} C_t \\ X_t \\ Y_t \\ T_t \end{bmatrix} = \begin{bmatrix} 0.7241 & 0.7241 \\ 1.2069 & 1.2069 \\ 1.7241 & 1.7241 \\ 0.5172 & 0.5172 \end{bmatrix}$$

$$\begin{bmatrix} G_t \\ I_t \end{bmatrix} + \begin{bmatrix} 0.3448 & 0 & 0 & 0 \\ 0.2414 & 0 & 0 & 0 \\ 0.3448 & 0 & 0 & 0 \\ 0.1034 & 0 & 0 & 0 \end{bmatrix} \begin{bmatrix} C_{t-1} \\ X_{t-1} \\ Y_{t-1} \\ T_{t-1} \end{bmatrix} + \mathbf{e}'_t \quad (2.16)$$

where $\mathbf{e}'_t = \mathbf{A}^{-1}\mathbf{e}_t$. This expression can be expanded to give the following four equations, one for each of the endogenous variables of the system:

$$\begin{aligned} C_t &= 0.7241G_t + 0.7241I_t + 0.3448C_{t-1} + e'_{1t} \\ X_t &= 1.2069G_t + 1.2069I_t + 0.2414C_{t-1} + e'_{2t} \\ Y_t &= 1.7241G_t + 1.7241I_t + 0.3448C_{t-1} + e'_{3t} \\ T_t &= 0.5172G_t + 0.5172I_t + 0.1034C_{t-1} + e'_{4t} \end{aligned} \quad (2.17)$$

In (2.17) e'_{1t}, ..., e'_{4t} are the elements in the $\mathbf{e}'_t$ vector of (2.16).

The set of expressions (2.17) is, of course, the *restricted* reduced form. The *unrestricted* reduced form of SYSTEM I would be a set of expressions of exactly the same form as (2.17). The coefficients would be different, however, since they would be estimated directly instead of being derived via the estimates of the parameters of the structural form.

To solve SYSTEM I for any specified set of values of the three predctermined variables, G_t, I_t and C_{t-1}, we have merely to substitute these values into the right-hand side of (2.17) together with a set of values for the structural-form residuals and hence for the reduced-form residuals. If all structural-form residuals are allotted the value zero for purposes of the solution, the same will be true of the reduced-form residuals since, as already pointed out, the latter are merely linear combinations of the former.

2.3 Solution of non-linear systems

In the previous section we have seen that, in the case of a linear system, one can obtain the solution of the system, for any set of values of the predetermined variables, simply by substituting these values into the system's solution expressions (reduced form). Unfortunately, this simple solution procedure cannot be applied to non-linear systems since, in general, solution expressions cannot be derived in the non-linear case, i.e. in general there is no reduced form of a non-linear system. The alternative is to employ one of the numerous numerical or iterative procedures which have been devised by mathematicians for the purpose of solving sets of non-linear simultaneous equations. In this section we shall give a brief description of two such procedures – the Gauss–Seidel method and the Newton–Raphson method, both of which are nowadays widely applied to the solution of non-linear KK systems.

To explain these solution procedures we shall make use of the following simple illustrative non-linear KK system to which we shall refer as SYSTEM II:

$$C_t = 0.6X_t + 0.2C_{t-1} + e_{1t} \tag{2.18}$$

$$X_t \equiv Y_t - T_t \tag{2.19}$$

$$Y_t \equiv C_t + G_t + I_t \tag{2.20}$$

$$T_t \equiv R_t Y_t \tag{2.21}$$

$$R_t = 0.04 + 0.00004Y_t + e_{2t} \tag{2.22}$$

The first three equations are identical to those of SYSTEM I. The simple linear tax function of the earlier system has been replaced, however, by a pair of relationships. The first of these, equation (2.21), is definitional in that net tax collections is given as the product of the average tax rate (denoted by R_t – the only new variable introduced) and real gross domestic product. Since it involves a product of endogenous variables, this equation is non-linear in the variables which means that SYSTEM II is a non-linear system. The other equation (2.22) explains the average tax rate R_t as a linear function of real gross domestic product.

Once again the numbers in the above illustrative KK system are to be regarded as parameter estimates which have been made from the appropriate statistical data.

Gauss–Seidel method

To explain the Gauss–Seidel method consider the following general representation of a non-linear KK system:

$$\begin{aligned} y_{1t} &= f_1(y_{2t}, y_{3t}, \ldots, y_{nt}, \bar{x}_{1t}, \ldots, \bar{x}_{mt}) + e_{1t} \\ y_{2t} &= f_2(y_{1t}, y_{3t}, \ldots, y_{nt}, \bar{x}_{1t} \ldots, \bar{x}_{mt}) + e_{2t} \\ &\vdots \\ y_{nt} &= f_n(y_{1t}, y_{2t}, \ldots, y_{n-1,t}, \bar{x}_{1t}, \ldots, \bar{x}_{mt}) + e_{nt} \end{aligned} \tag{2.23}$$

This representation differs from (2.12) in two respects. First, it is written with a specific 'normalisation' in mind. The first equation is regarded as explaining the endogenous variable y_{1t}, the second y_{2t}, and so on. Second, in the interests of clarity of exposition, the distinction between the lagged endogenous variables and the current and lagged exogenous variables has been suppressed – all the predetermined variables are embraced by the x_{it}. The bars over the x_{it} are designed to emphasise that they stand for the particular values of the predetermined variables for which the solution is being generated; $f_1, f_2, \ldots, f_n$ stand for specified numerical functional forms. In general, all are non-linear; in practice many will be linear.

Like all iterative solution procedures, the Gauss–Seidel method calls for a set of 'starting values' – for each endogenous variable of the system. These take the form of a set of guesses about the solution values of the endogenous variables. Most often, the guess for a particular endogenous variable will be its observed or historical value in period t. (When, as in forecasting applications, discussed in Chapter 9, the observed value is not available, a lagged value is used.) Denote the starting values for the endogenous variables in period t by:

$$y_{1t}^0, y_{2t}^0, \ldots, y_{nt}^0$$

The Gauss–Seidel iterations proceed from these starting values according to:

$$\begin{aligned}
y_{1t}^{i+1} &= f_1(y_{2t}^i, \quad y_{3t}^i, \quad \ldots, \quad y_{nt}^i, \quad x_{1t}, \ldots, x_{mt}) + e_{1t} \\
y_{2t}^{i+1} &= f_2(y_{1t}^{i+1}, \quad y_{3t}^i, \quad \ldots, \quad y_{nt}^i, \quad x_{1t}, \ldots, x_{mt}) + e_{2t} \\
&\vdots \\
y_{nt}^{i+1} &= f_n(y_t^{i+1}, \quad y_{2t}^{i+1}, \ldots, \quad y_{n-1,t}^{i+1}, \quad x_{1t}, \ldots, x_{mt}) + e_{nt}
\end{aligned} \qquad (2.24)$$

Initially i is set at zero and for subsequent iterations its value is successively 1, 2, 3 ...

The iterative process continues until the values of the endogenous variables in successive iterations converge to a pre-set level of tolerance, δ. That is, iteration ceases when:

$$\left| \frac{y_{jt}^{i+1} - y_{jt}^i}{y_{jt}^i} \right| < \delta \text{ for all } j = 1, 2, \ldots, n$$

(If any of the endogenous variables can have a solution value of zero, the denominator is replaced by $y_{jt}^i + 0.0001$ to ensure that the division is always defined.) It is conventional to set the tolerance level at one-tenth of 1 per cent ($\delta = 0.001$). Thus iterations continue until the proportionate change between successive iterations is smaller than 0.001 for every endogenous variable.

The Gauss–Seidel solution procedure can be illustrated by applying it to SYSTEM II. For this purpose we shall suppose that the values allotted to the three predetermined variables are:

$$I_t = \$534\text{m}$$
$$G_t = \$472\text{m} \quad (2.25)$$
$$C_{t-1} = \$2{,}147\text{m}$$

and that both e_{1t} and e_{2t} are put equal to zero.

As our starting values we shall use the period t historical values:

$$C_t^0 = \$2{,}375\text{m} \qquad X_t^0 = \$2{,}539\text{m} \qquad Y_t^0 = \$3{,}009\text{m}$$
$$T_t^0 = \$470\text{m} \qquad R_t^0 = 0.156 \quad (2.26)$$

As before, the zero superscript is used to denote 'initial guess about solution value'.

The first interation then procceds as follows. The new value of C_t, denoted by C_t^1, is calculated by substituting into the right-hand side of the consumption expenditure equation (2.18) the values of the endogenous variables given by the set of initial guesses and the value allotted to the predetermined variable C_{t-1}. This gives:

$$C_t^1 = 0.6X_t^0 + 0.2C_{t-1} = 1{,}952.8$$

A new value of X_t denoted by X_t^1, is calculated in a similar way from:

$$X_t^1 = Y_t^0 - T_t^0 = 2{,}539.0$$

When it comes to calculating the new value of Y_t, Y_t^1, we make use of the current iteration value of C_t (that is, C_t^1) rather than the initial guess C_t^0. Thus, the new value of Y_t is found from:

$$Y_t^1 = C_t^1 + G_t + I_t = 2{,}958.0$$

Similarly, having found a new value for Y_t, we can make use of this, rather than the initial value Y_t^0, when we come to calculate the new values for each of the two remaining endogenous variables T_t and R_t. The results are:

$$T_t^1 = R_t^0 Y_t^1 = 461.6$$
$$R_t^1 = 0.04 + 0.00004Y_t^1 = 0.158$$

The results of the second iteration are:

$$\begin{aligned}
C_t^2 &= 0.6X_t^1 + 0.2C_{t-1} &&= 1{,}952.8\\
X_t^2 &= Y_t^1 - T_t^1 &&= 2{,}497.2\\
Y_t^2 &= C_t^2 + G_t + I_t &&= 2{,}958.8\\
T_t^2 &= R_t^1 Y_t^2 &&= 468.5\\
R_t^2 &= 0.04 + 0.00004Y_t^2 &&= 0.158
\end{aligned}$$

Notice that the second iteration proceeds along exactly the same lines as the first. The only difference is that the 'old' values used in the C and X equations are those obtained from the first iteration rather than the initial guesses which were used in the first iteration. Similarly the results of the third iteration are:

$$\begin{aligned}
C_t^3 &= 0.6X_t^2 + 0.2C_{t-1} &&= 1{,}927.7\\
X_t^3 &= Y_t^2 - T_t^2 &&= 2{,}490.3\\
Y_t^3 &= C_t^3 + I_t + G_t &&= 2{,}933.7\\
T_t^3 &= R_t^2 Y_t^3 &&= 464.6\\
R_t^3 &= 0.04 + 0.00004Y_t^3 &&= 0.157
\end{aligned}$$

The iterative process is continued until the absolute proportionate change between successive iterations is smaller than 0.001 for every endogenous variable. Convergence, thus defined, is reached after eleven iterations. The corresponding (solution) values of the endogenous variables are:

$$\tilde{C}_t = 1{,}901.3 \qquad \tilde{X}_t = 2{,}454.2 \qquad \tilde{Y}_t = 2{,}907.3$$

$$\tilde{T}_t = 454.6 \qquad \tilde{R}_t = 0.156$$

We place a tilde (~) over each endogenous variable in this case to emphasise that the value shown is its (approximate) *solution* value – the value which satisfies all five relationships of the system (approximately) when the values of (2.25) are alloted to the predetermined variables and when both disturbances are put at zero.

The word 'approximate' in the preceding sentence deserves some emphasis. Whereas the solution values for a linear system are always exact, those for a non-linear system are always approximate because they are necessarily based on a finite number of iterations, i.e. of necessity the iterations are stopped before exact solution values are found. One can always derive more exact solution values by carrying the iterative process further, i.e. by lowering the level of tolerance. But so long as the level of tolerance is above zero (as in practice it must be) the solution values which finally emerge will never satisfy all relationships of the system exactly. The above applies, of course, to solutions generated by any iterative procedure – not only to Gauss–Seidel solutions.

That the values of $\tilde{C}_t$, etc., presented earlier do, indeed, represent an approximate solution of SYSTEM II for the specified set of values of the predetermined variables is easily verified. Substituting the solution value $\tilde{X}_t$ into the right-hand side of the first equation gives:

$$\begin{aligned} 0.6\tilde{X}_t + 0.2C_{t-1} &= 0.6(2{,}454.2) + 0.2(2{,}147) \\ &= 1{,}901.9 \end{aligned}$$

which is approximately equal to the solution value for C_t ($\tilde{C}_t = 1{,}901.3$). Similarly, for the remaining equations we have:

$$\begin{aligned} \tilde{Y}_t - \tilde{T}_t &= 2{,}907.3 - 454.6 \\ &= 2{,}452.7 \simeq \tilde{X}_t = 2{,}454.2 \\ \tilde{C}_t + G_t + I_t &= 1{,}901.3 + 472.0 + 534.0 \\ &= 2{,}907.3 = \tilde{Y}_t = 2{,}907.3 \\ \tilde{R}_t\tilde{Y}_t &= (0.156)\,(2907.3) \\ &= \;453.5 \simeq \tilde{T}_t = 454.6 \\ 0.04 + 0.00004\tilde{Y}_t &= 0.04 + 0.00004(2{,}907.3) \\ &= 0.156 = \tilde{R}_t = 0.156 \end{aligned}$$

Newton–Raphson method

An alternative representation of the general non-linear KK system is called for to explain the Newton–Raphson method of solving non-linear systems. This takes the following form:

$$\begin{array}{llllll} f_1(y_{1t}, y_{2t}, \ldots, y_{nt}, & \bar{x}_{1t}, \ldots, \bar{x}_{mt}) & + e_{1t} = 0 \\ f_2(y_{1t}, y_{2t}, \ldots, y_{nt}, & \bar{x}_{1t}, \ldots, \bar{x}_{mt}) & + e_{2t} = 0 \\ \vdots \quad \vdots \quad\quad \vdots & \quad\quad\quad \vdots & \;\vdots \quad\; \vdots \\ f_n(y_{1t}, y_{2t}, \ldots, y_{nt}, & \bar{x}_{1t}, \ldots, \bar{x}_{mt}) & + e_{nt} = 0 \end{array} \qquad (2.27)$$

Once again, no distinction is made between the three categories of predetermined variables – all are covered by the $\bar{x}_{1t}$. Likewise, $f_1, f_2, \ldots, f_n$

again stand for specified numerical functional forms. In this instance, however, no particular normalisation is used in the representation of the system. Indeed, as we shall see, one of the advantages that the Newton–Raphson method has over the Gauss–Seidel method is that no normalisation is required.

A more compact representation of the non-linear system is possible if we define the $(1 \times n)$ vector:

$$\mathbf{y} = [y_{1t}\ y_{2t}\ \ldots\ y_{nt}],$$

the $(1 \times m)$ vector:

$$\bar{\mathbf{x}} = [\bar{x}_{1t}\ \bar{x}_{2t}\ \ldots\ \bar{x}_{mt}]$$

and the $(n \times 1)$ vector-valued function:

$$\mathbf{f}(\mathbf{y}, \bar{\mathbf{x}}) = \begin{bmatrix} f_1(\mathbf{y}, \bar{\mathbf{x}}) \\ f_2(\mathbf{y}, \bar{\mathbf{x}}) \\ \vdots \quad \vdots \\ f_n(\mathbf{y}, \bar{\mathbf{x}}) \end{bmatrix}$$

The system is then:

$$\mathbf{f}(\mathbf{y}, \bar{\mathbf{x}}) + \mathbf{e} = \mathbf{0}$$

where $\mathbf{e}$ is the $(n \times 1)$ vector of residuals.

The next step is to define the so-called 'Jacobian matrix' of the system. The elements of the *first* row of the Jacobian matrix are the partial derivatives of the *first* equation with respect to the *first* endogenous variable, the *second* endogenous variable, and so on. Similarly, the elements of the *second* row are the partial derivatives of the *second* equation of the system with respect to the *first* endogenous variable, the *second* endogenous variable, and so on. The remaining rows of the Jacobian matrix are defined in a similar way for the remaining equations of the system. The form of the Jacobian matrix, a matrix of order $n \times n$, is therefore:

$$\mathbf{J} = \begin{bmatrix} \frac{\partial f_1}{\partial y_1} & \frac{\partial f_1}{\partial y_2} & \cdots & \frac{\partial f_1}{\partial y_n} \\ \frac{\partial f_2}{\partial y_1} & \frac{\partial f_2}{\partial y_2} & \cdots & \frac{\partial f_2}{\partial y_n} \\ \vdots & \vdots & & \vdots \\ \frac{\partial f_n}{\partial y_1} & \frac{\partial f_n}{\partial y_2} & \cdots & \frac{\partial fn}{\partial y_n} \end{bmatrix}$$

Note that, in general, since the f are non-linear functions, the elements of $\mathbf{J}$ are themselves functions of $\mathbf{y}$.

Like the Gauss–Seidel method, the Newton–Raphson procedure is an iterative method requiring starting values. These are denoted by:

$$\mathbf{y^0} = [y^0_{1t}\ y^0_{2t} \ldots y^0_{nt}]$$

When the Jacobian matrix is evaluated at these values of the endogenous variables and the specified values of the predetermined variables, the result is denoted by $\mathbf{J^0}$. The Newton–Raphson iterations then proceed according to:

$$\mathbf{y^{i+1}} = \mathbf{y^i} - [\mathbf{J^i}]^{-1}\{\mathbf{f}(\mathbf{y^i}, \bar{\mathbf{x}}) + \mathbf{e}\} \tag{2.28}$$

i being set initially at zero and then at 1, 2, ..., in successive iterations. The iterative process continues until the values of the endogenous variables in successive iterations converge to a pre-set level of tolerance, in the sense explained above in connection with the Gauss–Seidel method.

SYSTEM II can be used to illustrate the Newton–Raphson solution method. For this purpose we shall use the same values for the predetermined variables as were used in the explanation of the Gauss–Seidel method – those set out in (2.25). We shall also use the same 'starting values' and, as before, put both e_{1t} and e_{2t} equal to zero.

The first step in applying the Newton–Raphson method to SYSTEM II is to write the system in the form of (2.27). Thus:

$$\begin{aligned} C_t - 0.6X_t - 429.4 &= 0 \\ X_t - Y_t + T_t &= 0 \\ -C_t + Y_t - 1{,}006.0 &= 0 \\ -R_tY_t + T_t &= 0 \\ -0.00004Y_t + R_t - 0.04 &= 0 \end{aligned}$$

The next step is to form the Jacobian matrix of the system. This requires that the endogenous variables be numbered in some arbitrary fashion. We call C_t the first endogenous variable, X_t the second, Y_t the third, T_t the fourth and R_t the fifth. Thus the Jacobian of SYSTEM II, denoted by **J**, is:

$$\mathbf{J} = \begin{bmatrix} 1 & -0.6 & 0 & 0 & 0 \\ 0 & 1 & -1 & 1 & 0 \\ -1 & 0 & 1 & 0 & 0 \\ 0 & 0 & -R_t & 1 & -Y_t \\ 0 & 0 & -0.00004 & 0 & 1 \end{bmatrix} \tag{2.29}$$

It will be noticed that only two of the elements in the fourth row of **J** (the third and the fifth) involve endogenous variables. This is due to the fact that only the fourth equation is non-linear. The next step is to use the relevant starting values to convert these two elements into actual numbers to convert the Jacobian into a fully numerical matrix. This numerical Jacobian is $\mathbf{J}^0$. For $\mathbf{J}^0$, then, we have:

$$\mathbf{J}^0 = \begin{bmatrix} 1 & -0.6 & 0 & 0 & 0 \\ 0 & 1 & -1 & 1 & 0 \\ -1 & 0 & 1 & 0 & 0 \\ 0 & 0 & -0.156 & 1 & -3{,}009 \\ 0 & 0 & -0.00004 & 0 & 1 \end{bmatrix} \tag{2.30}$$

The third step is to find the inverse of $\mathbf{J}^0$, which is given by:

$$[\mathbf{J}^0]^{-1} = \begin{bmatrix} 1.76736 & 1.06042 & 0.76736 & -1.06042 & -3{,}190.78994 \\ 1.27893 & 1.76736 & 1.27893 & -1.76736 & -5{,}317.98323 \\ 1.76736 & 1.06042 & 1.76736 & -1.06042 & -3{,}190.78994 \\ 0.48843 & 0.29306 & 0.48843 & -0.70694 & 2{,}127.19329 \\ 0.00007 & 0.00004 & 0.00007 & -0.00004 & 0.87237 \end{bmatrix} \tag{2.31}$$

Next, we use the starting values and the specified values of the predetermined variables once again to evaluate the left-hand side of each equation of the system and arrange the results into a vector, the first element of which relates to the first equation, the second element to the second equation, and so on. This vector is designated $\mathbf{f}(\mathbf{y}^0, \bar{\mathbf{x}})$. (Recall that all elements of the vector $\mathbf{e}$ have been put at zero.) Thus $\mathbf{f}(\mathbf{y}^0, \bar{\mathbf{x}})$ is given by:

$$\mathbf{f}(\mathbf{y}^0, \bar{\mathbf{x}}) = \begin{bmatrix} 422.2 \\ 0 \\ -372.0 \\ 0.596 \\ -0.00436 \end{bmatrix} \tag{2.32}$$

We are now ready to carry out the first iteration. The vector of starting values $\mathbf{y}^0$ and the vector arising from the first iteration $\mathbf{y}^1$ are:

$$\mathbf{y}^0 = \begin{bmatrix} 2{,}375 \\ 2{,}539 \\ 3{,}009 \\ 470 \\ 0.156 \end{bmatrix} \qquad \mathbf{y}^1 = \begin{bmatrix} C_t^1 \\ X_t^1 \\ Y_t^1 \\ T_t^1 \\ R_t^1 \end{bmatrix} \tag{2.33}$$

$\mathbf{y}^1$ is evaluated from the following expression:

$$\mathbf{y}^1 = \mathbf{y}^0 - [\mathbf{J}^0]^{-1} \cdot \mathbf{f}(\mathbf{y}^0, \bar{\mathbf{x}}) \tag{2.34}$$

which is obtained by setting i to zero in (2.28). If we carry out the matrix operations indicated by this expression we find:

$$\mathbf{y}^1 = \begin{bmatrix} 1{,}900.9987 \\ 2{,}452.6646 \\ 2{,}906.9987 \\ 454.3342 \\ 0.1563 \end{bmatrix} \tag{2.35}$$

Further iterations proceed in the same way. The vector arising from the *second* iteration is given by:

$$\mathbf{y}^2 = \mathbf{y}^1 - [\mathbf{J}^1]^{-1} \cdot \mathbf{f}(\mathbf{y}^1, \bar{\mathbf{x}}) \tag{2.36}$$

Here $\mathbf{J}^1$ is the numerical Jacobian generated by means of the values which emerge from the *first iteration* instead of by means of the starting values, while $\mathbf{f}(\mathbf{y}^1, \bar{\mathbf{x}})$ is the vector of left-hand sides evaluated by means of the first-iteration values. By application of this expression we find that $\mathbf{y}^2$ is given by:

$$\mathbf{y}^2 = \begin{bmatrix} C_t^2 \\ X_t^2 \\ Y_t^2 \\ T_t^2 \\ R_t^2 \end{bmatrix} = \begin{bmatrix} 1{,}901.0291 \\ 2{,}452.7152 \\ 2{,}907.0291 \\ 454.3139 \\ 0.1563 \end{bmatrix} \tag{2.37}$$

The iterations proceed until the absolute proportionate change between successive iterations is smaller than the pre-set tolerance level for every endogenous variable. It we adopt one-tenth of 1 per cent ($\delta = 0.001$) as our tolerance level we find that, for SYSTEM II, convergence is reached after the second iteration. Thus the (approximate) solution of SYSTEM II, for the given values of the predetermined variables, may be written as:

$$\tilde{C}_t = 1{,}901.0 \qquad \tilde{X}_t = 2{,}452.7 \qquad \tilde{Y}_t = 2{,}907.0$$

$$\tilde{T}_t = 454.3 \qquad \tilde{R}_t = 0.156$$

We shall now conclude this discussion of the procedures which are nowadays used to solve non-linear KK systems by briefly mentioning certain difficulties to which they are subject, especially when the system, as is usual, is both large and complex.

One important feature of the Gauss–Seidel method is that it is sensitive to the way in which the relationships are ordered. That is, the Gauss–Seidel iterations may converge fairly rapidly when the relationships are evaluated in one particular order and converge very slowly or not at all when they are ordered in a different way. If the initial ordering of the system is one which involves convergence problems, there may be trouble because there will be no way of determining what sort of adjustment to the ordering will be worth trying.

The Newton–Raphson method is not subject to this particular difficulty but it may be sensitive to the choice of starting values. That is, the Newton–Raphson iterations may converge reasonably rapidly for one set of starting values and only slowly, or not at all for a different, equally plausible set. If the initial starting values give rise to convergence problems, the situation could be troublesome because here, too, there will be no clear pointers as to ways in which the starting values should be changed.

The Gauss–Seidel method is also sensitive to the way in which the equations of the system are normalised. That is, the Gauss–Seidel iterations may not converge with the system written in a particular way but may converge when the system is written in a different but algebraically equivalent way. Once again there is no way of knowing (apart from trying out the alternatives) which alternative normalisation, if any, will work. The Newton–Raphson method does not require normalisation at all and, for this reason, is not subject to the same potential difficulty.

Another limitation of the Newton–Raphson method is that, in general, it is not applicable to very large systems. This is bound up with the fact that the method calls for inversion of a matrix, of order equal to the number of relationships in the system, at every iteration. For systems of more than moderate size this inversion operation will not be computationally feasible unless the system can be appropriately decomposed.

Finally, we should note that, in practical implementations of the Gauss–Seidel and Newton–Raphson methods, the algorithms are modified in various ways to speed up the rate of convergence, to provide some insurance against the possibility that they fail to converge at all or to reduce the total computational burden and hence the cost of the procedure. These modifications vary from one implementation to another and need not concern us here. See, however, Hughes-Hallett (1981) for a discussion of some of these issues.

Reference and further reading

Hughes-Hallet, A. J. (1981) 'Some Extensions and Comparisons in the Theory of Gauss–Seidel Iterative Techniques for Solving Large Equation Systems', in E. G. Charatsis (ed.), *Proceedings of the Econometric Society European Meeting 1979*, North-Holland, Amsterdam.

Part II Construction of KK Systems

3 SPECIFICATION OF KK SYSTEMS

3.1 The Keynesian macro-analytical system

The purpose of this and the following three chapters is to consider in some detail the *construction* of modern KK macroeconometric systems. Once a KK system has been constructed it normally goes through a lengthy process of validation and is then put to work in a variety of ways. Validation of KK systems will be dealt with in Part III and their applications in Part IV.

For purposes of discussion the construction of a KK system can be broken down into two distinct stages. The first comprises the specification of the system. Under this head falls the tasks of setting out the relationships of the system in explicit mathematical form and classifying the variables which appear in those relationships into the 'endogenous' and 'predetermined' groups so that the system is complete in the sense that the number of endogenous variables is exactly equal to the number of relationships. The second stage comprises the estimation of the sytem. Here the various parameters which give the stochastic relationships of the system their mathematical form are replaced by actual numbers. This is usually done by applying some statistical technique (frequently of a highly sophisticated kind) to time-series data on the variables of the system. Stage 1 (specification) will be discussed in the present chapter, and stage 2 (estimation) in Chapters 4, 5 and 6.

As far as specification is concerned, the most important antecedent of modern KK macroeconometric systems is the macro-analytical system put forward by Keynes (1936) in *The General Theory of Employment, Interest and Money*. This system still forms a useful point of departure for a discussion of specification in modern KK systems, even though they have evolved over the last three decades to the point where their origin in *The General Theory* is no longer easy to detect.

The system of *The General Theory* may be set out as follows:

$$C = C(Y) \tag{3.1}$$

$$I = I(i) \tag{3.2}$$

$$Y = C + I + \bar{G} \tag{3.3}$$

$$M_d = M_d(Y, i) \qquad (3.4)$$

$$M_d = \bar{M}_s \qquad (3.5)$$

$$Y = Y(N) \qquad (3.6)$$

$$\frac{dY}{dN} = \bar{W}/P \qquad (3.7)$$

where C = consumption expenditure
I = investment expenditure
G = government expenditure
Y = aggregate income or output
i = rate of interest
N = employment
W = money wage level
P = price level
M_d = stock of money demanded
M_s = actual stock of money

The endogenous variables in this system are C, Y, I, i, P, N and M_d. The predetermined variables (all exogenous) are the three which appear with a bar, namely $\bar{G}$, $\bar{W}$ and $\bar{M}_s$.

The first three relationships deal with the product market: (3.1) and (3.2) are relationships which determine, respectively, the aggregate demand for consumption goods and the aggregate demand for investment goods, while (3.3) equates the aggregate demand for final goods and services as a whole with the available supply of such goods and services, i.e. (3.3) imposes market-clearing in the goods market. The fourth and fifth relationships are concerned with the money market: (3.4) determines the stock of money balances which individuals and firms in the aggregate wish to hold, while (3.5) equates the desired stock of money balances with the actual stock, i.e. (3.5) imposes market-clearing in the money market. The last two relationships apply to the labour market: (3.6) is a short-run aggregate production function, while (3.7), in which the marginal physical product of labour and the real wage are equated, is the condition for profit maximisation under perfect competition.

The key features of the Keynesian macro-analytical system, (3.1)–(3.7), may be listed as follows:

1. The use of a threefold categorisation of aggregate demand in the goods-market component.
2. The treatment of G, W and M_s as exogenous.
3. The absence of 'open-economy' variables and relationships.
4. The absence of lags in the behavioural relationships.

5. The absence of any explicit 'expectational variables'.
6. The absence of specific mathematical form in the case of relationships (3.1), (3.2), (3.4) and (3.6).

In the sections which follow, discussion of the specification of KK systems will be arranged around these six standpoints. By treating the topic in this way, we are deliberately restricting ourselves to a broad discussion of the main issues. To go further and attempt to give an appreciation of the detail would be futile. The only way in which this can be obtained is by taking the equations of one or more of the systems listed in Table 1.2 and working carefully through them.

3.2 Disaggregation of aggregate demand

For all practical purposes the KK system-builder is never content with the threefold division of aggregate demand from domestic sources on which the goods-market component of the Keynesian macro-analytical system is based – the division into consumption expenditure, investment expenditure and government expenditure. This is hardly surprising in view of the heterogeneous nature of each of these three components. Typically the consumption-expenditure category is split at the very least into two smaller categories and the investment-expenditure category into three smaller categories. The minimum split in the consumption-expenditure category in modern KK systems is usually into (i) expenditure on non-durable consumer goods, and (ii) expenditure on durable consumer goods, while the minimum split in the investment-expenditure category is usually into (i) expenditure on new buildings, (ii) expenditure on industrial plant and equipment, and (iii) expenditure on inventory accumulation.

The disaggregation outlined in the previous paragraph is a minimum only. Frequently disaggregation is taken a good deal further. For example, a split of government expenditure into (a) capital expenditure, and (b) consumption expenditure, and a further split of each of these two components, are quite common in working KK systems. Again one often finds expenditure on non-durable consumer goods split into (a) expenditure on food, (b) expenditure on rent, and (c) expenditure on other non-durables, while expenditure on durables may be broken down into (a) expenditure on new motor-vehicles, and (b) expenditure on other consumer durable goods. Finally, one sometimes finds expenditure on new buildings split into (a) expenditure on new dwellings, and (b) expenditure on other building and construction, while in some systems both expenditure on industrial plant and equipment and expenditure on inventory accumulation are split into (a) farm, and (b) non-farm.

Once the decision on the degree of disaggregation of the expenditure categories has been taken, the system-builder must decide whether the expenditure variables in the list are to be expressed: (a) in terms of constant prices throughout the system; or (b) in terms of current prices throughout; or (c) in terms of constant prices in some relationships and current prices in others. The decision which the system-builder takes in this matter varies from case to case, but for all practical purposes (a) or (c) is opted for.

Having settled this question, the system-builder must next decide which of the new set of expenditure variables is to be treated as endogenous and which as predetermined. To make this decision the endogenous–predetermined distinction is invoked and applied to each of the new expenditure variables in turn. Recall that, by definition, the predetermined variables of a KK system are those variables which do not interact with other variables in the system; they determine 'this period's' values of other variables *via* the relationships of the system, but are not themselves determined by this period's values of other variables. Evidently, all lagged variables have this property because their values will have been settled before 'this period' begins. Thus all lagged variables must be classified as predetermined. In addition, all variables which are contemporaneous with the endogenous variables (which belong to 'this period') but whose values may be regarded, in some sense, as being determined *outside* the system are candidates for the predetermined class. Such variables are usually labelled 'unlagged exogenous'.

In the nature of the case all of the new set of expenditure variables must belong to 'this period' – none can be lagged. Thus in the light of the discussion of the previous paragraph the question 'Which of them is to be treated as endogenous and which as predetermined?' can therefore be stated more specifically as: 'Which are to be treated as endogenous and which as unlagged exogenous?' Further, from the discussion of the last paragraph it will be clear that this question is equivalent to: Which of the new expenditure variables may be legitimately regarded as being determined *outside* the system (imposed on the system) in some sense and which may not be legitimately so regarded? In making this decision the system-builder will be forced to rely on judgement; there are no hard-and-fast rules to be appealed to. For each variable a judgement will have to be made as to whether there is a significant 'feedback' from other variables in the system or whether the feedback is so slight as to be virtually non-existent. In the former case the variable will be treated as endogenous; in the latter case it will be treated as 'externally determined' and be placed in the predetermined (unlagged exogenous) category. Naturally, what appears to one system-builder as a 'virtually non-existent' feedback may not appear so to another. Thus, while certain expenditure variables are obvious candidates for the predetermined group and are usually found there, one cannot give a list of variables which are always treated in this way. Likely candidates for an exogenous treatment include government-expenditure variables, variables which relate to the farm sector and, at least in the case of systems designed for small open economies, export variables.

Since a KK system must include as many relationships as there are endogenous variables for a solution to be possible (see section 2.1), it is necessary for the KK system-builder to provide a relationship for each of the new expenditure variables to which it is decided to give an endogenous treatment – a relationship which 'explains' the variable concerned. Usually but not necessarily each new relationship will give some new endogenous expenditure variable as a specific function (e.g. a linear function) of certain 'explanatory variables' and a random disturbance.

Some of the explanatory variables which appear in the relationships introduced to explain the new endogenous expenditure variables will have to be treated as endogenous in line with the earlier discussion.An additional relationship will be required to explain each of these new endogenous variables. Certain explanatory variables will be introduced in the process of specifying these relationships. Typically some of these will be new. If any of these new explanatory variables are placed in the endogenous category, further relationships will be needed to explain *them*. And so on. The additional relationships which originate in the explanatory variables of the new expenditure relationships and which are a direct consequence of basic decisions taken about the desirable degree of disaggregation of expenditure categories and about the endogeneity of particular variables may be quite numerous – possibly running into hundreds.

3.3 Specification of individual equations

We turn now to the more specific question of the process by which the relationships which are included in the system as the outcome of the decisions described in the previous section are specified. The task of specifying the explanatory variables, the lag structure and the mathematical form of these relationships are usually carried out together. Typically there are two distinct stages. In the first stage a preliminary version of the relationship is laid down, using an argument based on generally accepted economic theory. This preliminary version will be specific as regards explanatory variables, lag structure and mathematical form. In the second stage various econometric procedures are applied to this 'first-draft' relationship in an attempt to discover helpful *ad hoc* (non-theoretical) modifications. We shall consider each stage in turn.

The first stage is best explained by means of an illustration. The illustration we take is the relationship governing expenditure on motor-vehicles which appears in NIF–10. NIF–10 is the most recent version of NIF (NIF for 'National Income Forecasting'), an Australian KK system for which the Australian Treasury and the Australian Bureau of Statistics are jointly responsible. See Department of the Treasury (1981).

We begin by presenting the necessary notation as follows:

CMV	=	expenditure on motor-vehicles in constant prices
CMV^*	=	desired flow of services from motor-vehicles in constant prices
$PCMV$	=	deflator for motor-vehicle purchases
$PCON$	=	deflator for total consumption expenditure
$PCDR$	=	deflator for expenditure on consumer durables
$YDO\$$	=	household disposable income in current prices
$\$LFIN$	=	lending by finance companies in current prices
KMV	=	end-period actual stock of motor-vehicles
KMV^*	=	end-period desired stock of motor-vehicles.

The preliminary version of the NIF-10 relationship for expenditure on motor-vehicles is developed by means of the following theoretical argument. The first step is to lay down a relationship for CMV^*, the desired flow of services from motor-vehicles, namely:

$$CMV^*_t = \{a_0 + a_1(PCMV/PCON)_t + a_2[(PCDR_t - PCDR_{t-4})/PCDR_{t-4}]\}(YDO\$/PCON)_t + a_3(\$LFIN/PCDR)_t \quad (3.8)$$

The foundation for this relationship is the traditional utility-maximising theory of consumer demand, according to which the individual consumer's demand for any good is determined by real income, by the price of the good in question and by the prices of all other goods. This suggests that three of the explanatory variables in a relationship for CMV^* should be aggregate real income, an index of the prices of motor-vehicles and an index of the prices of consumer goods in general. The first is taken care of by the composite variable ($YDO\$/PCON$) and the second and third by the composite relative-price variable ($PCMV/PCON$). Theory suggests a positive sign for a_0, the parameter which measures the response of CMV^* to a change in ($YDO\$/PCON$), and a negative sign for a_1. The variable $(PCDR_t - PCDR_{t-4})/PCDR_{t-4})$ is intended to capture the influence on CMV^* of the *expected* rate of increase in the prices of consumer durables. One would expect the parameter a_2 to have a positive sign since the higher the expected rate of increase in the prices of consumer durables, the stronger the incentive for consumers to buy now rather than later, even if they have to incur costs (e.g. interest payments on additional borrowing) in order to do so. (Note that the real-income variable has both a direct influence on CMV^* via a_0 and an indirect influence via a_1 and a_2; in effect it acts as a scale factor for these parameters and so introduces a non-linearity into the response of CMV^* to changes in the relative-price and expectations variables.) Finally, the composite variable ($\$LFIN/PCDR$) is introduced to cater for the impact of the availability of finance on CMV^*. Other things being equal, CMV^* will be higher, the more readily available is consumer finance, i.e. the expected sign of a_3 is positive.

The next step in the argument is to postulate a relationship of proportionality between the desired flow of services from motor-vehicles and the desired stock of motor-vehicles:

$$KMV_t^* = a_4\, CMV_t^* \tag{3.9}$$

Next, a relationship specifying that the actual stock adjusts to the desired stock via a 'partial-adjustment' process is postulated:

$$KMV_t - KMV_{t-1} = a_5\,(KMV_t^* - KMV_{t-1}) \tag{3.10}$$

Finally, a relationship specifying the connection between the beginning-period and end-period stocks of motor-vehicles is laid down. This takes the form:

$$KMV_t = (KMV_{t-1} + CMV_t) - a_6(KMV_{t-1} + CMV_t/2) \tag{3.11}$$

The parameter a_6 is the rate of physical depreciation. On the assumption that the stock grows linearly over the period $KMV_{t-1} + CMV_t/2$ is the average of the stocks at the beginning of the period, the end of the period and any other number of equally spaced points between. Recalling the definition of a_6, it can be therefore seen that the second term in (3.11) represents the depreciation of motor-vehicles which occurs in the period. Thus (3.11) merely says that the actual (*after*-depreciation) end-period stock is the end-period stock *before* depreciation, i.e. $KMV_{t-1} + CMV_t$, *less* depreciation.

When relationships (3.8), (3.9), (3.10) and (3.11) are combined we get:

$$\begin{aligned} CMV_t = {} & [2a_5/(2 - a_6)][a_4\{a_0 + a_1(PCMV/PCON)_t \\ & + a_2(PCDR_t - PCDR_{t-4})/PCDR_{t-4}\}(YDO\$/PCON)_t] \\ & + a_3(\$LFIN/PCDR)_t + [2(a_6 - a_5)/(2 - a_6)]KMV_{t-1} \end{aligned} \tag{3.12}$$

Equation (3.12) is the preliminary version of the NIF–10 relationship for expenditure on motor-vehicles.

We said earlier that the process of individual-relationship specification usually proceeds in two stages. Having explained the first – use of theory to suggest a preliminary version which is specific as regards the explanatory variables, the lag structure and the mathematical form – with the help of an illustration drawn from NIF, we now proceed to deal with the second. As already indicated, this consists of the application of various econometric techniques to the 'first-draft' relationship with a view to uncovering possibly helpful *ad hoc* modifications.

Typically the exploratory work which comprises the second stage begins with a preliminary estimation of the first-draft relationship. Almost always the estimator used at this point will be OLS (ordinary least squares). This can be attributed to the computational simplicity of OLS and applies even when the intention is eventually to use one of the more sophisticated estimators discussed in the next chapter. For reasons to be explained in Chapter 4, OLS is not necessarily the best choice of estimator in this context. A strong case can be made for using an IV (instrumental variable) estimator. Nevertheless, OLS is the estimator commonly used in practice. Using the output of the preliminary estimation the system-builder will attempt to assess the 'first-draft' relationship in terms of econometric quality. Those parts of the output given most weight in this connection are: (a) the parameter estimates; (b) $\bar{R}^2$; (c) the *t*-ratios; and (d) the D–W, *h* and Wallis autocorrelation statistics. Parameter estimates should be 'sensible' in terms of sign and size, $\bar{R}^2$ should be close to unity, there should be 'healthy' *t*-ratios – equal numerically to at least 2.0 – and the hypotheses of absence of first-order and fourth-order disturbance autocorrelation should be accepted at, say, the 5 or 1 per cent level of significance.

Assuming that the estimated relationship falls down in one or more of these respects, the system-builder will next draw up a list of *ad hoc* modifictions. Normally these will be of three types: (i) omission of explanatory variables; (ii) inclusion of explanatory variables; and (iii) changes to the lag structure.

Modifications of type (i) are commonly suggested by the statistics discussed above. In particular, a low *t*-ratio is a sign that the corresponding explanatory variable might well be dropped.

Modifications of type (ii) are frequently indicated by another part of the output of the preliminary estimation, namely the series of residuals. Examination of the residuals often reveals suggestive patterns. For example, they may be both typically positive and subject to an upward trend. This will suggest that the endogenous variable explained in the relationship is subject to an upward trend not captured by the existing set of explanatory variables. This in turn will suggest that some other explanatory variable with a strong trend component should be introduced. Again there may be a string of three or four unusually large, positive residuals at some point in the sample period. This may draw attention to some special factor, making for abnormally high values of the endogenous variable concerned, which was operating at this point. An appropriate dummy variable may well be a relevant addition to the existing list of explanatory variables. As a final example the residuals may exhibit a pronounced seasonal pattern of the same type as the variable being explained. This will suggest that a set of seasonal dummies could be added with advantage.

Finally, changes to the lag structure are often suggested by evidence from the D–W, *h* and Wallis statistics that disturbance autocorrelation is present. A significant change in lag structure, e.g. one which involves replacing a one-period delay on some explanatory variable by a three-period distributed lag, constitutes a fruitful approach to the problem of removing disturbance correlation because this particular deficiency in an estimated relationship usually reflects mis-specification, and not infrequently this takes the form of mis-specification of the lag structure.

By using the output from the estimation of the first-draft relationship in the above ways the system-builder will emerge with a list of potentially helpful *ad hoc* modifications, either to the explanatory variables or to the lag structure or both. Having incorporated these modifications the builder will next estimate the revised relationship, using the same 'preliminary' estimator – usually OLS – as before. It is to be hoped that the output of the estimation of the revised relationship will show it to be acceptable in terms of econometric quality. If not, the battery of econometric techniques already deployed will be called on a second time in the hope of finding further potentially helpful modifications. The exploratory estimation will continue until a modified form of the first-draft (theoretical) relationship which is satisfactory in terms of sign and size of parameter estimates, $\bar{R}^2$, *t*-ratios and the D–W, *h* and Wallis statistic has been derived.

At this point the system-builder has what might be called a 'second-draft' relationship and the next move might well be to undertake an assessment in terms of predictive success. In this event, the builder would shorten the sample period by dropping off, say, the ten most recent periods and then re-estimate the relationship from the shortened sample period. The re-estimated relationship would then be used to make an *ex post* prediction of the dependent variable for each of the ten periods which now lie outside the sample period. The procedure for so doing would be to substitute the *historical* values of the explanatory variables into the estimated relationship and then to use it to calculate the implied value of the dependent variable. Finally, each of the series of ten outside-sample, *ex post* predictions of the dependent variable would be compared with the corresponding historical value to get an assessment of the preliminary relationship in terms of predictive success.

Another way of assessing the second-draft relationship which the system-builder might well be in a position to exploit is a procedure known as 'dynamic simulation'. Applications of dynamic simulation will be possible provided the explanatory variables in the second-draft relationship include a lagged value of the *dependent* variable. For instance, this will be the case if the partial-adjustment hypothesis has been called on in the development of the relationship, as will be evident from the above discussion of the NIF–10 relationship for expenditure on motor-vehicles.

If feasible, a dynamic simulation would proceed in the following way. First, the estimated relationship would be used to predict the value of the dependent variable for the *first* of the periods which constitute the sample period. This would be done by substituting the historical values of the explanatory variables, *including the lagged dependent variable*, into that relationship. Then the estimated relationship would be used to predict the value of the dependent variable for the *second* of the periods comprising the sample period. This would be done by substituting the historical values of all explanatory variables *except the lagged dependent variable*. The value substituted for this variable would be, not the value actually observed for the first period, but the value *predicted* for the first period by the relationship. This procedure would be repeated, period after period, until the end of the sample period. Thus the output of a dynamic simulation would be a set of T rather special *within-sample, ex post* predictions of the dependent variable where T is the number of periods covered by the sample period. Each of these predictions would be compared with the corresponding historical value and further assessment in terms of predictive success thus obtained.

The system-builder may reasonably expect the 'second-draft' relationship to perform fairly well when evaluated in terms of predictive success along the lines just described, and as a rule this expectation is confirmed. Should this not be the case, however, the process of *ad hoc* modifiction will be continued until an acceptable version is arrived at or until it is realised that further experimentation will be fruitful only when the results of evaluating the system as a whole by means of the procedures discussed in Chapter 8 are available.

3.4 Endogenisation of *G*, M_s and *W*

Among the key features of the Keynesian macro-analytical system identified in section 3.1 is the exogenous treatment of the variables G, M_s and W. The KK system-builder must decide whether to follow suit and treat these variables as exogenous or whether, in view of the intended applications of the system, an endogenous treatment is more appropriate.

Treatment of G

Whether or not the variable G needs to be endogenised depends on: (i) whether it is expressed in constant prices or in current prices; and (ii) whether government expenditure plans are formulated in constant prices or in current prices. Suppose, for example, that expenditure plans are formulated in constant prices. Then G in constant prices is determined by political decisions (i.e. is 'externally determined') and so should be treated as exogenous. G in current prices should therefore be treated as endogenous. The position would be reversed, of course, if government expenditure plans are formulated in current prices.

Assume that the system-builder decides to include a relationship which introduces G in terms of current prices into the system. For example, the goods market-clearing relationship could be specified in terms of current prices. Suppose further that, following the argument of the proceeding paragraph, he decides to place this variable in the endogenous category. He will then need an additional 'endogenising' relationship. Typically this will be an identity which links constant-price G (treated as exogenous) with current-price G – an identity of the form:

current-price G = constant-price G *multiplied by* the government-expenditure implicit deflator

While this identity will serve to endogenise current-price G, it will do so only by introducing the implicit deflator of government expenditure. Should the system-builder decide to treat this new variable as endogenous, a further relationship will be required to explain the implicit deflator. Questions will then arise as to the appropriate explanatory variables, mathematical form and lag structure for this price relationship. The way in which these questions will be answered will be clear from earlier discussion. The first step will be to lay down a preliminary version of the relationship on the basis of relevant economic theory. This preliminary version will then be subjected to various *ad hoc* modifications – suggested by the output of a sequence of exploratory estimations and by the results of predictive exercises of various types.

In the above discussion it has been assumed that G, *aggregate* government expenditure, is the only government-expenditure variable in the system. As indicated earlier, however, one of the features of modern KK systems is that each of the three somewhat heterogeneous aggregate demand categories on which the Keynesian macro-analytical system is based is normally split into several relatively homogeneous components. In the case of the government-expenditure category, the disaggregation typically proceeds by type of *government* (e.g. national, state and local governments may be distinguished), or by type of *expenditure* (e.g. there may be a distinction between defence expenditure and non-defence expenditure or between consumption expenditure and capital expenditure), or both.

Suppose that the government-expenditure demand category is handled in this way. The above discussion will still apply in all essential respects. For example, the component variables will need to be endogenised if they are expressed in terms of current prices (constant prices) and if government expenditure plans are formulated in terms of constant prices (current prices). Should it be called for, the endogenisation will be effected, in a proximate sense, by means of a set of identities, one for each component, each of which links one current-price component with the corresponding constant-price component via the relevant implicit deflator. The set of implicit deflators introduced into the system in this way will, themselves, have to be endogenised, and this will be achieved by means of a set of price equations whose explanatory variables, mathematical form and lag structure will be determined in the manner already described.

Treatment of M_s

Modern KK system-builders invariably take the view that M_s should be given an endogenous treatment. To see that this view is justified one has merely to consider the so-called 'formation-table' identity – an identity which emerges from straightforward manipulations of the balance-sheets of the central bank and the trading banks. According to the formation-table identity the change in M_s between any two periods is the sum of: (i) the change in the central bank's holding of gold and foreign exchange; (ii) the change in the government debt held by the banking system as a whole; (iii) the change in the outstanding loans and advances of the trading banks; and (iv) the net change in bank assets and liabilities other than those covered by (i), (ii) and (iii). While these four changes are, in part, 'externally determined' – by economic developments outside the country and by political decisions inside the country – they also reflect in a complex way developments which are occurring contemporaneously within the economy concerned. Having regard to the formation-table identity, the same must be true of the change in M_s. And this means, in view of the discussion of section 3.1, that M_s itself cannot be regarded as exogenous.

Naturally, the question which then arises is the precise manner in which M_s should be endogenised. Usually, the KK system-builder addresses this question as part of the wider question of how the modelling of the monetary sector as a whole is to be approached. This wider question is a particularly important one because, as will be explained below, the monetary sector plays a vital integrating role in today's KK systems. A measure of the importance of the monetary sector is that, typically, a high proportion of the total number of equations appears there.

Although the details vary a great deal between systems, one approach to the modelling of the monetary sector has evolved to the point where it can be regarded as something of a norm for KK systems. This particular approach, to be found in such KK systems as the UK Treasury and Bank of England systems, the Canadian system RDX2 and the Australian system NIF–10, is based on the same view of the process of money formation as that captured by the formation-table identity, referred to above (see HM Treasury, 1980; Bank of England, 1979; Bank of Canada, 1976, 1977; and Department of the Treasury, 1981). Typically, the formation-table identity itself appears, together with a group of identities designed to identify the financing counterparts of the incomes and the expenditure decisions of various sectors or groups of economic agents. Known as 'flow-of-funds' identities, they serve to endogenise such key monetary-sector variables as the public-sector borrowing requirement, net overseas monetary movements, the change in private-sector primary liquidity and, perhaps as a residual, the financial asset portfolio of the financial sector, including the banks, building societies and other financial institutions.

The flow-of-funds identities highlight the net injection of liquidity from the public and overseas sectors into the private sector. As such, these identities provide a crucial link between the public sector's revenue collection and expenditure decisions (usually identified as the public sector or government budget deficit) and foreign exchange transactions by the private sector on the one hand, and the process of money formation on the other. It is in this sense that the monetary sector of a KK system plays the part of integrating other sectors of the system.

Having identified the financial flows for each sector, a further group of identities (in some instances, a single identity) is developed to endogenise the (financial) asset portfolio of the private sector. Typically these identities will call on the change in private-sector primary liquidity and will bring into the picture various forms of lending to the non-financial private sector by banks, building societies and other financial institutions. Where they are applicable, reserve deposit requirements (the Australian Statutory Reserve Deposit is an example) will also appear in these identities.

The final group of monetary-sector relationships is designed to explain the way in which the asset portfolio of the private sector is allocated. In fact, this group of equations constitutes a set of sub-systems or so-called 'portfolio models' – one for each of the types of financial institutions and groups of agents identified. Whereas nearly all of the monetary-sector relationships described so far are identities, most of the portfolio relationships are stochastic behavioural equations drawing their theoretical underpinnings from the theory of portfolio choice (see, for instance, Brainard and Tobin, 1968; Tobin, 1969; and Parkin, 1970). Among the more important explanatory variables to be found in the portfolio relationships are various interest rates and interest-rate, inflation and other expectations variables. Many of these explanatory variables will be endogenous and, as such, relationships will be needed to explain them. The level of detail involved in portfolio sub-systems varies considerably between KK systems, and in some instances is formidable. An adequate treatment of this interesting and important topic is impossible in the space available. However, the reader will find an excellent account in Department of the Treasury (1981, section 5).

Treatment of W

In recent years a sharp difference of opinion has emerged regarding the determination of money wages. On the one hand are those who take the view that the money-wage level depends almost entirely on non-economic forces – on such factors as the economic aspirations of wage-earners, the extent to which these aspirations are satisfied, the militancy of trade unions and the degree of inequality of wealth and income. On the other hand are those who look to explain the movement in money wages primarily (though not exclusively) in terms of economic variables such as the extent of excess demand in the labour market, the price level in the recent past, the level of labour productivity and the level of profits. The first view implies that it is legitimate to treat W as exogenous, the second that W must be treated as endogenous. That this is so is clear from the discussion of section 3.2.

The builders of modern KK systems have belonged, almost without exception, to the second of the two groups just distinguished. Thus, in the main, they have given an affirmative answer to the question 'Should W be given an endogenous treatment?' As usual this has given rise to the question of the relationships required to endogenise W and the further question of the mathematical form and the lag structure by which each of these relationships should be characterised. The problem has generally been handled by introducing a behavioural relationship to explain W and then introducing additional relationships to explain any of the explanatory variables in this relationship which needed to be treated as endogenous in accordance with the discussion of section 3.2.

The endogenising wage relationships which KK system-builders have introduced are extremely diverse. There would be few, however, which are not firmly based on the well-known Phillips relationship (Phillips, 1958). Thus the explanatory variables in the relationship introduced to endogenise W almost always include some proxy for labour-market excess demand. The proxy used by Phillips himself was, of course, the unemployment rate, and this variable is sometimes to be found in the wage relationship of modern KK systems also. It is more usual, however, to find some variable such as the difference between registered vacancies and registered unemployed, the hours of overtime worked in manufacturing industry and the capacity utilisation percentage being used instead of the unemployment rate as the excess-demand proxy.

Sometimes the Phillips relationship makes its presence felt in the *explained* variable of the endogenising wage relationship, as well as in the explanatory variables. That is, one frequently finds that the variable explained is the percentage rate of increase of W rather than the level of W, as in the relationship which Phillips originally proposed.

It would also be true to say that most of the relationships which have been introduced into KK systems for the purpose of endogenising W include among their explanatory variables some which are exogenous. Thus while the builders of modern KK systems have, by and large, adopted the second of the two views distinguished at the outset of this sub-section, they have made concessions (in some cases important concessions) to those economists who have argued in recent years that the process of wage determination is largely political and sociological in character.

3.5 Open-economy relationships

Open-economy variables and relationships are absent from the Keynesian macro-analytical system presented in section 3.1. By contrast, they are invariably present in great detail in modern KK systems since, by and large, these relate to advanced economies, and no advanced economy can seriously be treated as if it were closed. A corollary is that the approach adopted for modelling the monetary sector in most working KK systems (see section 3.4) requires that the financing counterparts of international transactions be modelled. Typically, it is a relatively straightforward matter to devise the relationships needed to explain trade flows and their consequences for output and expenditure. However, where floating exchange-rate regimes apply and where domestic financial markets are highly integrated with those of other countries, the explanation of the financial consequences of international transactions is likely to be a major task.

Consider first the relationships required to handle the direct impact of trade on output and expenditure. Clearly, the goods market-clearing condition (equation (3.3) in the Keynesian macro-analytical system) will need to be specified in open-economy form. The effect will be that aggregate exports minus aggregate imports will be added to the list of aggregate expenditure variables. Aggregate exports might be treated as exogenous for some countries (until recently this has been the tradition in Australian KK systems) but, in general, both variables will be given an endogenous treatment. Each of the aggregates will usually be disaggregated into reasonably homogenous categories, some of which may be treated as exogenous. Relationships will then be provided for the remaining endogenous categories. The level of disaggregation of exports and imports in the system built by the LBS for the UK economy (see London Business School, 1977) is fairly typical and provides a useful illustration. Aggregate exports are broken into exports of goods and exports of services. Exports of goods are divided into four endogenous sub-classes – exports of food, drink and tobacco; exports of fuels; exports of basic materials; and exports of manufactures – and a single exogenous sub-class. Exports of services are divided into shipping and other services, travel and civil aviation credits, and government services, all three of which are treated as endogenous. Aggregate imports are similarly broken up into imports of goods and imports of services. The former is not disaggregated further. (In fact, imports of goods is obtained as a residual. Stochastic equations are provided for aggregate imports and for each of the sub-classes of imports of services. This treatment is, however, peculiar to the LBS system.) Imports of services are divided into travel, civil aviation and shipping, government services, and other services, all of which are treated as endogenous.

As well as trade relationships, the open-economy relationships of a modern KK system will usually include identities which explain various balance-of-payments components, including net monetary movements. Where a floating exchange-rate regime applies, relationships will also usually be provided to endogenise the exchange rate. In most cases the task of developing the open-economy financial relationships is far from straightforward. For example, in the 1976 version of the Canadian model RDX2 a total of thirty-three relationships is required to model the financial aspects of international transactions. These include relationships which explain long-term capital flows, international portfolio positions, short-term capital flows, the official and private (excess) demand for exchange and the spot and forward exchange rates. (Two variants of RDX2 are actually provided – a fixed exchange-rate variant and a floating exchange-rate variant.)

One of the features of the modelling of exchange-rate determination and capital flows (short-term capital flows in particular) in modern KK systems is that expectational variables are prominent among the explanatory variables, a matter to which we now turn.

3.6 Expectational variables

One of the features of the Keynesian macro-analytical system noted in section 3.1 was the absence of expectational variables. It will already be clear from the preceding discussion that variables of this type are not at all uncommon in today's working KK systems. In particular, such variables as interest-rate, exchange-rate and inflation expectations play an important role in modelling the monetary sector, capital flows and exchange-rate determination. Expectational variables are also important in the explanation of consumer durables expenditure and movements in money wages and some prices. Whether they appear explicitly or implicitly, expectational variables have found a permanent place in working KK systems. Nevertheless variables like 'the expected inflation rate' and 'the expected spot exchange rate' are hard to find in the variable listings of working KK systems. To see the reason for this it is necessary to examine the methods which are available for the modelling of expectations in KK systems. These methods fall into three groups:

1. Use of subsidiary hypotheses,
2. Use of observed expectations data,
3. *Ad hoc* methods.

When expectations are modelled by means of a subsidiary hypothesis, the system-builder postulates some mechanism governing the formation of the expectation concerned. One possibility is to postulate that the expectation is formed rationally. As we have seen in section 1.5, this approach gives rise to special problems of estimation and system solution (see Minford, 1980); and since it takes us outside the KK class into the MS class it will not be considered further in the present context. Some discussion of a quasi-rational treatment of expectations, which is sometimes called on by KK system-builders, is, however, appropriate.

Consider the problem of dealing with ${}_tp^e_{t+1}$, the expectation of the inflation rate formed at the beginning of period t for period $t + 1$ in a KK system in which $\mathbf{x}_t = [x_{1t}\ x_{2t}\ \dots\ x_{kt}]$ denotes the vector of all exogenous variables. If ${}_tp^e_{t+1}$ is formed rationally, then:

$$ {}_tp^e_{t+1} = E[p_{t+1}|\mathbf{x}_t] \qquad (3.13) $$

where p is the actual inflation rate. That is, the expectation of the inflation rate formed at the beginning of period t for period $t + 1$ is the expected value of next period's actual inflation rate, conditional on the information available at the beginning of this quarter, as embodied in the vector of exogenous variables. In the quasi-rational method of treatment of ${}_tp^e_{t+1}$, (3.13) is regarded as providing support for a reduced-form-like relationship between ${}_tp^e_{t+1}$, and the vector of exogenous variables, $\mathbf{x}_t$. This relationship takes the form:

$$ {}_tp^e_{t+1} = \beta_1x_{1t} + \beta_2x_{2t} + \dots + \beta_kx_{kt} + \epsilon_t \qquad (3.14) $$

where ϵ_t represents a random disturbance. Since it is generally impractical to use the full set of exogenous variables, the quasi-rational treatment proxies the expectational variable in question by a linear combination of a small sub-set of the exogenous variables.

Postulating that expectations are formed rationally is not the only method of modelling expectations which falls under the heading 'use of subsidiary hypotheses'. Another method is to propose that expectations are formed according to some hypothesis, like the extrapolative or adaptive mechanisms, in which only past values of the actual counterpart of the expectation are involved. Suppose, for instance, that the expectational variable in question is the expected inflation rate, denoted by ${}_tp^e_{t+1}$, and the actual inflation rate is once again denoted by p_t. Then a first-order *adaptive* mechanism:

$$ {}_tp^e_{t+1} = {}_{t-1}p^e_t + \gamma(p_{t-1} - {}_{t-1}p^e_t) \quad (0 < \gamma < 1) \tag{3.15}$$

or a second-order *extrapolative* mechanism:

$$ {}_tp^e_{t+1} = \alpha p_{t-1} + \beta p_{t-2} \tag{3.16}$$

might be proposed. The expectational variable could then be eliminated altogether by substitution (and where necessary appropriate transformation), its place being taken by a distributed lag on the analogous 'actual' variable. Alternatively, the subsidiary hypothesis could be used to endogenise the expectational variable provided that the system-builder is prepared to impose values of the parameters which appear in the process governing the formation of expectations (γ in (3.15), α and β in (3.16)).

The approach described in the preceding paragraph has been taken in several places in the UK Treasury model (HM Treasury, 1980). For instance, the series for consumer price expectations (*PEXPP*) is formed from the following equation, which also serves as the endogenising relationship for *PEXPP*:

$$ PEXPP_t = 0.565(100\ \Delta_4\ \ell\text{n}\ PCXIR_t) - 0.497(100\ \Delta_4\ \ell\text{n}\ PCXLR_{t-1}) + 0.932\ PEXPP_t \tag{3.17}$$

Here *PCXIR* denotes the deflator for consumers' expenditure and the effect of the '100 Δ_4 ln' operation is to produce a percentage rate of change over the same quarter of the previous year. The subsidiary hypothesis for *PEXPP*, embodied in equation (3.17), will be recognised as a mixed adaptive-extrapolative process. More complex subsidiary hypotheses are used to form series for, and explain the index of, expected price inflation (*PEXPF*), the inflation expectation index (*PEXPER*) and the expected rate of growth of output (*YEXPER*) in the UK Treasury model. It is left to the interested reader to follow these up.

A more sophisticated version of the use of subsidiary hypothesis modelling approach can be found in the Canadian model RDX2 (Bank of

Canada, 1976). The variable in question is the expected rate of change in the consumer price index (expected inflation rate), denoted by *PCPICE*. Although the details are quite complicated, the main idea is that the real and nominal supply prices of capital differ by the expected inflation rate. A group of equations is provided to explain the real and nominal supply prices. The explanatory variables in these equations include finite-length distributed lags on the actual rate of price change. By suitable manipulation of these equations, it is possible to extract the distributed-lag weights in:

$$PCPICE_t = \sum_{i=0}^{p} w_i \, \mathrm{J4P}(PCPI)_{t-i} \tag{3.18}$$

where J4P (*PCPI*) denotes the four-quarter percentage rate of change in the consumer price index. This relationship is used as the endogenising equation for *PCPICE*.

The second main group of methods which are available for the modelling of expectational variables in KK systems, labelled above 'use of observed expectations data', are methods which make use of an 'observed' series for the expectational variable in question. Although by no means readily available, such series exist for certain expectations variables. Typically, they are based on survey data. Often the source data are qualitative, and special methods are used to transform the responses into an observation on the expectational variable. (See Carlson and Parkin (1975) for an application to inflation expectations.) Given the availability of an appropriate 'observed' expectations series, the expectational variable concerned can be dealt with in the same way as any other variable. In particular, the KK system-builder must decide whether the expectational variable should be classified as exogenous or endogenous. If an endogenous treatment is opted for, a relationship must be specified explaining the expectational variable concerned in the familiar way.

Another way of forming 'observed' series for expectational variables which is sometimes used in building KK systems is to employ proxy measures. For instance, the Bank of England's (1979) UK system has among the endogenous variables used in modelling the determination of the exchange rate between sterling and the US dollar the *expected pressure on the exchange rate*. The required series for this variable is formed as a weighted average (the weights being fixed by the system-builders) of the change in the (actual) exchange rate and the change in foreign exchange reserves, each expressed as a percentage of the exchange rate. The equation which is thus used to form the proxy series for the expectational variable does double duty since it also acts as the endogenising relationship.

A still cruder method of providing a proxy 'observed' series for an expectational variable is to create a dummy or synthetic variable. The relationship for the motor-vehicles category of private final consumption expenditure in the Australian NIF–10 model (Department of the Treasury, 1981) provides an example. Here an (exogenous) variable, the expectation of exchange-rate adjustment, was called for to capture the effects on motor-vehicles expenditure of widely held expectations of price increases (decreases) when a devaluation (appreciation) of the Australian dollar was anticipated. In this instance, the system-builders identified those quarters in which press commentary suggested that an exchange-rate change was widely anticipated. A series for the expectation of exchange-rate adjustment was then formed by allotting the variable a value between plus and minus unity in these quarters and zero in all others. The particular value chosen in each quarter was designed to reflect the intensity of expectations held in each case. Synthetic variables may be formed in more sophisticated ways but this example serves to illustrate the general idea.

Finally, expectational variables may be dealt with by methods which are purely *ad hoc*. These methods involve the replacement of the expectational variable wherever it appears with one or more variables (these may be endogenous, exogenous or a mixture of both) which are regarded by the system-builder as being important causal influences on the expectation in question. It will now be clear that the quasi-rational treatment of expectational variables, discussed above, can be viewed as an *ad hoc* method of treatment. There are, however, many other methods of this type which are used by the KK system-builder. One common device is to substitute the analogous 'actual' variable for the expectational variable. The NIF–10 motor-vehicles expenditure equation referred to above provides an example of this approach. The four-quarter percentage change in the durables deflator is used as an explanatory variable in place of the expectation of the four-quarter rate of increase of durables prices. (It should be noted that this device is inapplicable if a particular expectational variable appears as an explanatory variable in a relationship whose 'dependent' variable is the corresponding 'actual' variable.) Another commonly used device is to replace an inflation-expectation variable by some general indicator of liquidity, such as the broadly defined volume of money, or its rate of change. The possibilities for *ad hoc* treatments of expectations are limited only by the system-builders' views on the determination of expectations. However, the examples already provided should be sufficient to illustrate the main ideas.

3.7 General observations

At the outset of this chapter the Keynesian macro-analytical system was introduced as a useful point of departure for considering the specification of a KK system. A question which arises quite naturally from the discussion of the specification task in the preceding six sections is the following: What are the significant differences between the parent and the children – between the simple macro-analytical system made famous by Keynes in his *General Theory* and the modern KK systems which have evolved from this system? We propose to conclude the chapter by briefly discussing this question. In doing so, we shall repeat one or two points already made in Chapter 1. Our main points, however, will be new and will feature prominently in the chapters to follow.

One difference between the parent and the children that will be obvious from the discussion of earlier sections is that the latter are formulated in a much more specific way. Apart from the two market-clearing relationships, the relationships in (3.1)–(3.7) are arbitrary as regards mathematical form and are silent on the question of lags. By contrast, the relationships of a modern KK system are always given specific mathematical form and a specific lag structure.

A second difference is that the parent is deterministic whereas the children are stochastic. Thus in KK systems a random disturbance is included in the right-hand side of all relationships apart from identities to take account of the random (non-systematic) elements in economic behaviour.

Third, the children are invariably much larger than the parent; in modern KK systems the relationships typically number not half a dozen but some (often many) hundreds. As will be clear from earlier discussion, this vast increase in size is intimately connected with the fact that modern KK systems typically identify many more than the three aggregate demand categories which appear in the Keynesian macro-analytical system, that some categories of government expenditure are treated as endogenous, that a full monetary sector is included, that money wages are endogenous and that open-economy relationships and variables appear prominently.

A fourth difference, closely associated with the third, is that the relationships of the offspring display much more variety than those of the parent. In the typical KK system one finds numerous examples of all of the main types of econometric relationship – behavioural, institutional, technological and market-clearing relationships, identities and equilibrium conditions. In (3.1)–(3.7), on the other hand, some of these equation types are not represented at all – for example, there are no institutional relationships and no identities – and others have no more than token representation.

The Keynesian macro-analytical system features only one policy instrument, namely government expenditure, and incorporates none of the variables which nowadays are generally regarded as the prime targets of economic policy – variables such as the inflation rate, the unemployment rate and the level of overseas reserves. By contrast, the KK systems to which it has given birth typically feature all major policy instruments – government expenditure, the various elements of the tax and transfer-payments structure, monetary instruments, the exchange rate and other external instruments, and so on – and all major policy targets. This is a fifth important difference between the parent and the offspring. It means that the policy questions which can be put to the latter are much more varied, much more detailed and much more fundamental than those which can be addressed by the former. This will become clear as this book proceeds.

A sixth notable difference between the macro-analytical system set out in (3.1)–(3.7) and the KK systems which have been built in recent years is that whereas the supply side of the macro economy is largely ignored in the former it is typically modelled with varying degrees of detail in the latter. When we refer to 'the supply side of the macro economy' we have in mind the forces which determine the availability of the primary factors of production – the services of capital and labour. The Keynesian macro-analytical system sidesteps the supply-side problem by treating both the supply of capital services and the supply of labour services as exogenous, at least implicitly. That the supply of capital services is implicitly treated as exogenous is evident from the fact that there is no capital variable in (3.6), the aggregate production function. To see that the supply of labour services is implicitly exogenous we have merely to note that N is defined as 'employment'. Strictly speaking, since N is determined, in effect, by feeding output into the production function it represents the demand for labour, not employment. The fact that it is defined, nevertheless, as employment must mean that the system contains another relationship, not made explicit, in which the demand for labour cannot exceed the exogenous supply of labour.

By contrast, it is typical of modern KK systems that the supply-side problem is squarely faced. The supply of capital services is almost always made endogenous, a common endogenising procedure being to accumulate the stock of, say, business plant and equipment from some arbitrary initial figure by feeding (endogenous) investment in plant and equipment into an equation which says in effect that the change in the capital stock is equal to the gain via investment less the loss via (endogenous) wear and tear. Likewise the supply of labour services is invariably endogenised – usually by means of relationships which explain the 'participation rate', i.e. the proportion of the (exogenous) population of working age which is available for work.

A final important way in which modern KK systems differ from their Keynesian parent is that, to a much greater extent, they are long run in character. This comes out in two main ways.

In the first place, as we have noted previously, the money supply, the supply of capital services and the supply of labour services are all treated as exogenous in the parent system. This procedure represents a legitimate shortcut in a model intended for short-run applications but not otherwise. Thus the list of exogenous variables in the parent system immediately stamps it as strictly short run in character. None of this applies to the children, however, since, as we have seen, their creators invariably go to considerable lengths to ensure that the three variables in question are treated endogenously.

The second way in which the comparatively long-run character of modern KK systems manifests itself is in the formulation of the behavioural relationships. Whereas the formulation of three behavioural relationships in (3.1)–(3.7) is, to a large extent, *ad hoc*, one often finds the behavioural relationships in modern KK systems (or at least their 'first drafts') formulated in two distinct stages: (i) a relationship showing the determinants of the *desired or long-run level* of the variable concerned; and (b) a relationship showing the mechanism by which the *actual* level of the variable adjusts to its desired level. The formulation of the equation for *CMV* in NIF–10 (discussed in section 3.3) provides a good illustration of this two-stage procedure. Thus the long-run position of the macro economy is, so to speak, embedded in modern KK systems so that they can be regarded as depicting a macro economy which never actually reaches its long-run position but which is, nevertheless, continuously on the move towards it. None of this is true of the Keynesian parent.

References and further reading

BANK OF CANADA (1976) *The Equations of RDX2 Revised and Estimated to 4Q72*, Bank of Canada Technical Report 5, Ottawa.

BANK OF CANADA (1977) *Sectoral Analysis of RDX2 Estimated to 4Q72*, Bank of Canada Technical Report 6, Ottawa.

BANK OF ENGLAND (1979) *Bank of England Model of the UK Economy*, Discussion Paper No. 5, London.

BRAINARD, W.C. and TOBIN, J. (1968) 'Pitfalls in Financial Model Building', *American Economic Review*, vol. 58, pp. 92–122.

CARLSON, J.A. and PARKIN, M. (1975) 'Inflation Expectations', *Economica*, vol. 42, pp. 123–38.

DEPARTMENT OF THE TREASURY (1981) *The NIF–10 Model of the Australian Economy*, Australian Government Publishing Service, Canberra.

HM TREASURY (1980) *Macroeconomic Model Equation and Variable Listing (December 1980 Version)*, London.

KEYNES, J.M. (1936) *The General Theory of Employment, Interest and Money*, Macmillan, London.

LONDON BUSINESS SCHOOL (1977) *The London Business School Quarterly Econometric Model of the United Kingdom Economy*, London.

MINFORD, A.P. (1980) 'A Rational Expectations Model of the United Kingdom Under Fixed and Floating Exchange Rates', in K. Brunner and A.H. Meltzer (eds), *On the State of Macro-Economics*, North-Holland, Amsterdam.

PARKIN, J.M. (1970) 'Discount House Portfolio and Debt Selection', *Review of Economic Studies*, vol. 37, pp. 469–97.

PHILLIPS, A.W. (1958) 'The Relation Between Unemployment and the Rate of Change of Money Wage Rates in the United Kingdom, 1861–1957', *Economica*, vol. 25, pp. 283–99.

TOBIN, J. (1969) 'A General Equilibrium Approach to Monetary Theory', *Journal of Money, Credit and Banking*, vol. 1, pp. 15–29.

4 ESTIMATION METHODS

4.1 The information content of a system

Once a KK system has been fully specified the next task is to replace the unknown parameters which appear in its behavioural relationships with actual numbers. The process by which this task is completed is known as *estimation*. Many methods are available for undertaking the estimation job and the next three chapters are concerned in one way or another with these methods.

In this chapter our aim will be twofold: (i) to describe the available methods; and (ii) to give details of the main results which have been established by econometricians in relation to these methods. As regards the latter we concentrate on giving an accurate statement of the results and of the conditions under which they hold. No attempt will be made to present proofs, though in all cases a reference to a work in which a proof can be found will be given.

All of the results to be discussed in the present chapter are so-called *asymptotic* results. While these results are the most important component of our knowledge about the methods which are available for the estimation of KK systems, they are by no means the sum total. Another significant component are what are called *finite-sample* results. These results will be discussed in Chapter 5.

In Chapter 6 we turn from what is known to what is done – from theory to practice. The two are, of course, closely connected. Here, as elsewhere in life, what is done is governed, in part, by what is known. Chapter 6 will show, however, that, at present, estimation knowledge provides a somewhat dubious guide to the choice of estimation technique and will discuss the more practical considerations on which the modern KK system-builder is forced to rely in making the estimation decision.

At the outset it must be emphasised that our concern throughout will be with the *true* KK system, the true structural form and the true reduced form (see section 2.2). In the interests of readability, however, we propose to omit 'true' and leave it to the reader to insert 'true' before 'KK systems', whenever it appears, and similarly for 'structural form' and 'reduced form'. There is little danger of confusion in this shortcut since, in most cases, it will be perfectly clear from the context that the system under discussion is the true system, not the numerical (estimated) system which we have had in mind hitherto whenever we have referred to a 'KK system'.

The procedures which have been developed for the estimation of KK systems represent an application of classical statistical inference. The system is regarded as holding for each of a succession of T time periods (months, quarters, years). We number this succession 1, 2, ..., T, and we say that the system holds over the T *sample points:* 1, 2, ..., T. All variables appearing in the system are observed at each of the T sample points, the resulting time series, each of length T, being referred to as the *sample data.* We choose an *estimator* and apply the chosen estimator to the sample data to obtain actual numbers or *estimates* of each of the parameters which appear in the system. Formally an estimator is a procedure (usually summed up in a mathematical formula) by which an estimate for each of the system's parameters is inferred from the sample data.

The structural form of a KK system contains certain special kinds of information which is exploited in the estimation process. To assist in understanding the nature of the information embodied in a KK system, we introduce the following simple illustrative *linear* KK system consisting of two stochastic equations and one identity in the endogenous variables y_1, y_2 and y_3 and the predetermined variables x_1, x_2, x_3 and x_4; u_1 and u_2 are, respectively, the random disturbances for the first and second equations, while the αs and the βs are the unknown parameters. The fact that this illustrative system is a *true* KK system is evident from the fact that its stochastic equations contain disturbances rather than residuals and from the fact that its parameters are unknown, as opposed to actual, numbers. (The third equation, being an identity, is deterministic – it can be regarded as having a disturbance which is always zero.) The variables are observed at T sample points: 1, 2, ..., T.

$$\left.\begin{aligned} y_{1t} &= \alpha_1 y_{2t} + \alpha_2 y_{3t} + \alpha_3 x_{1t} + u_{1t} \\ y_{2t} &= \beta_1 y_{1t} + \beta_2 x_{2t} + \beta_3 x_{3t} + u_{2t} \\ y_{3t} &\equiv y_{1t} + y_{2t} + x_{4t} \end{aligned}\right\} \quad (\mathrm{t} = 1, 2, \ldots, T) \qquad \begin{aligned}(4.1)\\(4.2)\\(4.3)\end{aligned}$$

For ease of reference, this illustrative system will be referred to as SYSTEM III. Clearly SYSTEM III does not encompass all the essential features of working KK systems, such as those referred to in Table 1.2. For instance, it is neither large nor non-linear. On the other hand, it does typify the general simultaneous system for which most of the estimators intended for use in KK systems were developed, and it represents a suitable vehicle for a discussion of the information content of a system.

As will be clear from Chapter 2, a linear KK system of n equations in n endogenous and k exogenous variables can be given the following matrix representation:

$$\mathbf{A}\mathbf{y}_t = \mathbf{B}_0\mathbf{x}_t + \mathbf{B}_1\mathbf{x}_{t-1} + \dots + \mathbf{B}_q\mathbf{x}_{t-q} + \mathbf{C}_1\mathbf{y}_{t-1} + \mathbf{C}_2\mathbf{y}_{t-2} + \dots + \mathbf{C}_p\mathbf{y}_{t-p} + \mathbf{u}_t \quad (t = 1, 2, \dots, T) \tag{4.4}$$

$\mathbf{y}_t$ and $\mathbf{u}_t$ are, respectively, $n \times 1$ vectors of endogenous variables and disturbances at sample point t; $\mathbf{x}_t$ is a $k \times 1$ vector of exogenous variables; p and q are, respectively, the longest lags on any endogenous and on any exogenous variable; $\mathbf{A}$, $\mathbf{C}_1, \dots, \mathbf{C}_p$ are all $n \times n$ matrices of (unknown) coefficients of the current and lagged endogenous variables; and $\mathbf{B}_0$, $\mathbf{B}_1, \dots \mathbf{B}_q$ are all $n \times k$ matrices of (unknown) coefficients of the current and lagged exogenous variables. The pre-sample period values of the endogenous variables, $\mathbf{y}_0, \mathbf{y}_{-1}, \dots, \mathbf{y}_{1-p}$, are assumed known.

For present purposes, a simpler representation of the system will suffice. Define a new vector $\mathbf{z}_t$ of *predetermined* variables at sample point t:

$$\mathbf{z}_t = \begin{bmatrix} \mathbf{x}_t \\ \mathbf{x}_{t-1} \\ \vdots \\ \mathbf{x}_{t-q} \\ \mathbf{y}_{t-1} \\ \vdots \\ \mathbf{y}_{t-p} \end{bmatrix}$$

The order of $\mathbf{z}_t$ is $[k(q + 1) + np] \times 1$. Similarly, define a new coefficient matrix $\mathbf{B}$, of order $n \times [k(q + 1) + np]$, made up from the coefficient matrices in (4.4) in the following way:

$$\mathbf{B} = [-\mathbf{B}_0 - \mathbf{B}_1 \dots -\mathbf{B}_q \; -\mathbf{C}_1 \; -\mathbf{C}_2 \dots -\mathbf{C}_p]$$

Then the alternative representation of the sytem is:

$$\mathbf{A}\mathbf{y}_t + \mathbf{B}\mathbf{z}_t = \mathbf{u}_t \quad (t = 1, 2, \dots, T) \tag{4.5}$$

SYSTEM III, being linear, can be expressed in the form of (4.5). In this case the vectors $\mathbf{y}_t$, $\mathbf{z}_t$ and $\mathbf{u}_t$ take the form:

$$\mathbf{y_t} = \begin{bmatrix} y_{1t} \\ y_{2t} \\ y_{3t} \end{bmatrix} \quad \mathbf{z_t} = \begin{bmatrix} x_{1t} \\ x_{2t} \\ x_{3t} \\ x_{4t} \end{bmatrix} \quad \mathbf{u_t} = \begin{bmatrix} u_{1t} \\ u_{2t} \\ 0 \end{bmatrix}$$

while the coefficient matrices are:

$$\mathbf{A} = \begin{bmatrix} 1 & -\alpha_1 & -\alpha_2 \\ -\beta_1 & 1 & 0 \\ -1 & -1 & 1 \end{bmatrix} \quad \mathbf{B} = \begin{bmatrix} -\alpha_3 & 0 & 0 & 0 \\ 0 & -\beta_2 & -\beta_3 & 0 \\ 0 & 0 & 0 & -1 \end{bmatrix}$$

It is most important to note that the system represented in (4.5) contains both exogenous and lagged endogenous variables. Since all working KK systems include lagged endogenous variables, there is little point in discussing a system in which all predetermined variables are, in fact, exogenous (as econometrics texts commonly do).

The information embodied in a KK system is of two types. First, there is so-called *prior information.* This is the information contained in the structural form of the system. In general, the prior-information content of a KK system takes the form of the lists of endogenous and predetermined variables, information about which variables enter each equation, about which equations are identities, and about which variable a given equation is regarded as determining. The nature of prior information can best be understood by considering the following very general way of writing SYSTEM III in which all variables in the list (y_1, y_2, y_3, x_1, x_2, x_3 and x_4) enter every equation and in which the variables appear on the left and the disturbances on the right of each equation:

$$\gamma_1 y_{1t} + \gamma_2 y_{2t} + \gamma_3 y_{3t} + \gamma_4 x_{1t} + \gamma_5 x_{2t} + \gamma_6 x_{3t} + \gamma_7 x_{4t} = u_{1t} \tag{4.6}$$

$$\theta_1 y_{1t} + \theta_2 y_{2t} + \theta_3 y_{3t} + \theta_4 x_{1t} + \theta_5 x_{2t} + \theta_6 x_{3t} + \theta_7 x_{4t} = u_{2t} \tag{4.7}$$

$$\delta_1 y_{1t} + \delta_2 y_{2t} + \delta_3 y_{3t} + \delta_4 x_{1t} + \delta_5 x_{2t} + \delta_6 x_{3t} + \delta_7 x_{4t} \equiv 0 \tag{4.8}$$

The only information used in setting out (4.6), (4.7) and (4.8) are the lists of endogenous and predetermined variables and the fact that the third equation is an identity. To obtain SYSTEM III in the form (4.1), (4.2) and (4.3), further information must be supplied. This consists of two sets of restrictions on the γs, θs and δs. There are the restrictions $\gamma_1 = 1$, $\theta_2 = 1$, $\delta_3 = 1$. These restrictions are called *normalisations*. They indicate, for each equation, which endogenous variable is regarded as the 'dependent' variable – the variable the equation in question is regarded as determining. The other restrictions necessary to collapse (4.6) – (4.8) into (4.1) – (4.3) are $\gamma_5 = 0$, $\gamma_6 = 0$, $\gamma_7 = 0$, $\theta_3 = 0$, $\theta_4 = 0$, $\theta_7 = 0$, $\delta_4 = 0$, $\delta_5 = 0$ and $\delta_6 = 0$. These are known as *zero restrictions*. Their function is simply to indicate which variables from the full list enter each equation by excluding those variables which do not. Imposing the normalisations $\gamma_1 = 1$, $\theta_2 = 1$ and $\delta_3 = 1$ and the zero restrictions $\gamma_5 = 0$, $\gamma_6 = 0$, $\gamma_7 = 0$, $\theta_3 = 0$, $\theta_4 = 0$, $\theta_7 = 0$, $\delta_4 = 0$, $\delta_5 = 0$ and $\delta_6 = 0$ on the general form of the system (4.6) – (4.8) and recognising that $\gamma_2 = -\alpha_1$, $\gamma_3 = -\alpha_2$, $\gamma_4 = -\alpha_3$, $\theta_1 = -\beta_1$, $\theta_5 = -\beta_2$, $\theta_6 = -\beta_3$, $\delta_1 = -1$, $\delta_2 = -1$ and $\delta_7 = -1$ produces the form of SYSTEM III shown in (4.1)–(4.3).

In short, the information contained in the illustrative KK system specified in (4.1)–(4.3) consists of:

(a) the lists of endogenous and predetermined variables;
(b) the fact that (4.3) is an exact relationship;
(c) the normalisation for each equation; and
(d) the zero restrictions for each equation.

This is the prior-information content of SYSTEM III.

The second general type of information embodied in a system consists of information about the degree of correlation of disturbances within and across equations. This information is set out systematically in the *covariance matrix of the system*. To explain this concept, consider the vector of disturbances of the system formed by arranging, in order, the disturbance of the first equation for each sample point, that of the second equation for each sample point, and so on. In the case of SYSTEM III, this vector, denoted by $\mathbf{u}^*$, takes the form:

$$\mathbf{u}^* = \begin{bmatrix} u_{11} \\ u_{12} \\ \vdots \\ u_{1T} \\ u_{21} \\ u_{22} \\ \vdots \\ u_{2T} \\ 0 \\ 0 \\ \vdots \\ 0 \end{bmatrix}$$

In the interest of brevity, let us now suppose that there are just three sample points ($T = 3$). Then $\mathbf{u}^*$ will be:

$$\mathbf{u}^* = \begin{bmatrix} u_{11} \\ u_{12} \\ u_{13} \\ u_{21} \\ u_{22} \\ u_{23} \\ 0 \\ 0 \\ 0 \end{bmatrix} \tag{4.9}$$

The zeros in $\mathbf{u}^*$ appear because the third equation in SYSTEM III is an identity.

The covariance matrix of the system is that associated with the system disturbance vector $\mathbf{u}^*$. It is obtained by taking the expected values of the elements of the matrix formed by post-multiplying the vector $\mathbf{u}^*$ by its transpose. All the entries in this matrix are either variances or covariances. The covariance matrix of SYSTEM III with $T = 3$ is:

$$\boldsymbol{\Sigma} = \left[\begin{array}{ccc|ccc|ccc}
\text{var}(u_{11}) & \text{cov}(u_{11}u_{12}) & \text{cov}(u_{11}u_{13}) & \text{cov}(u_{11}u_{21}) & \text{cov}(u_{11}u_{22}) & \text{cov}(u_{11}u_{23}) & \text{cov}(u_{11}\ 0) & \text{cov}(u_{11}\ 0) & \text{cov}(u_{11}\ 0) \\
\text{cov}(u_{12}u_{11}) & \text{var}(u_{12}) & \text{cov}(u_{12}u_{13}) & \text{cov}(u_{12}u_{21}) & \text{cov}(u_{12}u_{22}) & \text{cov}(u_{12}u_{23}) & \text{cov}(u_{12}\ 0) & \text{cov}(u_{12}\ 0) & \text{cov}(u_{12}\ 0) \\
\text{cov}(u_{13}u_{11}) & \text{cov}(u_{13}u_{12}) & \text{var}(u_{13}) & \text{cov}(u_{13}u_{21}) & \text{cov}(u_{13}u_{22}) & \text{cov}(u_{13}u_{23}) & \text{cov}(u_{13}\ 0) & \text{cov}(u_{13}\ 0) & \text{cov}(u_{13}\ 0) \\
\hline
\text{cov}(u_{21}u_{11}) & \text{cov}(u_{21}u_{12}) & \text{cov}(u_{21}u_{13}) & \text{var}(u_{21}) & \text{cov}(u_{21}u_{22}) & \text{cov}(u_{21}u_{23}) & \text{cov}(u_{21}\ 0) & \text{cov}(u_{21}\ 0) & \text{cov}(u_{21}\ 0) \\
\text{cov}(u_{22}u_{11}) & \text{cov}(u_{22}u_{12}) & \text{cov}(u_{22}u_{13}) & \text{cov}(u_{22}u_{21}) & \text{var}(u_{22}) & \text{cov}(u_{22}u_{23}) & \text{cov}(u_{22}\ 0) & \text{cov}(u_{22}\ 0) & \text{cov}(u_{22}\ 0) \\
\text{cov}(u_{23}u_{11}) & \text{cov}(u_{23}u_{12}) & \text{cov}(u_{23}u_{13}) & \text{cov}(u_{23}u_{21}) & \text{cov}(u_{23}u_{22}) & \text{var}(u_{23}) & \text{cov}(u_{23}\ 0) & \text{cov}(u_{23}\ 0) & \text{cov}(u_{23}\ 0) \\
\hline
\text{cov}(0\ u_{11}) & \text{cov}(0\ u_{12}) & \text{cov}(0\ u_{13}) & \text{cov}(0\ u_{21}) & \text{cov}(0\ u_{22}) & \text{cov}(0\ u_{23}) & \text{var}(0) & \text{cov}(0\ 0) & \text{cov}(0\ 0) \\
\text{cov}(0\ u_{11}) & \text{cov}(0\ u_{12}) & \text{cov}(0\ u_{13}) & \text{cov}(0\ u_{21}) & \text{cov}(0\ u_{22}) & \text{cov}(0\ u_{23}) & \text{cov}(0\ 0) & \text{var}(0) & \text{cov}(0\ 0) \\
\text{cov}(0\ u_{11}) & \text{cov}(0\ u_{12}) & \text{cov}(0\ u_{13}) & \text{cov}(0\ u_{21}) & \text{cov}(0\ u_{22}) & \text{cov}(0\ u_{23}) & \text{cov}(0\ 0) & \text{cov}(0\ 0) & \text{var}(0)
\end{array}\right] \qquad (4.10)$$

Σ is a symmetric matrix which is partitioned into blocks by the dotted lines. Because the covariance of a random variable with a constant is zero, the last three rows and the last three columns of Σ contain only zeros. Exploiting the partitioning of Σ, it may be written:

$$\Sigma = \left[\begin{array}{c|c|c} \mathbf{A} & \mathbf{B} & \mathbf{C} \\ \hline \mathbf{D} & \mathbf{E} & \mathbf{F} \\ \hline \mathbf{G} & \mathbf{H} & \mathbf{J} \end{array}\right] \tag{4.11}$$

where **A, B, ..., J** each stands for the analogous (3×3) block in (4.10).

Bearing in mind that the first subscript attached to u indicates the equation number while the second refers to the sample point, it can be seen that block **A** contains the *within-equation* variances and covariances for the first equation. The variances of the disturbances at the three sample points for equation (4.1) are arranged along the leading diagonal. The off-diagonal elements are the covariances of the equation (4.1) disturbances at different sample points. If the disturbance u_1 is not autocorrelated, all these off-diagonal elements in block **A** will be zero. If u_1 is homoskedastic (exhibits the same variance at all sample points), the leading diagonal elements of block **A** will be identical. Blocks **E** and **J** hold the analogous within-equation variances and covariances for the disturbances of the second and third equations respectively. Of course, since the third equation is an identity and consequently has no disturbance, block **J** is a null matrix.

Blocks **B** and **D** are each other's transpose. Both contain the covariances between the disturbances of equations (4.1) and (4.2) at the same and at different sample points. These are described as the *across-equations* covariances. Elements along the leading diagonal of blocks **B** and **D** are the across-equations covariances of the disturbances of (4.1) with those of (4.2) at the *same* sample point. For instance, the first leading diagonal element, cov $(u_{11}u_{21})$, is the covariance between u_1 and u_2 at sample point 1. The leading diagonal elements of blocks **B** and **D** indicate the degree of across-equations *contemporaneous* disturbance correlation between equations (4.1) and (4.2). When the extent of such correlation is the same at every sample point, the leading diagonal elements of blocks **B** and **D** will all be identical. The off-diagonal elements of blocks **B** and **D** are the across-equations covariances of the disturbances of (4.1) with those of (4.2) at *different* sample points. They indicate the degree of across-equations *non-contemporaneous* disturbance correlation between (4.1) and (4.2). In the absence of this form of across-equations disturbance correlation, all off-diagonal elements of blocks **B** and **D** would be zero.

Blocks **C** and **G** are analogous to blocks **B** and **D** except that they relate to covariances of the disturbance of (4.1) with the (identically zero) disturbance of (4.3). Similarly blocks **F** and **H** contain the across-equations covariances between the disturbances of (4.2) and (4.3). As before, covariances between disturbances at the same sample point, indicating the degree of across-equations contemporaneous disturbance correlation, lie along the leading diagonals of these blocks. Off the leading diagonals are found the covariances between the disturbances at different sample points, indicating the degree of across-equations non-contemporaneous disturbance correlation.

With $T = 3$, Σ, the covariance matrix of the disturbances of SYSTEM III, is of order 9×9 and (taking into account its symmetry) contains forty-five distinct elements. Since the sample to which it relates contains only three points per endogenous variable, i.e. nine data points in total, it is impossible to estimate all forty-five elements, together with the six structural parameters, as is necessary if the information contained in this covariance matrix is to be exploited. In general, a KK system of n equations with T sample points available has a covariance matrix of order $nT \times nT$ in which $nT(nT + 1)/2$ distinct elements appear. Since $nT(nT + 1)/2$ will always exceed nT, there are never sufficient degrees of freedom available to exploit fully the information embodied in the covariance matrix. For this reason it is the practice to reduce the number of unknown elements of the covariance matrix by making various assumptions about the behaviour of the system disturbances. This practice amounts to injecting further information about the system into the covariance matrix. Commonly, but not necessarily, a set of assumptions is made which can usefully be thought of as generalising the well-known classical assumptions for the disturbance of a single relationship, while explicitly permitting across-equations contemporaneous disturbance correlation, an essential feature of KK, and indeed of all, systems of stochastic equations. Specifically, the usual assumptions are:

(a) absence of within-equation disturbance autocorrelation;
(b) within-equation homoskedasticity of disturbance;
(c) absence of across-equations non-contemporaneous disturbance correlation; and
(d) presence of across-equations contemporaneous disturbance correlation, the extent of which is the same at all sample points.

(The first of these assumptions is sometimes replaced with one which permits within-equation disturbance autocorrelation conforming to a specified process.)

The effect of the first of these assumptions is to diagonalise those *blocks* which lie along the leading diagonal of the covariance matrix. For example, in the case of SYSTEM III with $T = 3$, blocks **A, E** and **J** are diagonal matrices when assumption (a) applies. Assumption (b) makes the leading diagonal elements of these blocks identical. Assumption (c) diagonalises all blocks other than those which lie along the leading diagonal of the covariance matrix, while assumption (d) ensures that their leading diagonal elements are identical. Thus under assumptions (a)–(d) the covariance matrix of SYSTEM III with $T = 3$ takes the form:

$$\mathbf{\Sigma} = \left[\begin{array}{ccc|ccc|ccc} \sigma_{11} & 0 & 0 & \sigma_{12} & 0 & 0 & 0 & 0 & 0 \\ 0 & \sigma_{11} & 0 & 0 & \sigma_{12} & 0 & 0 & 0 & 0 \\ 0 & 0 & \sigma_{11} & 0 & 0 & \sigma_{12} & 0 & 0 & 0 \\ \hline \sigma_{12} & 0 & 0 & \sigma_{22} & 0 & 0 & 0 & 0 & 0 \\ 0 & \sigma_{12} & 0 & 0 & \sigma_{22} & 0 & 0 & 0 & 0 \\ 0 & 0 & \sigma_{12} & 0 & 0 & \sigma_{22} & 0 & 0 & 0 \\ \hline 0 & 0 & 0 & 0 & 0 & 0 & 0 & 0 & 0 \\ 0 & 0 & 0 & 0 & 0 & 0 & 0 & 0 & 0 \\ 0 & 0 & 0 & 0 & 0 & 0 & 0 & 0 & 0 \end{array}\right] \tag{4.12}$$

In (4.12) σ_{11} denotes the constant variance of u_1, the disturbance of the first equation of SYSTEM III, σ_{22} is the constant variance of the disturbance of u_2 and σ_{12} is the common contemporaneous covariance of u_1 with u_2. (4.12) can be written more compactly as follows, with $\mathbf{I}_3$ denoting a 3×3 identity matrix and $\mathbf{0}$ a 3×3 null matrix:

$$\mathbf{\Sigma} = \left[\begin{array}{c|c|c} \sigma_{11}\mathbf{I}_3 & \sigma_{12}\mathbf{I}_3 & \mathbf{0} \\ \hline \sigma_{12}\mathbf{I}_3 & \sigma_{22}\mathbf{I}_3 & \mathbf{0} \\ \hline \mathbf{0} & \mathbf{0} & \mathbf{0} \end{array}\right] \tag{4.13}$$

Equivalently:

$$\mathbf{\Sigma} = \begin{bmatrix} \sigma_{11} & \sigma_{12} & 0 \\ \sigma_{12} & \sigma_{22} & 0 \\ 0 & 0 & 0 \end{bmatrix} \otimes \mathbf{I}_3 \tag{4.14}$$

where $\otimes$ denotes the Kronecker product. Defining:

$$\boldsymbol{\Omega} = \begin{bmatrix} \sigma_{11} & \sigma_{12} & 0 \\ \sigma_{12} & \sigma_{22} & 0 \\ 0 & 0 & 0 \end{bmatrix} \tag{4.15}$$

(4.14) can be written still more compactly:

$$\boldsymbol{\Sigma} = \boldsymbol{\Omega} \otimes \mathbf{I}_3 \tag{4.16}$$

The matrix $\boldsymbol{\Omega}$ can be interpreted and will be described as the covariance matrix of the disturbances *at a single sample point*, given assumptions (a) to (d). Whereas $\boldsymbol{\Sigma} = E(\mathbf{u}^*\mathbf{u}^{*\prime})$ is the covariance matrix associated with $\mathbf{u}^*$, the vector of system disturbances at all sample points, $\boldsymbol{\Omega} = E(\mathbf{u}\mathbf{u}')$ is the covariance matrix associated with $\mathbf{u}$, where:

$$\mathbf{u} = \begin{bmatrix} u_{1t} \\ u_{2t} \\ 0 \end{bmatrix} \tag{4.17}$$

is the vector of system disturbances at the given sample point t ($t = 1, 2, 3$). (Recall that $\mathbf{u}$ appears in (4.5).)

Finally, it is important to note that, unlike $\boldsymbol{\Sigma}$, the order of $\boldsymbol{\Omega}$ is independent of the number of sample points. In general, $\boldsymbol{\Omega}$ is of order $n \times n$ for a system of n equations. As long as the number of data points (nT) exceeds the number of distinct, non-zero elements of $\boldsymbol{\Omega}$ plus the number of structural parameters, there is in principle no problem involved in estimating the elements of $\boldsymbol{\Omega}$ and thereby exploiting the information it contains.

4.2 System estimators

The above discussion of the information content of KK systems motivates a useful classification of the estimators which are applicable in the system context. A basic distinction can be made between

(a) those estimators which use no more information than is contained in one equation of the system; and
(b) those which use information relating to the system as a whole.

An estimator which falls in group (a) calls only on the zero restrictions and normalisation of a single equation. On the other hand, a group (b) estimator calls on the zero restrictions and normalisations of more than one equation, and perhaps on the covariance matrix $\mathbf{\Omega}$ as well.

Group (b) can usefully be subdivided into:

(i) those estimators which use only *a limited amount* of the available whole-system information; and
(ii) those which use the *full* whole-system information.

Those estimators which fall in group (a) will be described in this book by the acronym SIEs (single-equation information estimators). Estimators from group (bi) will be called LISEs (limited information relating to the whole-system estimators), while those from group (bii) will be labelled FISEs (full information relating to the whole-system estimators).

In the remaining sections of this chapter this classification will be used as a basis for describing the estimators which are available in the system context and for presenting the main results relating to those estimators.

4.3 Single-equation information estimators

As the name suggests, SIEs are estimators which have been developed for the specific purpose of estimating the parameters of a single stochastic equation. Accordingly, when a SIE is used in the system context it is applied to the stochastic equations one at a time and proceeds in any application as though the equation concerned stands alone – the fact that the equation is surrounded by others in a complete system is ignored.

The best known SIE is *ordinary least squares* (OLS). OLS has been developed for the estimation of a single stochastic equation which is linear in the parameters and variables or which can be made so by an appropriate transformation. Accordingly, in the system context OLS can be applied only to such of the stochastic equations as meet this requirement.

Most readers will be familiar with the OLS estimator already. Consequently, it will be given no more than a brief treatment. If we denote by $\boldsymbol{\beta}_i$, the $h \times 1$ vector of parameters in the particular stochastic equation of interest (the ith equation), then the OLS estimator of $\boldsymbol{\beta}_i$, $\hat{\boldsymbol{\beta}}_i$ is given by

$$\hat{\boldsymbol{\beta}}_i = (\mathbf{X}_i'\mathbf{X}_i)^{-1}\mathbf{X}_i'\mathbf{y}_i \tag{4.18}$$

where $\mathbf{X}_i$ is the $T \times h$ matrix of observations of endogenous and predetermined variables included on the right-hand side of the equation, and $\mathbf{y}_i$ is the $T \times 1$ vector of observations on the dependent (left-hand-side endogenous) variable. The covariance matrix of $\hat{\boldsymbol{\beta}}_i$ (not to be confused with either $\mathbf{\Sigma}$ or $\mathbf{\Omega}$) is:

$$\text{cov}(\hat{\boldsymbol{\beta}}_i) = \sigma_{ii}(\mathbf{X}_i'\mathbf{X}_i)^{-1} \tag{4.19}$$

where σ_{ii} is the variance of the disturbance of the equation of interest (as defined in (4.12)). The covariance matrix of $\hat{\boldsymbol{\beta}}_{\mathbf{i}}$ is estimated from:

$$\hat{\text{cov}}(\hat{\boldsymbol{\beta}}_{\mathbf{i}}) = (T - h)^{-1} S_i (\mathbf{X}_{\mathbf{i}}'\mathbf{X}_{\mathbf{i}})^{-1} \tag{4.20}$$

where $S_i = (\mathbf{y}_{\mathbf{i}} - \mathbf{X}_{\mathbf{i}}\hat{\boldsymbol{\beta}}_{\mathbf{i}})'(\mathbf{y}_{\mathbf{i}} - \mathbf{X}_{\mathbf{i}}\hat{\boldsymbol{\beta}}_{\mathbf{i}})$ is the sum of squared OLS residuals from the estimation of the ith stochastic equation.

A great deal is known about the properties of OLS, much more than about any of the LISEs or FISEs. In particular, it is known that OLS is a powerful estimator when certain requirements regarding the variables on the right-hand side of the equation of interest (the regressors) and the disturbance of the equation are met. Under the classical assumptions, for instance, OLS is unbiased, consistent and efficient.[1]* See Intriligator (1978, pp. 106–9). Crucial among the classical assumptions are those which require the regressors to be non-stochastic and the disturbance spherical. However, the equation of interest will, in general, include one or more endogenous variables on the right-hand side.[2] These endogenous-variable regressors are clearly stochastic in nature. Although OLS is no longer unbiased, consistency and asymptotic efficiency are retained in the presence of stochastic regressors provided that the disturbance is spherical and contemporaneous correlation between regressors and disturbance is absent (see Kmenta, 1971, pp. 533–4). However, an essential feature of systems of stochastic equations is that, in general, each endogenous variable is contemporaneously correlated with *every* disturbance. Hence the condition that contemporaneous correlation between the regressors and the disturbance be absent cannot be met. This means, in turn, that the minimum requirements for consistency cannot be satisfied. In general, therefore, OLS is inconsistent in the KK-system context. A direct proof of this proposition, and of the finite-sample bias of OLS in the system context, can be found in Intriligator (1978, pp. 375–7). See also Dhrymes (1978, pp. 287–9).

The conclusion, then, is that, when applied to KK systems, OLS produces parameter estimates which lack the minimum desirable properties. The same is true of the other SIEs, most of which are derivatives of OLS, to which we now turn.

Aside from OLS, the SIEs which are in regular use in KK systems can be placed in three main groups. One group comprises those designed to handle the estimation of *distributed-lag* equations. A second group encompasses SIEs designed to handle estimation in the presence of *autocorrelation*, which is generally regarded as the most important source

---

* Notes are to be found at the end of each chapter, before the References and Further Reading.

of non-sphericalness of the disturbance in the context of KK estimation. In the third group are those estimators designed to undertake the estimation of equations which are not in the linear in parameters and variables form and which are not amenable to transformation. As explained earlier, OLS cannot be applied in this situation.

As regards the first group, a distributed-lag equation may be defined as a stochastic equation whose right-hand side includes one or more terms of the form:

$$\sum_{j=0}^{m} w_j \, x_{t-j}$$

where x is a variable which can be either endogenous or exogenous. Distributed lags are quite common in working KK systems and the SIEs which are used to estimate them are known as distributed-lag estimators.

The distributed-lag estimator most frequently encountered in KK systems is the *polynomial distributed lag* (PDL), or Almon, estimator. Here the distributed-lag weights w_0, w_1, ..., w_m are required to lie on a polynomial of specified degree r (often $r = 2$ or 3). By an appropriate transformation, the problem of estimating the w_j is then turned into an application of OLS in which the regressors are linear combinations of x_t, x_{t-1}, ..., x_{t-m}. (In fact PDL is just a special case of the restricted least squares estimator: see Kmenta, 1971, pp. 492–5.)

The starting-point for SIEs designed to handle autocorrelation is the hypothesis that the disturbance of the equation of interest is generated by a particular process. In the simplest case this process is an autoregressive process of the form:

$$u_{it} = \rho u_{it-s} + \epsilon_{it} \tag{4.21}$$

where u_{it} is the (structural) disturbance in the equation of interest and ϵ_{it} is another non-autocorrelated disturbance. An estimator which makes use of this hypothesis is the Cochrane–Orcutt (CO) estimator. This uses an iterative non-linear method to estimate jointly the parameters of the stochastic equation of interest and the parameter ρ of the disturbance process. (See Kmenta, 1971, pp. 287–9, for details.)

A more sophisticated SIE from the second group is the autoregressive moving average exogenous (ARMAX) estimator. In this case the starting-point is a more general mixed autoregressive moving average process of the form:

$$u_{it} = \rho_1 u_{it-1} + \rho_2 u_{it-2} + \ldots + \rho_s u_{it-s} + \epsilon_{it} + \theta_1 \epsilon_{it-1} + \ldots + \theta_v \epsilon_{it-v} \quad (4.22)$$

where u_{it} and ϵ_{it} are defined as before and s and v are specified integers (usually no greater than 2). The ARMAX estimator then uses non-linear techniques to estimate jointly the structural parameters appearing in the equation of interest, together with the ρs and θs of (4.22). (See Pagan, 1974, for details).

Turning now to the third group, as explained in section 1.2, it is common to find non-linearities in the stochastic equations of a KK system. Sometimes these can be eliminated with the aid of suitable transformations. (See Kmenta, 1971, pp. 451–60, for a discussion of these transformation procedures.) There are many non-linear relationships, however, for which no transformation exists. These are described as *intrinsically* non-linear and the SIE used to deal with their estimation is non-linear least squares (NLLS).

To illustrate, suppose the stochastic equation of interest is:

$$y_{it} = \alpha x_{1t}^{\beta} + \gamma x_{2t} + u_{it} \quad (t = 1, 2, \ldots, T) \quad (4.23)$$

y_i is an endogenous variable and x_1 and x_2 may be either endogenous or predetermined variables. (Recall that SIEs take no account of the role which particular right-hand-side variables play in the system.) u_{it} is a disturbance. As with OLS, the first step in NLLS is to form the residual sum of squares function. For (4.23), this is:

$$S = \sum_{t=1}^{T} (y_{it} - \hat{\alpha} x_{1t}^{\hat{\beta}} - \hat{\gamma} x_{2t})^2 \quad (4.24)$$

where $\hat{\alpha}$, $\hat{\beta}$ and $\hat{\gamma}$ denote estimates of the corresponding parameters. The NLLS estimators are those values of $\hat{\alpha}$, $\hat{\beta}$ and $\hat{\gamma}$ which minimise S. The problem now is one of minimisation of a non-linear function. Iterative numerical methods, which are closely related to the Newton–Raphson method described in section 2.3 in connection with the solution of a system of non-linear equations, are used to achieve the minimization of S with respect to $\hat{\alpha}$, $\hat{\beta}$ and $\hat{\gamma}$.

One method of tackling the minimisation of (4.24) is to set out the necessary conditions for a minimum of S by taking its partial derivatives with respect to $\hat{\alpha}$, $\hat{\beta}$ and $\hat{\gamma}$ and equating each to zero. The result will be three non-linear equations which must be solved for the three unknowns $\hat{\alpha}$,

$\hat{\beta}$ and $\hat{\gamma}$. The solution can be achieved by application of the Newton–Raphson method. The solution values are the NLLS estimates of the parameters. This approach calls for analytical partial derivatives with respect to each of the structual parameters. Other more direct methods are available which obviate this requirement. An account of these methods can be found in Draper and Smith (1966, ch. 10).

Before leaving the SIEs, a further remark on their properties is in order. Under classical assumptions, suitably modified to reflect a correctly specified distributed-lag relationship, the PDL estimator is unbiased, consistent and efficient. This follows from the fact that PDL is simply OLS applied to a suitably transformed relationship. Similarly, the CO and ARMAX estimators are consistent and asymptotically efficient under generalised classical assumptions, one of which is that the disturbance is generated by a process of the type and order specified. One approach to the proof of this proposition (applicable if the disturbances are normally distributed) relies on the CO and ARMAX estimators being maximum likelihood estimators. (See Kmenta, 1971, pp. 282–8.) An alternative method of proof regards them as approximating the Aitken (generalised least squares) estimator. (See Johnston, 1972, pp. 208–10, 259–65.) Finally, NLLS is consistent and asymptotically efficient under assumptions which resemble the classical assumptions with a correctly specified regression function. (See Malinvaud, 1970, pp. 329–38.) The asymptotic properties of these SIEs will not be affected by the replacement of the non-stochastic regressors assumption with one which admits stochastic regressors contemporaneously uncorrelated with the structural disturbance. However, as we have seen, this requirement is untenable in the system context. Consequently, PDL, CO, ARMAX and NLLS, like OLS, are inconsistent when applied to the estimation of an individual stochastic equation of a KK system. Ultimately, their disadvantages, like those of OLS, are associated with their being SIEs, i.e. with their neglect of whole-system information.

4.4 Limited information relating to the whole-system estimators

The second main group of estimators applicable in the system context are the *limited* information relating to the whole-system estimators, the LISEs. These estimators resemble the SIEs in that they are applied to the stochastic equations one at a time. Indeed, if desired, a solitary equation from the system can be estimated using a LISE without it being necessary to tackle the estimation of the remainder of the system.[3]

Unlike the SIEs, LISEs recognise that the equation of interest is part of the system and some, though limited, reference is made to the rest of the system and to the information it contains. Specifically, LISEs call on the list of endogenous variables and the list of predetermined variables from the full system, in addition to the normalisation and zero restrictions of the individual structural equation of immediate interest.

The LISE in most widespread use is two-stage least squares (2SLS). There are, however, several others, the best known being limited information maximum likelihood (LIML) and instrumental variables (IV).

As its name suggests, 2SLS consists of two separate applications of OLS.[4] The *first stage* is the OLS estimation of the (unrestricted) reduced-form equations (see section 2.2) for those endogenous variables which are included on the right-hand side of the stochastic equation of immediate interest. These first-stage OLS estimates are used to generate, for each sample point, the predicted value of each of the included endogenous variables. In the *second stage* of 2SLS, the stochastic equation of interest is estimated by OLS using the predicted values of the included endogenous regressors in place of their observed values. For a technical account of the 2SLS method see Intriligator (1978, pp. 384–93).

One important point which is clear from the above account is that 2SLS is applicable only when the KK system concerned is linear since it is only then that a reduced form exists (see section 2.2).

The first equation of SYSTEM III represents a suitable vehicle for demonstrating the 2SLS method. The equation of interest is:

$$y_{1t} = \alpha_1 y_{2t} + \alpha_2 y_{3t} + \alpha_3 x_{1t} + u_{1t} \quad (t = 1, 2, \ldots, T) \tag{4.25}$$

The endogenous variables included on the right-hand side are y_2 and y_3. Recalling that the full list of predetermined variables is x_1, x_2, x_3 and x_4, the unrestricted reduced-form equations of interest are:

$$\left.\begin{aligned} y_{2t} &= \pi_{21} + \pi_{22}x_{1t} + \pi_{23}x_{2t} + \pi_{24}x_{3t} + \pi_{25}x_{4t} + v_{1t} \qquad (4.26) \\ y_{3t} &= \pi_{31} + \pi_{32}x_{1t} + \pi_{33}x_{2t} + \pi_{34}x_{3t} + \pi_{35}x_{4t} + v_{2t} \qquad (4.27) \end{aligned}\right\} (t = 1, 2, \ldots, T)$$

v_{1t} and v_{2t} represent reduced-form disturbances. OLS is applied to (4.26) giving estimates $\hat{\pi}_{21}, \hat{\pi}_{22}, \ldots, \hat{\pi}_{25}$ of the reduced-form coefficients, and to (4.27) giving estimates $\hat{\pi}_{31}, \hat{\pi}_{32}, \ldots, \hat{\pi}_{35}$. These estimates are next used to generate the series of predicted values of y_2 and y_3 denoted by $\hat{y}_2$ and $\hat{y}_3$, respectively, from

$$\left.\begin{aligned}\hat{y}_{2t} &= \hat{\pi}_{21} + \hat{\pi}_{22}x_{1t} + \hat{\pi}_{23}x_{2t} + \hat{\pi}_{24}x_{3t} + \hat{\pi}_{25}x_{4t} \\ \hat{y}_{3t} &= \hat{\pi}_{31} + \hat{\pi}_{32}x_{1t} + \hat{\pi}_{33}x_{2t} + \hat{\pi}_{34}x_{3t} + \hat{\pi}_{35}x_{4t}\end{aligned}\right\} (t = 1, 2, \ldots, T) \quad \begin{aligned}(4.28)\\(4.29)\end{aligned}$$

This constitutes the first stage of the 2SLS procedure. The second stage is the application of OLS to (4.25) with $\hat{y}_{2t}$ and $\hat{y}_{3t}$ replacing y_{2t} and y_{3t} respectively. In other words the 2SLS estimates are obtained by applying OLS to:

$$y_{1t} = \alpha_1\hat{y}_{2t} + \alpha_2\hat{y}_{3t} + \alpha_3x_{1t} + u'_{1t} \quad (t = 1, 2, \ldots, T) \tag{4.30}$$

where u'_{1t} is a disturbance, different from u_{1t}. The resulting estimated equation is:

$$y_{1t} = \hat{\alpha}_1y_{2t} + \hat{\alpha}_2y_{3t} + \hat{\alpha}_3x_{1t} + e_{1t} \quad (t = 1, 2, \ldots, T) \tag{4.31}$$

where $\hat{\alpha}_1$, $\hat{\alpha}_2$ and $\hat{\alpha}_3$ are the 2SLS estimates of the corresponding parameters and e_{1t} represents the 2SLS residual for equation (4.25).

The 2SLS estimator of the parameters of the *i*th equation can be written (see Theil, 1971, p. 451):

$$\hat{\boldsymbol{\beta}}_\mathbf{i} = [\mathbf{X}'_\mathbf{i}\mathbf{Z}(\mathbf{Z}'\mathbf{Z})^{-1}\mathbf{Z}'\mathbf{X}_\mathbf{i}]^{-1}\mathbf{X}'_\mathbf{i}\mathbf{Z}(\mathbf{Z}'\mathbf{Z})^{-1}\mathbf{Z}'\mathbf{y}_\mathbf{i} \tag{4.32}$$

where, as before, $\boldsymbol{\beta}_\mathbf{i}$ is the $h \times 1$ vector of parameters in the *i*th equation, $\mathbf{X}_\mathbf{i}$ is the $T \times h$ matrix of observations on *all* variables included on the right-hand side of the *i*th equation and $\mathbf{y}_\mathbf{i}$ is the $T \times 1$ vector of observations on the dependent variable. The new matrix $\mathbf{Z}$ is the $T \times (kq + np)$ matrix of observations on all *predetermined* variables of the system. It can be formed from the vectors $\mathbf{z}_\mathbf{t}$ used in (4.5) as follows:

$$\mathbf{Z} = [\mathbf{z}'_1\ \mathbf{z}'_2\ \ldots\ \mathbf{z}'_{\mathbf{kq+np}}]$$

The asymptotic covariance matrix for the 2SLS estimator is estimated from:

$$\text{asy. }\hat{\text{cov}}(\hat{\boldsymbol{\beta}}_\mathbf{i}) = \sigma_{ii}[\mathbf{X}'_\mathbf{i}\mathbf{Z}(\mathbf{Z}'\mathbf{Z})^{-1}\mathbf{Z}'\mathbf{X}_\mathbf{i}]^{-1} \tag{4.33}$$

where $\sigma_{ii} = (T - h)^{-1}S_i$, and S_i is the sum of squared 2SLS residuals for the *i*th equation.

Although 2SLS is biased, it can be shown, under certain conditions, to be consistent. However, 2SLS does not achieve asymptotic efficiency. For proofs of these properties and a formal statement of the conditions on which the consistency of 2SLS depends see Theil (1971, pp. 497–9). The conditions can be stated informally as follows:

1. All stochastic equations are linear in the parameters and variables, and the equation of interest is correctly specified.
2. The full list of predetermined variables is correct.
3. There are sufficient zero restrictions on the system that, given the normalisations, the parameters of the stochastic equation of interest are identifiable.[5]
4. The expectation of every disturbance is zero at each sample point and its distribution has finite moments of every order.
5. The disturbances are identically distributed at each sample point and are independent over sample points.
6. The system is stable.
7. The moment matrix of the exogenous variables converges.
8. The pre-sample period values of the endogenous variables are constants.
9. The disturbances are contemporaneously uncorrelated with the predetermined variables.

Limited information maximum likelihood (LIML) was popular during the 1950s but is no longer encountered in working KK systems. Although LIML has the same asymptotic properties as 2SLS (in fact, both are members of a class of LISEs called the *k*-class: see Kmenta, 1971, pp. 565–71), it has been shown in finite-sample studies (the subject of the next chapter) that LIML has no finite moments (see Basmann, 1974; Mariano and Sawa, 1972). It has also been shown in these studies that LIML estimates are highly sensitive to small changes in the sample data, a difficulty which has its root in the one just mentioned. When LIML's computational difficulty is also taken into account (LIML makes considerably heavier computational demands than 2SLS, for example) its fall from grace is hardly surprising. In this light, and since LIML is not in current use in working KK systems, its mechanics will not be described. (See Johnston, 1972, pp. 384–7, for details.)

Instrumental variables (IV) is a method of estimation with quite widespread applications. IV is a class of estimator which is applicable when the equation of interest is linear and which includes OLS, 2SLS and LIML. Its mechanics are quite similar to those of OLS. The OLS estimator was given in (4.18). The IV estimator of the parameters of the *i*th equation is:

$$\hat{\boldsymbol{\beta}}_i = (\mathbf{W}_i'\mathbf{X}_i)^{-1}\mathbf{W}_i'\mathbf{y}_i \tag{4.34}$$

where, once again, $\boldsymbol{\beta}_i$ is the $h \times 1$ vector of parameters in the *i*th equation,

$\mathbf{X_i}$ is the $T \times h$ matrix of observations on all variables included on the right-hand side of the ith equation, and $\mathbf{y_i}$ is the $T \times 1$ vector of observations on the dependent variable; $\mathbf{W_i}$ is a $T \times h$ matrix of observations on a set of instrumental variables, each of which is associated with a particular right-hand-side variable of the ith equation – there is an association between columns of the $\mathbf{X_i}$ and $\mathbf{W_i}$ matrices.

The IV method hinges on the selection of an instrumental variable for each right-hand side variable. IV is consistent (see Intriligator, 1978, pp. 399–400) if the instruments satisfy:

(a) $\text{plim}\,(T^{-1}\mathbf{W_i}'\mathbf{u_i}) = 0$
(b) $\text{plim}\,(T^{-1}\mathbf{W_i}'\mathbf{X_i})$ exists and is non-singular

where $\mathbf{u_i}$ is the $T \times 1$ vector of the ith disturbance at the T sample points. Loosely speaking, (a) calls for the instruments to be contemporaneously uncorrelated with the structural disturbance, while (b) requires that they be correlated with the associated right-hand-side variable. Within the constraints imposed by these requirements, there is considerable scope for choosing the instruments. Since the predetermined variables satisfy both (a) and (b), predetermined variables included in the structural equation of interest are normally chosen to act as their own instruments. As for the included right-hand-side endogenous variables, their instruments are commonly selected from the predetermined variables excluded from the equation of interest. It is this which motivates the labelling of IV as a LISE.

The asymptotic covariance matrix for the IV estimator $\hat{\boldsymbol{\beta}}_\mathbf{i}$ is estimated from:

$$\text{asy. }\hat{\text{cov}}(\hat{\boldsymbol{\beta}}_\mathbf{i}) = \sigma_{ii}(\mathbf{W_i}'\mathbf{X_i})^{-1}(\mathbf{W_i}'\mathbf{W_i})(\mathbf{X_i}'\mathbf{W_i})^{-1} \quad (4.35)$$

where $\sigma_{ii} = (T - h)^{-1}S_i$, and S_i is the sum of squared IV residuals for the ith equation.

As mentioned above, 2SLS falls into the IV class. 2SLS has the special feature, however, that there is no scope for choice in the selection of instruments. 2SLS theory requires that the predetermined variables in the structural equation of interest must act as their own instruments and that the instruments for the included right-hand-side endogenous variables must be their predicted counterparts as derived from the estimated reduced form. In short 2SLS theory requires that each instrument must be a specific linear combination of the full set of predetermined variables. The fact that there is no arbitrariness in the choice of instruments is one compelling reason for preferring 2SLS to other members of the IV class. A still more important reason is that 2SLS is asymptotically the most efficient member of the sub-class of IV estimators whose instruments are linear combinations of the full set of predetermined variables. See Dhrymes (1970, pp. 296–303). (Note, however, that in general 2SLS is *not* asymptotically efficient.)

Other LISEs are those which belong to the fixed-point (FP) class. A feature of the three LISEs discussed so far is that they can be applied to the stochastic equations of a KK system one at a time. By contrast, the entire system must be estimated when a fixed-point estimator is employed, even if parameter estimates are required only for a single equation. There are several members of the FP class, examples being iterative instrumental variables (IIV), restricted reduced-form two-stage least squares (RRF2SLS), restricted reduced-form instrumental variables (RRFIV) and limited information iterated instrumental variables (LIIV). A comprehensive account of these estimators is given by Giles (1973). It should be noted that they are applicable only to linear KK systems.

The basic ideas underlying the FP class can be explained with reference to the LIIV estimator, the FP estimator which is potentially the most useful. Consider the representation of a linear KK system given as (4.5):

$$\mathbf{A}\mathbf{y}_t + \mathbf{B}\mathbf{z}_t = \mathbf{u}_t \quad (t = 1, 2, \ldots, T) \tag{4.36}$$

and the associated restricted reduced form (see section 2.2):

$$\mathbf{y}_t = -\mathbf{A}^{-1}\mathbf{B}\mathbf{z}_t + \mathbf{A}^{-1}\mathbf{u}_t \quad (t = 1, 2, \ldots, T) \tag{4.37}$$

The first step in LIIV estimation is to obtain initial estimates of the structural parameters (the elements of $\mathbf{A}$ and $\mathbf{B}$) by applying IV to each of the stochastic equations in (4.36) in turn. For this purpose, all included predetermined variables are used as their own instruments, while the instruments for the included endogenous variables are selected from the excluded predetermined variables. Denote the estimates of the structural coefficient matrices obtained in this way by $\hat{\mathbf{A}}$ and $\hat{\mathbf{B}}$. Next, $\hat{\mathbf{A}}$ and $\hat{\mathbf{B}}$ are substituted into the restricted reduced form to produce an estimate for each endogenous variable at each sample point. Denote the $(n \times 1)$ vector of estimates at sample point t by $\tilde{\mathbf{y}}_t$. Then $\tilde{\mathbf{y}}_t$ is given by:

$$\tilde{\mathbf{y}}_t = -\hat{\mathbf{A}}^{-1}\hat{\mathbf{B}}\mathbf{z}_t \quad (t = 1, 2, \ldots, T) \tag{4.38}$$

The stochastic equations are then re-estimated one by one by IV with the elements of the $\tilde{\mathbf{y}}_t$ acting as instruments for the included right-hand-side endogenous variables in each equation. (Included predetermined variables again act as their own instruments.) This produces the LIIV estimates of the structural parameters.

LIIV is consistent and has the same asymptotic covariance matrix as 2SLS (see Dhrymes, 1978, p. 312) under the same conditions as 2SLS except that condition (1) on page 88 is strengthened to read:

> All structural equations are linear in the parameters and variables, and are correctly specified.

Note that, like 2SLS, LIIV is not asymptotically efficient, though it shares with 2SLS the distinction of being asymptotically efficient relative to other LISEs.

A modification of LIIV consists of iterating the above procedure to convergence. The estimates obtained as above are regarded as 'first-round' estimates and used to form a new set of vectors $\tilde{\mathbf{y}}_t$. The IV estimation of the structural parameters is then repeated using the new elements of the $\tilde{\mathbf{y}}_t$ series as instruments. This process continues until the estimates converge relative to some specified tolerance level. Iteration of LIIV may be desirable in the interests of the small-sample properties of the estimator, though there is nothing to be gained in terms of asymptotic properties (see Dhrymes, 1978, p. 313).

The other FP estimators are broadly similar to LIIV. They differ in the way in which the initial estimates are obtained, the means by which the $\tilde{\mathbf{y}}_t$ vector is formed (in some variants, a Gauss–Seidel solution procedure is used to provide FP estimators applicable to non-linear systems) and the estimator used in the final step. See Giles (1973), Maddala (1971), Brundy and Jorgenson (1971), Dutta and Lyttkens (1970) and Salmon and Eaton (1975).

In general, the LISEs are consistent but not asymptotically efficient. They achieve consistency by taking account of some of the whole-system information. Equally they fail to achieve asymptotic efficiency because some of the whole-system information, that contained in the covariance matrix of the system, is ignored.

4.5 Full information relating to the whole-system estimators

The final group of system estimators, the full-information relating to the whole-system estimators, or FISEs, differ from the LISEs in two respects. The first is that it is not possible with any of the FISEs to estimate the parameters of just one equation. All equations of the system are estimated simultaneously. (Recall that the FP estimators are the only LISEs of which this is true.) The second is that the FISEs exploit the information contained in the covariance matrix of the system and, in particular, recognise that the disturbance of one equation may be contemporaneously correlated with those of others. A direct consequence of the fact that all equations are estimated at the one time is that the FISEs take account of the zero restrictions and normalisation of all equations in the estimation of each individual equation. Because they exploit more of the available information of the system than do the LISEs, the FISEs outrank the LISEs in terms of asymptotic properties.

The best-known FISEs are three-stage least squares (3SLS) and full information maximum likelihood (FIML). One of the fixed-point estimators, the full information iterated instrumental variables (FIIV) estimator, is also a FISE.

As its name suggests, 3SLS is an extension of 2SLS, and like 2SLS is applicable only to linear systems. To explain 3SLS, we shall again make use of SYSTEM III.

The first step in 3SLS is to apply 2SLS to each of the stochastic equations. In the case of SYSTEM III, the first step would be to produce:

$$\left.\begin{aligned} y_{1t} &= \hat{\alpha}_1 y_{2t} + \hat{\alpha}_2 y_{3t} + \hat{\alpha}_3 x_{1t} + e_{1t} \qquad (4.39) \\ y_{2t} &= \hat{\beta}_1 y_{1t} + \hat{\beta}_2 x_{2t} + \hat{\beta}_3 x_{3t} + e_{2t} \qquad (4.40) \end{aligned}\right\} \quad (t = 1, 2, \ldots, T)$$

$\hat{\alpha}_1$, $\hat{\alpha}_2$, $\hat{\alpha}_3$, $\hat{\beta}_1$, $\hat{\beta}_2$ and $\hat{\beta}_3$ are the 2SLS estimates of the corresponding parameters, while e_{1t} and e_{2t} are the 2SLS residuals. The next step is to impose assumptions (a) to (d) of section 4.1 and to use the 2SLS residuals to form an estimate of $\mathbf{\Omega}$ after deleting all rows and columns corresponding to the identities. In the case of SYSTEM III the estimate of $\mathbf{\Omega}$ takes the following form. (Note that failure to drop the identity (4.3) would leave a column and a row of zeros in $\mathbf{\Omega}$, making it singular.)

$$\hat{\mathbf{\Omega}} = \begin{bmatrix} \hat{\sigma}_{11} & \hat{\sigma}_{12} \\ \hat{\sigma}_{12} & \hat{\sigma}_{22} \end{bmatrix} \qquad (4.41)$$

where:

$$\hat{\sigma}_{11} = \frac{1}{T} \sum_{t=1}^{T} e_{1t}^2$$

$$\hat{\sigma}_{22} = \frac{1}{T} \sum_{t=1}^{T} e_{2t}^2$$

$$\hat{\sigma}_{12} = \frac{1}{T} \sum_{t=1}^{T} e_{1t} e_{2t}$$

The third step in 3SLS is to employ a simple device which makes it possible to look upon the entire system as if it were a single relationship. First, we form a vector of observations on the dependent variables of all stochastic equations (denoted by $\mathbf{y}^*$) and an observations matrix of all regressors in all such equations (denoted by $\mathbf{Z}^*$). We also form a variant of the $\mathbf{Z}^*$ matrix (denoted by $\hat{\mathbf{Z}}^*$) in which the observations used for the endogenous-variable regressors are the same as those used in the second stage of the 2SLS procedure, i.e. they are estimated values obtained from the OLS estimation of the corresponding unrestricted reduced-form equation. In the case of SYSTEM III $\mathbf{y}^*$ $\mathbf{Z}^*$ and $\hat{\mathbf{Z}}^*$ (recall that the identity (4.3) has been dropped) are:

$$\mathbf{y}^* = \begin{bmatrix} y_{11} \\ y_{12} \\ \vdots \\ y_{1T} \\ y_{21} \\ y_{22} \\ \vdots \\ y_{2T} \end{bmatrix} \qquad \mathbf{Z}^* = \begin{bmatrix} y_{21} & y_{31} & x_{11} & 0 & 0 & 0 & 0 \\ y_{22} & y_{32} & x_{12} & 0 & 0 & 0 & 0 \\ \vdots & \vdots & \vdots & \vdots & \vdots & \vdots & \vdots \\ y_{2T} & y_{3T} & x_{1T} & 0 & 0 & 0 & 0 \\ 0 & 0 & 0 & y_{11} & y_{21} & x_{21} & x_{31} \\ 0 & 0 & 0 & y_{12} & y_{22} & x_{22} & x_{32} \\ \vdots & \vdots & \vdots & \vdots & \vdots & \vdots & \vdots \\ 0 & 0 & 0 & y_{1T} & y_{2T} & x_{2T} & x_{3T} \end{bmatrix}$$

$$\hat{\mathbf{Z}}^* = \begin{bmatrix} \hat{y}_{21} & \hat{y}_{31} & x_{11} & 0 & 0 & 0 & 0 \\ \hat{y}_{22} & \hat{y}_{32} & x_{12} & 0 & 0 & 0 & 0 \\ \vdots & \vdots & \vdots & \vdots & \vdots & \vdots & \vdots \\ \hat{y}_{2T} & \hat{y}_{3T} & x_{1T} & 0 & 0 & 0 & 0 \\ 0 & 0 & 0 & \hat{y}_{11} & \hat{y}_{21} & x_{21} & x_{31} \\ 0 & 0 & 0 & \hat{y}_{12} & \hat{y}_{22} & x_{22} & x_{32} \\ \vdots & \vdots & \vdots & \vdots & \vdots & \vdots & \vdots \\ 0 & 0 & 0 & \hat{y}_{1T} & \hat{y}_{2T} & x_{2T} & x_{3T} \end{bmatrix}$$

Associated with these 'stacked' observations matrices is a vector of *all* parameters of the system ($\boldsymbol{\alpha}^*$) and a vector of disturbances at all sample points for all stochastic equations of the system ($\mathbf{u}^*$). For SYSTEM III $\boldsymbol{\alpha}^*$ and $\mathbf{u}^*$ (note, once again, that (4.3) has been dropped) are:[6]

$$\boldsymbol{\alpha}^* = \begin{bmatrix} \alpha_1 \\ \alpha_2 \\ \alpha_3 \\ \beta_1 \\ \beta_2 \\ \beta_3 \end{bmatrix} \qquad \mathbf{u}^* = \begin{bmatrix} u_{11} \\ u_{12} \\ \vdots \\ u_{1T} \\ u_{21} \\ u_{22} \\ \vdots \\ u_{2T} \end{bmatrix}$$

Using the vectors and matrices just introduced, we can represent the stochastic equations of the system by:

$$\mathbf{y}^* = \mathbf{Z}^*\boldsymbol{\alpha}^* + \mathbf{u}^* \tag{4.42}$$

The final step in 3SLS is to apply the Aitken estimator[7] to (4.42) using the previously derived estimate of $\boldsymbol{\Omega}$. (This is given in (4.41) for SYSTEM III.) Thus the 3SLS estimator is given by:

$$\hat{\boldsymbol{\alpha}}^* = (\hat{\mathbf{Z}}^{*\prime}\hat{\boldsymbol{\Omega}}^{-1}\hat{\mathbf{Z}}^*)^{-1}(\hat{\mathbf{Z}}^{*\prime}\hat{\boldsymbol{\Omega}}^{-1}\mathbf{y}^*) \tag{4.43}$$

The 3SLS asymptotic covariance matrix is estimated from:

$$\text{asy. }\hat{\text{cov}}(\hat{\boldsymbol{\alpha}}^*) = (\hat{\mathbf{Z}}^{*\prime}\hat{\boldsymbol{\Omega}}^{-1}\hat{\mathbf{Z}}^*)^{-1} \tag{4.44}$$

From the expression for the 3SLS estimator given in (4.43), it is clear that it is not possible to obtain the 3SLS estimates of the parameters which appear in any one stochastic equation without, at the same time, obtaining the estimates of all other structural parameters. It is in this sense that 3SLS undertakes the estimation of the complete system in 'one hit'. To obtain the full flavour of these remarks, it is helpful to write out the equations covered by (4.43) for SYSTEM III. This task is left to the reader, who will find that, for SYSTEM III, the 3SLS estimates are obtained by solving a system of six simultaneous equations in α_1, α_2, α_3, β_1, β_2 and β_3 as unknowns much like the normal equations which are solved to get the OLS estimates.

3SLS is consistent and asymptotically efficient if the following conditions are met. For a proof of these properties and a formal statement of the required conditions see Theil (1971, pp. 511–13).

1. All structural equations are linear in the parameters and variables, and are correctly specified.
2. There are sufficient zero restrictions on the system that, given the normalisations, all structural parameters are identifiable.
3. The expectation of every disturbance is zero at each sample point and its distribution has finite moments of every order.
4. The disturbances are identically distributed at each sample point with covariance matrix $\mathbf{\Omega}$ and are independent over sample points.
5. After deleting rows and columns which correspond to identities in the system, the remaining sub-matrix of $\mathbf{\Omega}$ is non-singular.
6. The system is stable.
7. The moment matrix of the exogenous variables converges.
8. The pre-sample period values of the endogenous variables are constant.
9. The disturbances are contemporaneously uncorrelated with the predetermined variables.

Note that condition (4) is stronger than is required to guarantee absence of within-equation autocorrelation, presence of within-equation homoskedasticity and absence of across-equations non-contemporaneous disturbance correlation, while admitting across-equations contemporaneous disturbance correlation.

We turn now to the second well-known FISE, namely the full information maximum likelihood (FIML) estimator. Although quite simple in conception, FIML is without question the most difficult to implement. It is distinguished from all other system estimators in that it tackles the estimation of the entire set of parameters at once without breaking the estimation task down into a sequence of stages. Unlike 3SLS, FIML can, in principle, be applied to any KK system, linear or otherwise. For purposes of explaining the method, however, a linear system, i.e.

$$\mathbf{A}\mathbf{y}_t + \mathbf{B}\mathbf{z}_t = \mathbf{u}_t$$

will be assumed.

The FIML estimates of a linear KK system are obtained by maximising the (log) likelihood function[8] for the entire system. Where the joint distribution of the disturbances is multivariate normal and where assumptions (a) to (d) of section 4.1 apply, it can be shown (Kmenta, 1971, pp. 578–9; Intriligator, 1978, pp. 413–14) that the log-likelihood function is:

$$L(\mathbf{A}, \mathbf{B}, \boldsymbol{\Omega}) = -\frac{Tn}{2}\,\ell n(2\pi) - \frac{T}{2}\,\ell n|\boldsymbol{\Omega}| + T\,\ell n||\mathbf{A}||$$

$$-\frac{1}{2}\left\{\sum_{t=1}^{T}(\mathbf{A}\mathbf{y}_t + \mathbf{B}\mathbf{x}_t)'\boldsymbol{\Omega}^{-1}(\mathbf{A}\mathbf{y}_t + \mathbf{B}\mathbf{x}_t)\right\} \tag{4.45}$$

As the notation indicates, the arguments of the likelihood function are the structural parameters (the elements of **A** and **B**) and the elements of the covariance matrix $\boldsymbol{\Omega}$. To find the elements of **A, B** and $\boldsymbol{\Omega}$ which maximise L in (4.45), it is necessary to evaluate the partial derivatives of L with respect to each element of **A, B** and $\boldsymbol{\Omega}$, set all of them equal to zero and solve the resulting set of equations simultaneously for the elements of **A, B** and $\boldsymbol{\Omega}$. In principle this set of equations is not unlike the OLS normal equations or the equations which are solved at the final stage of 3SLS. However, even for a system in which all equations are linear both in parameters and variables, the set of equations to be solved to obtain the FIML estimates are intrinsically highly non-linear. Some appreciation of the extent of non-linearity can be gained by inspection of (4.45). The partial derivatives of the final term in braces will clearly involve the structural parameters and covariance-matrix elements in a non-linear way. Still more difficult is the innocent looking term $\ell n\ ||\mathbf{A}||$, the double bars denoting the absolute value of the determinant. The partial derivative of $\ell n\ ||\mathbf{A}||$ with respect to a particular structural parameter is the element in the corresponding position of the inverse of **A**.[9] Since the inverse of **A** involves all of its elements in a complicated non-linear way, the partial derivatives of $\ell n\ ||\mathbf{A}||$ will be non-linear functions of all the structural parameters.

To further illustrate this point, consider the application of FIML to SYSTEM III. Since FIML makes use of the inverse of $\boldsymbol{\Omega}$, it is necessary at the outset to eliminate all identities from the system by substitution[10] to ensure that $\boldsymbol{\Omega}$ is non-singular. Substituting for y_{3t} in (4.1), using (4.3), and rearranging, SYSTEM III can be condensed to:[11]

$$\left.\begin{aligned} y_{1t} &= \eta_1 y_{2t} + \eta_2 x_{1t} + \eta_3 x_{4t} + u_{1t} \quad (4.46) \\ y_{2t} &= \beta_1 y_{1t} + \beta_2 x_{2t} + \beta_3 x_{3t} + u_{2t} \quad (4.47) \end{aligned}\right\} \quad (t = 1, 2, \ldots, T)$$

where $\eta_1 = (\alpha_1 + \alpha_2)(1 - \alpha_2)^{-1}$, $\eta_2 = \alpha_3(1 - \alpha_2)^{-1}$ and $\eta_3 = \alpha_2(1 - \alpha_2)^{-1}$.

(In the interests of clarity the subsequent discussion will concentrate on the estimation of the ηs and βs rather than on the αs and βs.)

$$\mathbf{A} = \begin{bmatrix} 1 & -\eta_1 \\ -\beta_1 & 1 \end{bmatrix} \qquad \mathbf{B} = \begin{bmatrix} -\eta_2 & 0 & 0 & -\eta_3 \\ 0 & -\beta_2 & -\beta_3 & 0 \end{bmatrix}$$

$$\mathbf{y_t} = \begin{bmatrix} y_{1t} \\ y_{2t} \end{bmatrix} \qquad \mathbf{u_t} = \begin{bmatrix} u_{1t} \\ u_{2t} \end{bmatrix}$$

$$\mathbf{z_t} = \begin{bmatrix} x_{1t} \\ x_{2t} \\ x_{3t} \\ x_{4t} \end{bmatrix}$$

The covariance matrix of the disturbances at a single sample point is:

$$\boldsymbol{\Omega} = \begin{bmatrix} \sigma_{11} & \sigma_{12} \\ \sigma_{12} & \sigma_{22} \end{bmatrix}$$

Thus, in the case of SYSTEM III, the information required to form the log likelihood is:

$$|\boldsymbol{\Omega}| = \sigma_{11}\sigma_{22} - \sigma_{12}^2$$

$$|\mathbf{A}| = 1 - \beta_1\eta_1$$

$$\boldsymbol{\Omega}^{-1} = \frac{1}{|\boldsymbol{\Omega}|} \begin{vmatrix} \sigma_{22} & -\sigma_{12} \\ -\sigma_{12} & \sigma_{11} \end{vmatrix}$$

The log-likelihood function for SYSTEM III is therefore:

$$L(\mathbf{A}, \mathbf{B}, \mathbf{\Omega}) = -\frac{Tn}{2}\,\ell n(2\pi) - \frac{T}{2}\,\ell n(\sigma_{11}\sigma_{22} - \sigma_{12}^2)$$

$$+ T\,\ell n|1 - \beta_1\eta_1| - \frac{1}{2}(\sigma_{11}\sigma_{22} - \sigma_{12}^2)^{-1} \times$$

$$\Big\{\sigma_{22}\sum_{t=1}^{T}(y_{1t} - \eta_1 y_{2t} - \eta_2 x_{1t} - \eta_3 x_{4t})^2$$

$$+ \sigma_{11}\sum_{t=1}^{T}(-\beta_1 y_{1t} + y_{2t} - \beta_2 x_{2t} - \beta_3 x_{3t})^2$$

$$- 2\sigma_{12}\sum_{t=1}^{T}(y_{1t} - \eta_1 y_{2t} - \eta_2 x_{1t} - \eta_3 x_{4t}) \times$$

$$(-\beta_1 y_{1t} + y_{2t} - \beta_2 x_{2t} - \beta_3 x_{3t})\Big\} \tag{4.48}$$

The necessary conditions for a maximum of L are:

$$\frac{\partial L}{\partial \eta_1} = 0 \qquad \frac{\partial L}{\partial \beta_1} = 0 \qquad \frac{\partial L}{\partial \sigma_{11}} = 0$$

$$\frac{\partial L}{\partial \eta_2} = 0 \qquad \frac{\partial L}{\partial \beta_2} = 0 \qquad \frac{\partial L}{\partial \sigma_{12}} = 0$$

$$\frac{\partial L}{\partial \eta_3} = 0 \qquad \frac{\partial L}{\partial \beta_3} = 0 \qquad \frac{\partial L}{\partial \sigma_{22}} = 0$$

The first of these equations is:

$$\frac{\partial L}{\partial \eta_1} = \frac{-T\beta_1}{|1 - \beta_1\eta_1|} + \frac{1}{2(\sigma_{11}\sigma_{22} - \sigma_{12}^2)}\Big\{\sigma_{22}\sum_{t=1}^{T} 2y_{2t}(y_{1t} - \eta_1 y_{2t} - \eta_2 x_{1t} - \eta_3 x_{4t})$$

$$+ 2\sigma_{12}\sum_{t=1}^{T} y_{2t}(-\beta_1 y_{1t} + y_{2t} - \beta_2 x_{2t} - \beta_3 x_{3t})\Big\} = 0 \tag{4.49}$$

It is left to readers with the necessary stamina to evaluate the remaining equations. The non-linearity of the necessary conditions is nevertheless clearly apparent from (4.49) and the difficulty of solving the relevant nine-equation system simultaneously for the ηs, βs and σs can also be appreciated. The interested reader is referred to Phillips and Wickens (1978, pp. 275–6, 343–9) for another fully worked example of FIML estimation.

Despite the intrinsic non-linearity of the equations to be solved to obtain the FIML estimates, the problem essentially is a computational one and can be solved by methods such as Newton–Raphson, albeit at a considerably higher computational cost than for 3SLS. On the other hand, because implementation of FIML demands that the problem of the solution of a set of non-linear equations be faced, irrespective of whether or not the structural form of the system is linear, it is *in principle* no more difficult to handle a non-linear system with FIML than it is a linear system, a remark that does not apply to any of the other estimators discussed apart from NLLS. (It should be said, however, that in practice there is an enormous increase in the computational burden associated with FIML if the system is non-linear in the endogenous variables. The reason lies in the fact that the term which replaces $T \ell n \|\mathbf{A}\|$ in (4.45) – the Jacobian of the transformation from $\mathbf{u}_t$ to $\mathbf{y}_t$ – is not constant from observation to observation when the system is non-linear. Consequently, it must be evaluated at every sample point within each iteration of the Newton–Raphson solution procedure. Other things equal, this increases the computational cost by a factor of T relative to the linear case.) Restrictions on the structural parameters both within equations and across different structural equations can also be accommodated without difficulty by FIML (and at a computational cost comparable with the linear case) but not by any of the other LISEs or FISEs so far discussed.

Since FIML is a maximum likelihood estimator, it is consistent and asymptotically efficient under the same set of conditions (1)–(9) as 3SLS with the additional requirement:

10. The distribution of the structural disturbances is multivariate normal.

It can also be shown that the asymptotic covariance matrix of FIML is the same as that for 3SLS (provided that there are no restrictions on the covariance matrix of the disturbances, $\mathbf{\Omega}$). See Theil (1971, p. 526). In practice, however, the asymptotic covariance matrix of FIML estimates will usually be estimated by forming the negative of the inverse of the information matrix (see Kmenta, 1971, p. 182).

The last estimator to be discussed is a FISE of the FP class. The estimator in question is full information iterated instrumental variables (FIIV). FIIV differs from LIIV in that (in a fashion similar to 3SLS) it takes account of the information contained in the covariance matrix of the disturbances at a single sample point. As with LIIV, FIIV begins by applying IV to the structural equations seriatum (equation by equation in order). In addition, however, the residuals from these estimations of the structural equations are used to form an estimate of the covariance matrix $\mathbf{\Omega}$ by the same method as that used in 3SLS. The $\tilde{\mathbf{y}}_t$ vectors are next formed in the same way as in LIIV. The final step in FIIV is to apply an instrumental-variables variant of the Aitken estimator to the stochastic structural equations using the elements of $\tilde{\mathbf{y}}_t$ vectors as instruments and the estimate of the covariance matrix $\mathbf{\Omega}$ described above. (As with 3SLS, the identities must be dropped[12] from the system at this stage to ensure the non-singularity of $\mathbf{\Omega}$.)

To illustrate the final step of FIIV, consider again the estimation of SYSTEM III. As in 3SLS, certain 'stacked' matrices and vectors are formed; $\mathbf{y}^*$, $\boldsymbol{\alpha}^*$, $\mathbf{Z}^*$ and $\mathbf{u}^*$ are defined as for 3SLS. In addition, the following is required:

$$\tilde{\mathbf{Z}}^* = \begin{bmatrix} \tilde{y}_{21} & \tilde{y}_{31} & x_{11} & 0 & 0 & 0 & 0 \\ \tilde{y}_{22} & \tilde{y}_{32} & x_{12} & 0 & 0 & 0 & 0 \\ \vdots & \vdots & \vdots & \vdots & \vdots & \vdots & \vdots \\ \tilde{y}_{2T} & \tilde{y}_{3T} & x_{1T} & 0 & 0 & 0 & 0 \\ 0 & 0 & 0 & \tilde{y}_{11} & \tilde{y}_{21} & x_{21} & x_{31} \\ 0 & 0 & 0 & \tilde{y}_{12} & \tilde{y}_{22} & x_{22} & x_{32} \\ \vdots & \vdots & \vdots & \vdots & \vdots & \vdots & \vdots \\ 0 & 0 & 0 & \tilde{y}_{1T} & \tilde{y}_{2T} & x_{2T} & x_{3T} \end{bmatrix}$$

The FIIV estimator of $\boldsymbol{\alpha}^*$ is then:

$$\hat{\boldsymbol{\alpha}}^* = (\tilde{\mathbf{Z}}^{*\prime}\hat{\mathbf{\Omega}}^{-1}\mathbf{Z}^*)^{-1}(\tilde{\mathbf{Z}}^{*\prime}\hat{\mathbf{\Omega}}^{-1}\mathbf{y}^*) \tag{4.50}$$

Like LIIV, FIIV can also be iterated, though as before this does not improve the asymptotic properties of the estimator.

FIIV is consistent and asymptotically efficient under the same conditions as 3SLS. The asymptotic covariance matrix of FIIV coincides, therefore, with that of 3SLS (see Dhrymes, 1978, p. 314).

To conclude this section, it will be useful to summarise the properties of the FISEs. Subject to certain requirements, the FISEs are, in general, consistent and asymptotically efficient. Their superiority over the LISEs rests therefore on the efficiency gain in large samples. On the other hand, there is a penalty to be paid in terms of the considerably higher computational costs of the FISEs relative to the LISEs.

Notes

1. Proofs of these results and most others given in the present chapter can be found in any econometrics textbook. See, for instance, Johnston (1972), Kmenta (1971), Goldberger (1964), Theil (1971), Theil (1978), Klein (1974), Wonnacott and Wonnacott (1979), Koutsoyiannis (1977), Dhrymes (1978) and Dutta (1975).
2. If this were not the case for any equation, the system would not be a simultaneous one and the estimation problem then becomes that of 'seemingly unrelated regressions'. See Intriligator (1978, p. 403). In terms of (4.5) this case occurs when the matrix **A** is an identity matrix.
3. An exception is the fixed-point class of estimators, discussed below.
4. The description of the 2SLS method given is the one which motivated its development and from which its name derives. In practice, more direct computational procedures are used.
5. Readers not familiar with the identification concept can consult Intriligator (1978, pp. 47–51) for a non-technical account. A complete treatment is given by Intriligator (1978, pp. 336–58).
6. $\mathbf{u}^*$ was shown earlier in (4.9) for SYSTEM III with (4.3) included and $T = 3$.
7. See Kmenta (1971, pp. 504–5).
8. For a general account of maximum likelihood estimation see Kmenta (1971, pp. 174–82).
9. The matrix-differentiation rule is:

$$\frac{\partial|\mathbf{A}|}{\partial\mathbf{A}} = \mathbf{A}^*$$

where $\mathbf{A}$ is $n \times n$ and $\mathbf{A}^*$ is its matrix of cofactors. Thus:

$$\frac{\partial \ell n|\mathbf{A}|}{\partial\mathbf{A}} = \frac{1}{|\mathbf{A}|}\mathbf{A}^*$$

using the rules for differentiating logarithms and a function of a function. Finally, from the relationship between the cofactors and the inverse of a matrix;

$$\frac{\partial \ell n|\mathbf{A}|}{\partial\mathbf{A}} = \frac{1}{\mathbf{A}}\mathbf{A}^* = \mathbf{A}^{-1}$$

See Dhrymes (1978, p. 533).

10. The reader may be puzzled as to why the identities are dropped from the system in the case of 3SLS but are 'worked in' by being substituted out in the case of FIML. The answer lies in the fact that since 2SLS achieves consistency, the 3SLS extension improves on 2SLS only by the attainment of asymptotic

efficiency. However, this extension calls only for information about the stochastic equations. Hence in the case of 3SLS the identities are not required to achieve asymptotic efficiency. On the other hand, since FIML estimation is undertaken in a single 'stage', dropping the identities would leave the system mis-specified and FIML would not then even achieve consistency.

11. In (4.46) the disturbance should strictly be distinguished from that of (4.1) since, if u_{1t} is the disturbance in (4.1) and u'_{1t} that in (4.46), $u'_{1t} = (1 - \alpha_2)^{-1} u_{1t}$. For convenience, however, the distinction is ignored.
12. See note 10.

References and further reading

BASMANN, R. L. (1974) 'Exact Finite Sample Distributions for Some Econometric Estimators and Test Statistics: A Survey and Appraisal', in M. D. Intriligator and D. A. Kendrick (eds), *Frontiers of Quantitative Economics*, vol. 11, North-Holland, Amsterdam.

BRUNDY, J. M. and JORGENSON, D. W. (1971) 'Efficient Estimation of Simultaneous Equations by Instrumental Variables', *Review of Economics and Statistics*, vol. 53, pp. 207–24.

DHRYMES, P. J. (1970) *Econometrics: Statistical Foundations and Applications*, Harper & Row, New York.

DHRYMES, P. J. (1978) *Introductory Econometrics*, Springer-Verlag, New York.

DRAPER, N. R. and SMITH, H. (1966) *Applied Regression Analysis*, Wiley, New York.

DUTTA, M. (1975) *Econometric Methods*, South-Western Publishing, Cincinnati, Ohio.

DUTTA, M. and LYTTKENS, E. (1970) 'Iterative Instrumental Variables and Estimation of a Large Simultaneous System', Discussion Paper No. 7, Bureau of Economic Research, Rutgers University.

GILES, D. E. A. (1973) 'Essays on Econometric Topics: From Theory to Practice', Research Paper No. 10, Reserve Bank of New Zealand, Wellington.

GOLDBERGER, A. S (1964) *Econometric Theory*, Wiley, New York.

INTRILIGATOR, M. D. (1978) *Econometric Models, Techniques and Applications*, Prentice-Hall, Englewood Cliffs, N. J.

JOHNSTON, J. (1972) *Econometric Methods*, 2nd edn, McGraw-Hill, New York.

KLEIN, L. R. (1974) *A Textbook of Econometrics*, 2nd edn, Prentice-Hall, Englewood Cliffs, N. J.

KMENTA, J. (1971) *Elements of Econometrics*, Macmillan, New York.

KOUTSOYIANNIS, A. (1977) *Theory of Econometrics*, 2nd edn, Macmillan, London.

MADDALA, G. S. (1971) 'Simultaneous Estimation Methods for Large- and Medium-Size Econometric Models', *Review of Economic Studies*, vol. 38, pp. 435–45.

MALINVAUD, E. (1970) *Statistical Methods of Econometrics*, 2nd edn, North-Holland, Amsterdam.

MARIANO, R. S. and SAWA. T. (1972) 'Exact Finite Sample Distribution of the Limited Information Maximum Likelihood Estimator in the Case of Two Included Endogenous Variables', *Journal of the American Statistical Association*, vol. 67, pp. 159–63.

PAGAN, A. R. (1974) 'A Generalized Approach to the Treatment of Autocorrelation', *Australian Economic Papers*, vol. 13, pp. 267–80.

PHILLIPS, P. C. B. and WICKENS, M. R. (1978) *Exercises in Econometrics*, Philip Allan, Oxford.

SALMON, M. H. and EATON, J. R. (1975) 'Estimation Problems in Large Econometric Models: An Application of Various Estimation Techniques to the London Business School Model', in G. A. Renton (ed.), *Modelling the Economy*, Heinemann, London.

THEIL, H. (1971) *Principles of Econometrics*, Wiley, New York.

THEIL, H. (1978) *Introduction to Econometrics*, Prentice-Hall, Englewood Cliffs, N. J.

WONNACOTT, R. J. and WONNACOTT, T. H. (1979) *Econometrics*, 2nd edn, Wiley, New York.

5 FINITE-SAMPLE PROPERTIES OF SYSTEM ESTIMATORS

5.1 Analytical results

In Chapter 4 we presented a number of results relating to the estimators which are presently available for use in relation to KK systems. All are asymptotic results, by which is meant that in every case the result was concerned with the conditions under which a particular estimator possesses various desirable asymptotic properties such as consistency and asymptotic efficiency and with the expression for the asymptotic covariance matrix of the estimator under those conditions.

The present chapter also deals with results for system estimators. The results to be considered here, however, are results relating to samples of finite size. They are loosely described as 'small-sample' results as opposed to the 'large-sample' (asymptotic) results of Chapter 4.

The finite-sample results considered in this chapter can be divided into two groups: (i) those derived by means of the analytical approach; (ii) those derived by means of the experimental approach. The first group will be discussed in the present section and the second group in section 5.2.

We begin by explaining the meaning of 'the analytical approach'. By this term is meant a process of deductive reasoning which has two essential ingredients. First, an environment or set of assumptions is specified. Then the logical consequences of the environment are deduced by means of an argument which conforms to the rules of mathematics and which calls on theorems from probability and statistics. All of the asymptotic results presented in Chapter 4 have been derived by this means. In fact it would be true to say that, to date, nearly all the major advances in econometric theory have been the product of the analytical approach.

It should be noted that results generated by the analytical approach have no validity outside the associated environment. For example, the analytical approach generates the result that the OLS estimator is best linear unbiased and has the multivariate normal distribution under the classical assumptions. This result ceases to hold if any one of these assumptions is not met. Again by application of the analytical approach it can be deduced that the 2SLS estimator is consistent under the assumptions listed as conditions (1) to (9) in section 4.4. This result has no validity if any one of these conditions is violated.

The output of the analytical approach in the 'finite-sample' area is very limited compared with what has been produced in the way of asymptotic results. The reason is that, in the nature of the case, the deductive process required to obtain expressions for the moments or form of the finite-sample distributions of estimators is practically intractable when applied to a system environment of any generality. Such progress as has been made with finite-sample results using the analytical approach has been possible only within quite limited environments. To make the deductive process tractable, workers in this field often have confined themselves to systems of only two or three equations, with small numbers of non-stochastic exogenous variables.

Perhaps the main achievement of the finite-sample analytical work has been to draw attention to the fact that not all moments of the finite-sample distributions of the system estimators exist. For instance, one of the earliest contributions of the so-called 'exact sampling studies' was Basmann (1961) in which it was shown that the mean of 2SLS exists but its variance does not, in a particular two-equation simultaneous system. Basmann (1961, p. 634) conjectured that the finite-sample moments of 2SLS exist up to the order of over-identification (see Intriligator, 1978, pp. 336–358) of a structural equation in question. Kinal (1980) has recently provided a proof of Basmann's conjecture as part of a wider result relating to the existence of moments of the *k*-class estimators. Aside from the intrinsic interest of such questions, these results have a particular importance which will be explained in connection with the experimental approach in section 5.2.

Finite-sample distributions (or their approximations), as well as expressions for such of their low-order moments as exist, have been derived for the *k*-class system estimators (which includes OLS, 2SLS and LIML). See Nagar (1959), Basmann (1961), Basmann (1963), Richardson (1968), Sargan and Mikhail (1971), Kadane (1971), Mariano and Sawa (1972), Basmann (1974) and Ullah and Nagar (1974). In all these studies the results are for particular cases in which at most three endogenous variables are included in the equation of interest. Kinal (1980) provides a generalisation of the results concerning the existence of moments of system estimators in the *k*-class for arbitrary numbers of included endogenous variables. Finally, Phillips (1980) obtains the exact finite-sample distribution of IV for the general case in which the structural equation includes an arbitrary number of endogenous variables. Analogous results for OLS and 2SLS are proved by Hillier (1981).

Two important limitations of these studies should be noted. First, all have concentrated on system estimators belonging to the SIE and LISE class. Very little work has been done on the FISEs. However, Sargan

(1978) has made some progress with the question of the existence of finite-sample moments of 3SLS. The second limitation of these studies is that all have assumed non-stochastic exogenous variables. For this reason they are not relevant to KK systems, in which the predetermined variables include lagged endogenous variables. Basmann, Richardson and Rohr (1974) conjecture that the exact finite-sample distributions of system estimators are unaffected by the presence of lagged endogenous variables. Although they provide some experimental evidence in support of this conjecture, it remains unproven.

A detailed survey and review of finite-sample analytical work is given by Basmann (1974); of particular interest are the comments by Kmenta, Madansky and Maddala which are appended. Another excellent survey is Mariano (1980). The interested reader is also referred to Christ (1966, pp. 469–73) and the surveys in Smith (1971) and Smith (1973, ch. 2).

Aside from its limited relevance to working KK systems, a major problem with the analytical method in the finite-sample area is that its results are invariably very complex and exceedingly difficult to interpret. Indeed it is frequently the case that comparative conclusions can be drawn from the results only by taking steps which effectively destroy their generality, e.g. by replacing unknown parameters with specific values. It is for this, among other reasons, that the experimental approach has proved to be the more fruitful method of obtaining finite-sample results, though the analytical approach has recently progressed at a remarkable rate. Having presented this brief discussion of the analytical approach, the alternative experimental approach is considered in the next two sections.

5.2 The Monte Carlo method

It was noted in the preceding section that the analytical approach is *deductive* in character. By contrast the experimental approach, usually known as the *Monte Carlo method* is *inductive.* The discoveries of the Monte Carlo approach are based on reasoning by inference.

The Monte Carlo method is the nearest thing to a controlled laboratory-type experiment in econometrics. In the KK context it may be described in broad terms as follows. The experimenter artificially sets up a system and specifies values for all exogenous variables and for the parameters. Values are then generated for the 'random' disturbances for some specified sample size and, using these values, values are calculated for the endogenous variables at each sample point. Next, it is pretended that the parameters are unknown and, using only the values of the endogenous and predetermined variables at each sample point, one or more estimators are applied to obtain an associated estimate of parameters. The process of generating values for the disturbances, calculating values for the endogenous variables and undertaking parameter estimation is then repeated, or *replicated*, a large number of times. The set of estimates of each parameter by each estimator can then be used to infer properties of the estimators for the given sample size and for the chosen values of the parameters. For instance, the mean value of each parameter estimate can be calculated as a basis for comparing the chosen estimators in terms of bias.

A useful way of explaining the experimental approach in more detail is by means of an illustrative Monte Carlo experiment. Suppose the objective is to examine the finite-sample behaviour of OLS and 2SLS as estimators of the parameters of SYSTEM III (see section 4.1), which is repeated below for convenience:

$$\left.\begin{aligned} y_{1t} &= \alpha_1 y_{2t} + \alpha_2 y_{3t} + \alpha_3 x_{1t} + u_{1t} \\ y_{2t} &= \beta_1 y_{1t} + \beta_2 x_{2t} + \beta_3 x_{3t} + u_{2t} \\ y_{3t} &\equiv y_{1t} + y_{2t} + x_{4t} \end{aligned}\right\} \quad (t = 1, 2, \ldots, T) \qquad \begin{aligned} (5.1) \\ (5.2) \\ (5.3) \end{aligned}$$

To set up the Monte-Carlo experiment, the following matters must be dealt with:

1. The sample size, T, must be specified.
2. Values must be assigned to each of the parameters, α_1, α_2, α_3, β_1, β_2, β_3.
3. Values must be assigned to each of the elements of $\mathbf{\Omega}$, the covariance matrix of the disturbances of the system at any given sample point (see section 4.1).
4. Values of the predetermined variables x_{1t}, x_{2t}, x_{3t} and x_{4t} must be specified for each sample point.
5. A method of generating values for the random disturbances u_{1t} and u_{2t} at each sample point must be chosen. Note that the chosen method must provide values of the disturbances which are consistent with the covariance matrix $\mathbf{\Omega}$, laid out in point (3).
6. Appropriate criteria on which the performance of the estimators under study, OLS and 2SLS, can be judged must be specified.

Each of these matters will now be considered in more detail.

The first task in a Monte Carlo experiment is to choose the sample size. For the purposes of our illustrative Monte Carlo experiment, T is set at 30. The second and third matters to be dealt with, selection of parameter values and covariance matrix elements, are known jointly as the *model design*. The model design for the illustrative Monte Carlo experiment is as follows:

$\alpha_1 = 1.8 \quad \alpha_2 = 1.2 \quad \alpha_3 = 0.7$
$\beta_1 = 1.5 \quad \beta_2 = 0.5 \quad \beta_3 = 0.3$

$$\Omega = \begin{bmatrix} 5.0 & 2.5 \\ 2.5 & 3.0 \end{bmatrix}$$

In specifying SYSTEM III no information was given on which of the four predetermined variables are lagged endogenous, unlagged exogenous and lagged exogenous. For convenience it will be assumed that all four are unlagged exogenous variables. Values for each of these variables were generated from the uniform (0, 1) distribution (see Kmenta, 1971, p. 54), using a standard computer algorithm[1] designed for the purpose. As such, the illustrative experiment is a fairly 'sterile' one. Some Monte Carlo experimenters have chosen historical values of particular economic variables (see, for instance, Summers, 1965, p. 9) in an attempt to give their experiment more real-life flavour. This is more the exception than the rule, however. The values generated by the computer algorithm are set out in Table 5.1.

The centrepiece of any Monte Carlo experiment is the generation of values for the random disturbances. Generally a two-stage process is used. Independent series of standard normal random deviates of the required length are first drawn. These series are then transformed into series for the random disturbances in such a way as to guarantee that they have the covariance matrix set out in the model design. Since this, and the subsequent computational steps in the experiment, must be replicated a large number of times, a computer is virtually essential. Aside from its computational efficiency, the use of a computer algorithm is recommended for the generation of standard normal random numbers. Among other advantages, this will produce sequences of pseudo-random numbers which are reproducible from a known 'seed' number. If this is not the case, it is impossible to subject a particular Monte Carlo experiment to independent verification. See Naylor (1971, pp. 381–2) for a discussion of the desirable properties of pseudo-random number generators.

Two random disturbances appear in SYSTEM III. The first step, therefore, is to call on the computer algorithm[2] to generate two independent series of standard normal random numbers. Denote these series by ϵ_{1t} and ϵ_{2t}; $t = 1, 2, \ldots, T$ (recall that T is 30 for the illustrative experiment). By definition, ϵ_{1t} and ϵ_{2t} have zero means, unit variances and zero covariance. The next step is to use a method presented in Nagar (1969, pp. 427–31) for transforming M independent series of standard normal random deviates, each of length T, into M series of random variables with zero means and a specified covariance matrix. In the present case, in which $M = 2$, we form:

Table 5.1 Values for the predetermined variables in the illustrative Monte Carlo experiment

t	x_{1t}	x_{2t}	x_{3t}	x_{4t}
1	0.28508	0.94831	0.90558	0.61016
2	0.27387	0.17105	0.15587	0.93019
3	0.97685	0.84180	0.67885	0.75914
4	0.94981	0.21021	0.46568	0.78397
5	0.53229	0.06258	0.61077	0.16985
6	0.20275	0.75568	0.13623	0.59258
7	0.67831	0.71730	0.66407	0.43865
8	0.39397	0.70293	0.94922	0.36762
9	0.52977	0.17809	0.54358	0.60015
10	0.89517	0.07856	0.97066	0.78181
11	0.12315	0.37152	0.91725	0.84847
12	0.78899	0.13356	0.27575	0.26620
13	0.57152	0.74396	0.56510	0.96569
14	0.61512	0.76500	0.69421	0.34633
15	0.24664	0.32600	0.59697	0.72635
16	0.22582	0.01188	0.21836	0.75086
17	0.33556	0.60568	0.04102	0.63022
18	0.76615	0.63325	0.35365	0.03828
19	0.69178	0.03859	0.76366	0.31373
20	0.66638	0.62711	0.82373	0.88963
21	0.81626	0.81477	0.40494	0.08543
22	0.90324	0.82791	0.76178	0.86797
23	0.67556	0.65309	0.19505	0.04834
24	0.14966	0.45519	0.13633	0.43425
25	0.28334	0.35856	0.24001	0.37204
26	0.01267	0.29130	0.79285	0.85149
27	0.02069	0.85982	0.49807	0.92232
28	0.79361	0.00731	0.13718	0.37868
29	0.25366	0.92859	0.52648	0.50500
30	0.18659	0.74992	0.55439	0.49467

$$s_{22} = +\sqrt{\sigma_{22}}$$

$$s_{21} = \sigma_{12}/s_{22}$$

$$s_{11} = +\sqrt{(\sigma_{11} - s_{21}^2)}$$

where σ_{11} and σ_{22} are, respectively, the specified variances of u_{1t} and u_{2t}, and σ_{12} is the specified covariance. The two random disturbances are then obtained from:

$$\left.\begin{aligned} u_{1t} &= s_{11}\,\epsilon_{1t} + s_{21}\epsilon_{2t} \\ u_{2t} &= s_{22}\epsilon_{2t} \end{aligned}\right\} \quad (t = 1, 2, \ldots, T)$$

It is readily verified[3] that the disturbances produced in this way have zero means and the required covariance matrix Ω.

The two series of standard normal random deviates drawn in the *first replication* of the illustrative Monte Carlo experiment are set out in Table 5.2. Given the values $\sigma_{11} = 5.0$, $\sigma_{12} = 2.5$ and $\sigma_{22} = 3.0$ laid down as the elements of Ω in the model design, we find that $s_{22} = 1.7321$, $s_{21} = 1.4434$ and $s_{11} = 1.7078$. The two random disturbance series are therefore formed using:

$$\left.\begin{aligned} u_{1t} &= 1.7078\epsilon_{1t} + 1.4434\epsilon_{2t} \\ u_{2t} &= 1.7321\epsilon_{2t} \end{aligned}\right\} (t = 1, 2, \ldots, T)$$

The series generated in this way are set out in Table 5.3.

Table 5.2 Standard normal random deviates drawn in the first replication of the illustrative Monte Carlo experiment

t	ϵ_{1t}	ϵ_{2t}
1	1.82019	0.59921
2	−0.17380	−0.80894
3	2.23871	−0.63431
4	−0.14689	−0.78881
5	−1.16833	−0.35575
6	−0.49143	0.19195
7	−0.30545	0.41851
8	1.17816	1.00262
9	0.91613	−1.21783
10	−1.19818	−0.22989
11	1.34125	0.09729
12	0.57034	0.79764
13	−1.48271	0.98229
14	1.76671	0.92469
15	0.28003	0.50696
16	1.17538	−0.01584
17	−0.05445	−0.54286
18	0.15289	0.73165
19	0.35756	0.18319
20	0.91692	1.75688
21	0.22037	0.35796
22	−0.82587	−0.38167
23	2.42323	−0.84914
24	0.60150	−1.06797
25	−1.74325	−0.04383
26	−1.15381	0.59732
27	1.39755	0.24051
28	0.11444	0.64826
29	−1.14704	1.58108
30	−0.40430	−0.94493

Table 5.3 Random disturbances generated for the first replication of the illustrative Monte Carlo experiment

t	u_{1t}	u_{2t}
1	3.973	1.038
2	−1.464	−1.401
3	2.908	−1.099
4	−1.389	−1.366
5	−2.509	−0.616
6	−0.562	0.332
7	0.082	0.725
8	3.459	1.737
9	−0.193	−2.109
10	−2.378	−0.398
11	2.431	0.169
12	2.125	1.382
13	−1.114	1.701
14	4.352	1.602
15	1.210	0.878
16	1.984	−0.027
17	−0.877	−0.940
18	1.317	1.267
19	0.875	0.317
20	4.102	3.043
21	0.893	0.620
22	−1.961	−0.661
23	2.913	−1.471
24	−0.514	−1.850
25	−3.040	−0.076
26	−1.108	1.035
27	2.734	0.417
28	1.131	1.123
29	0.323	2.739
30	−2.054	−1.637

Having generated the required random disturbances, the next step in a Monte Carlo experiment is to generate the implied values of the endogenous variables. In a linear system such as SYSTEM III this is most conveniently performed using the restricted reduced form (see section 2.2) corresponding to the model design. An appropriate iterative procedure (see section 2.3) will be required, however, for a non-linear system. Written in the form of (2.15), SYSTEM III appears as follows:

$$\mathbf{A y_t} = \mathbf{B x_t} + \mathbf{u_t}$$

where, for the model design set out above:

$$\mathbf{A} = \begin{bmatrix} 1 & -1.8 & -1.2 \\ -1.5 & 1 & 0 \\ -1 & -1 & 1 \end{bmatrix} \qquad \mathbf{B} = \begin{bmatrix} -0.7 & 0 & 0 & 0 \\ 0 & -0.5 & -0.3 & 0 \\ 0 & 0 & 0 & -1 \end{bmatrix}$$

(The matrix $\mathbf{C}_1$ in (2.15) is null in this case.)

The restricted reduced form of SYSTEM III corresponding to the model design is therefore (see (2.17)):

$$\left.\begin{aligned} y_{1t} &= 0.1489x_{1t} + 0.3191x_{2t} + 0.1915x_{3t} + 0.2553x_{4t} + v_{1t} \\ y_{2t} &= 0.2234x_{1t} - 0.0213x_{2t} - 0.0128x_{3t} + 0.3830x_{4t} + v_{2t} \\ y_{3t} &= 0.3723x_{1t} + 0.2979x_{2t} + 0.1787x_{3t} - 0.3617x_{4t} + v_{3t} \end{aligned}\right\} (t = 1, 2, \ldots, T)$$

where

$$v_{1t} = -0.2128u_{1t} - 0.6383u_{2t}$$

$$v_{2t} = -0.3191u_{1t} + 0.0426u_{2t}$$

$$v_{3t} = -0.5319u_{1t} - 0.5957u_{2t}$$

Since, by definition, these expressions provide the values of the endogenous variables at each sample point in terms of the predetermined variables and the structural disturbances, they can be used immediately to generate the required values of the endogenous variables, as in Table 5.4.

The final step in each replication is the calculation of the OLS and 2SLS estimates of the structural parameters. For this purpose we imagine that only the specification of SYSTEM III (equations (5.1)–(5.3)) and the series over $T = 30$ sample points for y_{1t}, y_{2t}, y_{3t}, x_{1t}, x_{2t}, x_{3t} and x_{4t} are known – that is, that no more data are available than would be the case in an ordinary estimation situation. Estimation is then performed in the usual way. For the purposes of the illustrative experiment the calculations were carried out using TSP, a widely available econometric software package (see Hall and Hall, 1979). The estimates obtained in the first replication were as follows:[4]

	$\hat{\alpha}_1$	$\hat{\alpha}_2$	$\hat{\alpha}_3$	$\hat{\beta}_1$	$\hat{\beta}_2$	$\hat{\beta}_3$
OLS	−0.458	0.823	−0.553	0.362	−0.189	−0.182
2SLS	1.566	0.295	0.435	0.079	−0.427	−0.413

Table 5.4 Values of the endogenous variables generated for the first replication of the illustrative Monte Carlo experiment

t	y_{1t}	y_{2t}	y_{3t}
1	−2.182	−1.490	−3.062
2	0.843	−0.004	1.769
3	−0.655	−1.457	−1.353
4	0.670	−0.117	1.337
5	0.668	0.600	1.437
6	−0.541	−0.061	−0.010
7	−1.049	−0.291	−0.902
8	−2.403	−1.232	−3.267
9	0.994	−0.366	1.229
10	0.216	0.257	1.255
11	−1.154	−1.102	−1.407
12	−1.615	−0.891	−2.240
13	−1.526	−0.046	−0.607
14	−2.505	−1.566	−3.725
15	−1.258	−0.668	−1.200
16	−0.676	−0.969	−0.894
17	0.375	−0.063	0.942
18	−1.483	−0.534	−1.979
19	−0.730	−0.530	−0.947
20	−3.499	−1.645	−4.255
21	−1.067	−0.451	−1.432
22	0.073	0.091	1.032
23	−0.040	−1.145	−1.137
24	0.986	−0.103	1.317
25	0.398	0.772	1.542
26	−0.889	0.085	0.048
27	−1.456	−1.188	−1.722
28	−1.201	−0.634	−1.456
29	−2.381	−0.210	−2.086
30	0.982	0.378	1.855

This completes the first replication of the illustrative Monte Carlo experiment. A new set of standard normal random deviates is now drawn; these are transformed into random disturbances with the required covariance matrix set down in the model design and the implied values of the endogenous variables are generated. Together with the values for the predetermined variables (which are the same in *all* replications), these values are used to calculate a new set of OLS and 2SLS estimates of the structural parameters. Since the standard normal deviates will differ from the original set,[5] the new set of estimates will differ from the original set. These steps constitute the second replication. They are now repeated a large number of times. In principle the larger the number of replications, the better. In practice computing costs are the main constraint. Typically the number of replications will be 500 to 1,000. In the case of the illustrative experiment only 100 replications were performed. Table 5.5 shows a selection of the results of the experiment.

The only matter remaining to be dealt with is the sixth in the list set out above – the selection of criteria with which to judge the performance of the estimators under study. Superficially this would appear to be quite straightforward and largely determined by the preferences of the Monte Carlo experimenter. Potential criteria might include the bias of the estimators, their variances, mean square error (MSE) or mean absolute error (MAE). If there are m replications in the experiment and $\hat{\theta}_i$ denotes the estimate obtained in the i-th replication using estimator $\hat{\theta}$ of the parameter θ, then these measures are defined as follows:

$$\text{Bias } (\hat{\theta}) = \bar{\hat{\theta}} - \theta \text{ where } \bar{\hat{\theta}} = m^{-1} \sum_{i=1}^{m} \hat{\theta}_i$$

$$\text{Var } (\hat{\theta}) = m^{-1} \sum_{i=1}^{m} (\hat{\theta}_i - \bar{\hat{\theta}})^2$$

$$\text{MSE } (\hat{\theta}) = m^{-1} \sum_{i=1}^{m} (\hat{\theta}_i - \theta)^2 = \text{Var } (\hat{\theta}) + [\text{Bias } (\hat{\theta})]^2$$

$$\text{MAE } (\hat{\theta}) = m^{-1} \sum_{i=1}^{m} |\hat{\theta}_i - \theta|$$

With the exception of the last, each of these measures has a population counterpart. In these cases, the value obtained from the results of a Monte Carlo experiment represents an *estimate* of the corresponding population concept. It makes no sense to attempt to estimate something that does not exist, and we know from the analytical research on the system estimators that not all of their finite-sample moments exist. However, the measures set out above, with the exception of MAE, are estimates either of finite-sample moments or of measures whose existence depends upon the existence of one or more moments. Thus var $(\hat{\theta})$ is an estimate of the second finite-sample moment of the estimator $\hat{\theta}$, while bias $(\hat{\theta})$ is an estimate of a measure, the existence of which hinges on the existence of the first finite-sample moment of $\hat{\theta}$. MSE $(\hat{\theta})$ estimates a measure whose existence depends on the existence of both first and second finite-sample moments of $\hat{\theta}$. It is in this connection that the finite-sample analytical studies have the special significance alluded to in section 5.1. It is sensible to adopt some particular measure as the criterion against which to judge the performance of estimators only if the finite-sample moments on which

Table 5.5 Results from selected replications and summary statistics for the illustrative Monte Carlo experiment

Replication	Estimator	$\hat{\alpha}_1$	$\hat{\alpha}_2$	$\hat{\alpha}_3$	$\hat{\beta}_1$	$\hat{\beta}_2$	$\hat{\beta}_3$
1	OLS	−0.458	0.823	−0.553	0.362	−0.189	−0.182
	2SLS	1.566	0.295	0.435	0.079	−0.427	−0.413
2	OLS	−1.199	−1.016	−0.614	−0.747	−0.164	0.014
	2SLS	−1.274	−0.106	−0.473	−0.721	−0.235	0.146
3	OLS	0.248	2.535	0.691	0.606	0.543	−0.541
	2SLS	0.616	0.825	0.174	0.491	0.589	−0.625
4	OLS	−0.736	−1.565	−0.501	−0.835	0.169	−0.129
	2SLS	−1.130	−0.320	−0.082	−0.808	0.183	−0.079
5	OLS	−0.505	3.172	0.672	0.606	−0.502	0.770
	2SLS	−1.482	3.406	0.887	0.272	−0.244	0.311
⋮							
99	OLS	−0.770	3.843	0.758	0.546	0.002	0.120
	2SLS	−0.413	4.762	1.054	0.482	−0.003	0.130
100	OLS	−0.521	−1.605	−0.414	−0.900	0.091	−0.088
	2SLS	−0.936	−0.429	−0.140	−0.980	−0.027	−0.198
Bias	OLS	−2.397	−0.361	−0.657	−1.661	−0.382	−0.398
	2SLS	−2.404	−0.252	−0.706	−1.552	−0.339	−0.388
Variance	OLS	0.027	6.046	0.311	0.594	0.149	0.142
	2SLS	0.633	2.044	0.224	0.884	0.256	0.240
MSE	OLS	5.770	6.175	0.743	3.254	0.295	0.300
	2SLS	6.411	2.108	0.721	3.291	0.371	0.391
MAE	OLS	2.397	2.444	0.661	1.631	0.461	0.469
	2SLS	2.404	1.179	0.750	1.598	0.504	0.516

its existence depends are known to exist. In the earliest Monte Carlo studies, mean square error was commonly chosen as the criterion for judgement of estimator performance – one estimator was preferred to another if its MSE was the smaller. It was later shown that in some of these studies one or both of the first two finite-sample moments of the estimators under study did not exist, thus calling into question the interpretation placed on the results of their experiments by the investigators concerned. It can be argued, however (Malinvaud, 1970, p. 720), that the existence of the finite-sample moments is irrelevant for comparisons between estimators based on the *same* sample size. This argument is based upon the observation that the operational significance of the discovery that a given finite-sample moment does not exist is that an estimate of that moment (or of some related measure) will increase without limit as the sample size increases. Hence, provided that comparisons are made between estimators calculated from the same sample size, the interpretations placed on the results of the early Monte Carlo studies will hold.

The estimators of interest in the illustrative Monte Carlo experiment are OLS and 2SLS. Standard textbook theory assures us that the first two finite-sample moments of OLS exist for the parameters of both stochastic equations of SYSTEM III (see Intriligator, 1978, pp. 107–8). The first of these equations is over-identified by order 1, the order of over-identification being the excess of the number of predetermined variables excluded from the equation over the number of included endogenous variables less one (see Intriligator, 1978, p. 348). Basmann's conjecture then tells us that the first finite-sample moment of 2SLS will exist but the second will not. Hence for the parameters of (5.1) it makes sense to compare OLS and 2SLS using the results of a Monte Carlo experiment in terms of their performance against the criterion of bias but not against the variance or mean square error criteria. The second equation in SYSTEM III (5.2) is also over-identified by order 1, so the same remarks apply. However, in line with the argument of the previous paragraph, since the illustrative experiment relates to a single sample size ($T = 30$), all four criteria mentioned above are provided in Table 5.5.

It will be seen from the table that both OLS and 2SLS exhibit relatively large bias and mean absolute error. Furthermore, there is no clear ranking of the estimators. In the case of some parameters OLS performs better, in others 2SLS. It is also the case that different rankings arise from different criteria. Judged against the bias criterion, OLS ranks ahead of 2SLS for only two of the six parameters. However, OLS ranks ahead of 2SLS for four of the six parameters when judged against the MAE criterion.

It must be stressed that our experiment was designed simply for purposes of illustration; it was not intended as a serious piece of Monte Carlo work. Thus no particular weight can be given to the above conclusions. They do serve, however, to draw attention to the fact that great care is required in interpreting the results of Monte-Carlo experiments.

What has been described above represents a single Monte Carlo experiment, the results of which relate to just one model design for a particular system. One of the reasons why the results of this experiment are not at all illuminating is that they relate to only one system and then to just one point in its parameter space. Clearly no attempt at generalising the results could be justified on the basis of this single sample point. In practice Monte Carlo investigators would attempt inferences of a general kind only after a large number of model designs had been systematically considered.

The emphasis so far has been on Monte Carlo experiments as a means of comparing the finite-sample behaviour of estimators. In section 5.3 we will see that the Monte Carlo method has a number of other important uses. One interesting question which the method can be used to address is just how big the sample size must be before (analytical) asymptotic results become relevant. 2SLS, although biased, is consistent. Does the bias diminish sufficiently fast as the sample size increases that fifty sample points is adequate, or is one hundred called for, or must the sample size be larger still? Another important use of Monte Carlo experiments is in investigating the distribution of an individual estimator. Carefully designed experiments can provide us with a lot of useful information about the finite-sample distribution of an estimator. Also of interest is the effect of changes in the environment on the behaviour of one or more estimators. Monte Carlo experiments have been used to investigate the effect on the system estimators of various forms of mis-specification, of the presence of multicollinearity and of autocorrelation of the structural disturbances. Another important use of Monte Carlo experiments is investigation of the power of tests of hypotheses. Specifically, they help us to determine, for a given finite-sample size, whether, as intended, a particular test procedure leads to the rejection of a true null hypothesis the proportion of times indicated by the chosen level of significance.

5.3 Monte Carlo studies of system estimators

Many Monte Carlo studies of the behaviour of the system estimators are now available. In the present context the most important of these are Summers (1965), Cragg (1967), and Mosbaek and Wold (1970). One of the major problems facing the reader of such studies is that of assimilating the voluminous evidence which these studies have accumulated. Fortunately, some excellent reviews of this literature are available. In particular, the reader is urged to consult Johnston (1972), Smith (1973) and Intriligator (1978). These sources will also provide a comprehensive bibliography for the interested reader, a task which will not be attempted here. See also Sowey (1973).

Almost all the Monte Carlo studies have concentrated on quite small systems. The main finding of the studies is that, in the absence of departures from 'textbook' assumptions, the finite-sample behaviour of the system estimators is broadly in line with that indicated by the analytical asymptotic results. OLS has the largest bias. In fact its bias is sufficiently large to ensure that its mean square error exceeds that of the LISEs, its relatively small variance notwithstanding. On both bias and mean square error criteria, the FISEs outrank the LISEs. Within the classes of estimators there are no clear preferences of one estimator over any other. In the FISE class, for instance, FIML will outrank 3SLS in some model designs but the ranking will be reversed in others. Although the Monte Carlo evidence is very limited for the fixed-point estimators (the study of Mosbaek and Wold (1970) is the only one in which a fixed-point estimator has been included), there appears to be a preference among the LISEs for 2SLS over a fixed-point estimator, reinforced by the finding that the bias of fixed-point, unlike 2SLS, is quite sensitive to the parameter values. It must be emphasised that these broad conclusions apply only to small systems (two or three equations) in which 'textbook' assumptions apply. Specifically, the systems concerned are linear, have structural disturbances free of autocorrelation, no lagged endogenous variables among the predetermined variables and are free of both specification and measurement error of any kind. When departures from these assumptions occur, the ranking of the estimators may change. In the rest of the chapter, we shall consider briefly the Monte Carlo evidence relating to various important forms of departure from the textbook assumptions.

Lagged endogenous variables

Surprisingly perhaps, in view of its overwhelming importance to working systems, this departure from the textbook assumptions has received very little attention in Monte Carlo work. Most studies have used predetermined variables which were all exogenous, their values being generated in broadly the same way as in the illustrative experiment described in section 5.2. Such evidence as there is (see Hendry and Harrison, 1974; Mosbaek and Wold, 1970) suggests that, in the absence of autocorrelation, the general picture which emerges when the textbook assumptions apply carries over to the situation in which the predetermined variables include lagged endogenous variables. However, the available evidence is scanty and applies only to the SIEs and LISEs; no study has yet considered the performance of the FISEs when lagged endogenous variables are present. The Monte Carlo evidence here is consistent with the analytical asymptotic results which show that the properties and rankings of the system estimators are unaffected by the appearance of lagged endogenous variables, provided that conditions (6)–(8) of sections 4.4 and 4.5 are satisfied.

Autocorrelation

The presence of autocorrelation in the structural disturbances leaves unchanged the ranking of the system estimators established under textbook assumptions, and appears to have little effect on their bias (see Cragg, 1967). However, as the analytical results for the single-equation case (see Kmenta, 1971, pp. 273–82) might lead us to suspect, there are problems with statistical inference when the autocorrelation is strong, because the *t*-ratios are biased (see Simister, 1969; Johnston, 1972).

Another important question under this head has been investigated by Goldfeld and Quandt (1972). KK system-builders are often faced with the practical difficulty that they can handle either simultaneity or autocorrelation but not both together. This difficulty arose originally because theory was not sufficiently well developed. Nowadays the theory has been fully developed but the computer software required to implement a particular system estimator which takes account of autocorrelation in a working KK system is not always available. (Hendry (1976) provides a useful summary of system estimators of this type.) The Monte Carlo evidence from Goldfeld and Quandt's (1972) study suggests that, for the model designs considered, if the technology required to implement a system estimator which takes account of autocorrelation is unavailable, attention should be focused on whichever of the two problems is the more severe. With weak autocorrelation it is preferable in these circumstances to use a system estimator and ignore the autocorrelation. When autocorrelation is strong, the choice of an appropriate SIE like CO or ARMAX can probably be justified over a LISE or FISE.

Non-linearity

Because non-linearity in the parameters is much less prominent in KK systems than non-linearity in the variables, the behaviour of the system estimators in systems which are linear in the parameters but non-linear in endogenous variables is of particular interest to KK system-builders. It is fortunate, therefore, that the only Monte Carlo study which has embraced non-linearity, that of Goldfeld and Quandt (1972), focuses on non-linearity in the variables. Only three estimators are considered in this study, but the broad conclusion is that, once again, the picture which emerges for textbook assumptions, itself in line with the analytical asymptotic results, is undisturbed by non-linearity in the variables. Against the bias criterion, FIML outranks a form of 2SLS modified to handle the non-linearity (the estimator in question, NL2SLS, due to Kelejian (1971), will be considered in Chapter 6), which in turn outranks OLS.

Specification error

A number of Monte Carlo studies have dealt with the effects on the behaviour of the system estimators of various types of mis-specification. The most important contribution is that of Cragg (1968), who provides a very careful and systematic treatment of five types of specification error. In Chapter 4 we saw that the consistency of 2SLS depends, among other things, on the correctness of the specification of the equation of interest and on the correctness of the list of predetermined variables for the entire system. The consistency of the FISEs requires that the entire system be correctly specified. In this light we might expect that the effects of specification error would be isolated to the parameters appearing in the mis-specified equation in the case of 2SLS (except where the mis-specification involves the complete omission of a predetermined variable from the system), while all parameter estimates will be affected when a FISE is the estimator used. Broadly speaking, the Monte Carlo evidence confirms this expectation. The ranking of the FISEs deteriorates sufficiently that the LISEs outperform the FISEs when specification errors occur. However, the omission of an exogenous variable does not appear to have a particularly serious effect on 2SLS.

Measurement error

Measurement error in the variables was one of the earliest problems (see Ladd, 1956) considered in Monte Carlo studies of system estimators, and the problem has been a concern of several studies. Once again, the most significant contribution is that of Cragg (1966). The performance of all system estimators deteriorates when measurement error is present. However, the effects on OLS are less serious than those on the LISEs and FISEs. Although this is not sufficient to upset the rankings of the system estimators established for the case of textbook assumptions, there is a tendency for the grounds for preferring either the LISEs or FISEs over OLS to weaken.

There is also Monte Carlo evidence on a number of issues which are not, strictly speaking, departures from the textbook assumptions but which are nevertheless of some importance to the question of the choice of estimator for use in working KK systems. The chapter will be concluded with a brief discussion of these matters.

Multicollinearity

The Monte Carlo evidence on the effects of multicollinearity on system estimators is somewhat mixed, the question having been considered by Summers (1965), Quandt (1962), Schink and Chiu (1966), Cragg (1967), Mosbaek and Wold (1970) and Sasser (1973). If a general conclusion is possible, it is probably that multicollinearity is not a major problem for system estimators other than 2SLS, the performance of which may deteriorate markedly in some circumstances.

Sparseness

A distinguishing feature of working KK systems is that the coefficient matrix for the endogenous variables (the matrix **A** in equation (4.4) is *sparse*. A sparse matrix is one which has a high percentage of elements which are zero. Some relevant analytical results are available. If the matrix **A** is diagonal (i.e. very sparse), OLS is both unbiased and consistent, though not efficient even asymptotically. (This is the case of seemingly unrelated regressions; see Intriligator, 1978, pp. 165–73, 403.) When **A** is triangular (a little less than 50 per cent sparseness), OLS is again consistent. (In this case, the system is described as *recursive*; see Intriligator, 1978, pp. 358–61.) In all other cases OLS is inconsistent. An interesting question, and an important one for KK model-builders, is whether the LISEs and FISEs retain their superiority of performance over OLS when the matrix **A** is sparse (though neither diagonal nor triangular). Quandt (1962; 1965) and Mosbaek and Wold (1970) provide some evidence on this question. The bias of both OLS and 2SLS decreases with increasing sparseness. In highly sparse systems, there is little to put 2SLS ahead of OLS.

Sample size

The effects of increasing sample size on the behaviour of system estimators depend on the size of the system and on the model design. The most definitive conclusions under this head are those of Mosbaek and Wold (1970), who find that the bias of OLS, 2SLS and FP decreases with increasing sample size.

Model size

There is very little Monte Carlo evidence on the effects of model size (number of equations) on the relative performance of the system estimators. The studies of Mosbaek and Wold (1970) and Smith (1973, Ch. 5) suggest that the case for preferring the LISEs and FISEs over OLS is weakened rapidly as the number of equations in the system increases. Experimenting with three linear KK models with six, sixteen and thirty-four equations respectively, Smith (1973, Ch. 5) finds that 2SLS outranks OLS in the smallest system but OLS is the better estimator in the larger system.

Two final points should be made. The first is that, with the exception of considerations relevant to large systems (model size and sparseness), there is little in the Monte Carlo evidence just discussed to disturb the picture which emerges from experiments which call on textbook assumptions. However, most studies have considered individual departures from the textbook assumptions in isolation. There is very little evidence relating to several such departures occurring together. Second, it is interesting to note once again that the Monte Carlo evidence is very much in line with the conclusions which can be drawn on the basis of analytical asymptotic theory, particularly when this is combined with some intelligent intuition (see Hendry, 1973).

Notes

1. The IMSL sub-routine GGUBS was used for this purpose. See International Mathematical and Statistical Libraries (1980). We are grateful to Anne Lakin, who undertook the programming required for the Monte Carlo experiment.
2. IMSL sub-routine GGNML was used.
3. Using the fact that $E(\epsilon_{1t}) = E(\epsilon_{2t}) = 0$:

$$E(u_{1t}) = s_{11}E(\epsilon_{1t}) + s_{21}E(\epsilon_{2t}) = 0$$

$$E(u_{2t}) = s_{22}E(\epsilon_{2t}) = 0$$

Using var (ϵ_{1t}) = var $(\epsilon_{2t}) = 1$:

$$\text{var }(u_{1t}) = s_{11}^2 \text{ var }(\epsilon_{1t}) + s_{21}^2 \text{ var }(\epsilon_{2t})$$
$$= s_{11}^2 + s_{21}^2 = \sigma_{11} - s_{21}^2 + s_{21}^2 = \sigma_{11}$$
$$\text{var }(u_{2t}) = s_{22}^2 \text{ var }(\epsilon_{2t}) = s_{22}^2 = \sigma_{22}$$

Since ϵ_{1t} and ϵ_{2t} are independent, $E(\epsilon_{1t}\epsilon_{2t}) = 0$. Hence:

$$\text{cov }(u_{1t}u_{2t}) = E[(s_{11}\epsilon_{1t} + s_{21}\epsilon_{2t})(s_{22}\epsilon_{2t})]$$
$$= s_{11}s_{22}E(\epsilon_{1t}\epsilon_{2t}) + s_{21}s_{22}E(\epsilon_{2t}^2)$$
$$= s_{21}s_{22} \text{ var }(\epsilon_{2t})$$
$$= s_{21}s_{22} = (\sigma_{12}/s_{22})s_{22} = \sigma_{12}$$

Thus:

$$\begin{bmatrix} \text{var }(u_{1t}) & \text{cov }(u_{1t}u_{2t}) \\ \text{cov }(u_{2t}u_{1t}) & \text{var }(u_{2t}) \end{bmatrix} = \begin{bmatrix} \sigma_{11} & \sigma_{12} \\ \sigma_{12} & \sigma_{22} \end{bmatrix} = \Omega$$

as required.

4. Sufficient date are available in Table 5.1 and 5.4 for the interested reader to undertake the calculation of the OLS and 2SLS estimates.
5. A property required of the pseudo random number generator used is that it be non-repeating for any desired length. See Naylor (1971, pp. 381–2).

References and further reading

Basmann, R. L. (1961) 'A Note on the Exact Finite Sample Frequency Functions of Generalized Classical Linear Estimators in Two Leading Overidentified Cases', *Journal of the American Statistical Association*, vol. 56, pp. 619–36.

Basmann, R. L. (1963) 'A Note on the Exact Finite Sample Frequency Functions of Generalized Classical Linear Estimators in a Leading Three-Equation Case', *Journal of the American Statistical Association*, vol. 58, pp. 161–71.

Basmann, R. L. (1974) 'Exact Finite Sample Distributions for Some Econometric Estimators and Test Statistics: A Survey and Appraisal', in M. D. Intriligator and D. A. Kendrick (eds), *Frontiers of Quantitative Economics*, vol. II, North-Holland, Amsterdam.

Basmann, R. L., Richardson D. H., and Rohr, R. J. (1974) 'An Experimental Study of Structural Estimators and Test Statistics Associated With Dynamical Econometric Models', *Econometrica*, vol. 42, pp. 717–30.

Christ, C. F. (1966) *Econometric Models and Methods*, Wiley, New York.

Cragg, J. G. (1966) 'On the Sensitivity of Simultaneous Equation Estimators to the Stochastic Assumptions of the Models', *Journal of the American Statistical Association*, vol. 61, pp. 136–51.

Cragg, J. G. (1967) 'On the Relative Small-Sample Properties of Several Structural-Equation Estimators', *Econometrica*, vol. 35, pp. 89–110.

Cragg, J. G. (1968) 'Some Effects of Incorrect Specification on the Small-Sample Properties of Several Simultaneous-Equation Estimators', *International Economic Review*, vol. 9, pp. 63–86.

Goldfeld, S. M. and Quandt, R. E. (1972) *Nonlinear Methods in Econometrics*, North-Holland, Amsterdam.

Hall, B. H. and Hall, R. E. (1979) *Time Series Processor Version 3.3*, Stanford, California.

Hendry, D.F. (1973) 'On Asymptotic Theory and Finite Sample Experiments', *Economica,* vol, 160, pp. 210–17.

Hendry, D. F. (1976) 'The Structure of Simultaneous Equations Estimators', *Journal of Econometrics*, vol. 4, pp. 51–88.

Hendry, D. F. and Harrison, R. W. (1974) 'Monte Carlo Methodology and the Small Sample Behaviour of Ordinary and Two-Stage Least Squares', *Journal of Econometrics*, vol. 2, pp. 151–74.

Hillier, G. H. (1981) 'Exact Marginal Densities for the Two-Stage and Ordinary Least Squares Estimators for the Coefficient of an Endogenous Variable in a Structural Equation Containing $n + 1$ Endogenous Variables', mimeo, Monash University, Melbourne.

International Mathematical and Statistical Libraries (1980) *IMSL Library Reference Manual*, 8th edn, Houston, Texas.

Intriligator, M. D. (1978) *Econometric Models, Techniques and Applications,* Prentice-Hall, Englewood Cliffs, N.J.

Johnston, J. (1972) *Econometric Methods*, 2nd edn, McGraw-Hill, New York.

Kadane, J. B. (1971) 'Comparison of k-Class Estimators when the Disturbances are Small', *Econometrica*, vol. 39, pp. 723–38.

Kelejian, H. H. (1971) 'Two Stage Least Squares and Econometric Systems Linear in Parameters but Non-Linear in the Endogenous Variables', *Journal of the American Statistical Association*, vol. 66, pp. 373–4.

Kinal, T. W. (1980) 'The Existence of Moments of k-Class Estimators', *Econometrica*, vol. 48, pp. 241–9.

Kmenta, J. (1971) *Elements of Econometrics*, Macmillan, New York.

Ladd, G. W. (1956) 'Effects of Shocks and Errors in Estimation: An Empirical Comparison', *Journal of Farm Economics*, vol. 38, pp. 485–95.

Malinvaud, E. (1970) *Statistical Methods of Econometrics*, 2nd edn, North-Holland, Amsterdam.

Mariano, R. S. (1980) *'Analytical Small-Sample Distribution Theory in Econometrics: The Simultaneous-Equations Case'* Discussion Paper 8026, Centre for Operations Research and Econometrics, Université Catholique de Louvain.

Mariano, R. S. and Sawa, T. (1972) 'Exact Finite Sample Distribution of the Limited Information Maximum Likelihood Estimator in the Case of Two Included Endogenous Variables', *Journal of the American Statistical Association*, vol. 67, pp. 159–63.

Mosbaek, E. and Wold, H. O. (1970) *Interdependent Systems: Structure and Estimation*, North-Holland, Amsterdam.

NAGAR, A. L. (1959) 'The Bias and Moment Matrix of the General *k*-Class Estimators of the Parameters in Simultaneous Equations', *Econometrica*, vol. 27, pp. 575–95.

NAGAR, A. L. (1969) 'Stochastic Simulation of the Brookings Econometric Model', in J. S. Duesenberry, G. Fromm, L. R. Klein and E. Kuh (eds), *The Brookings Model: Some Further Results*, Rand McNally, Chicago.

NAYLOR, T. H. (1971) *Computer Simulation Experiments with Models of Economic Systems*, Wiley, New York.

PHILLIPS, P. C. B. (1980) 'The Exact Distribution of Instrumental Variable Estimators in an Equation Containing $n + 1$ Endogenous Variables', *Econometrica*, vol. 48, pp. 861–77.

QUANDT, R. E. (1962) 'Some Small Sample Properties of Certain Structural Equation Estimators', Research Memorandum No. 48, Econometric Research Program, Princeton University.

QUANDT, R. E. (1965) 'On Certain Small Sample Properties of *k*-Class Estimators', *International Economic Review*, vol. 6, pp. 92–104.

RICHARDSON, D. H. (1968) 'The Exact Distribution of a Structural Coefficient Estimator', *Journal of the American Statistical Association*, vol. 63, pp. 1214–26.

SARGAN, J. D. (1978) 'On the Existence of the Moments of 3SLS Estimators', *Econometrica*, vol. 46, pp. 1329–50.

SARGAN, J. D. and MIKHAIL, W. M. (1971) 'A General Approximation to the Distribution of Instrumental Variable Estimators', *Econometrica*, vol. 39, pp. 131–69.

SASSER, W. E. (1973) *A Finite-Sample Study of Various Simultaneous Equation Estimators*, Duke University Press, Durham, N. C.

SCHINK, W. A. and CHIU, J. S. (1966) 'A Simulation Study of Effects of Multicollinearity and Autocorrelation on Estimates of Parameters', *Journal of Financial and Quantitative Analysis*, vol. 1, pp. 36–67.

SIMISTER, L. T. (1969) 'Monte Carlo Studies of Simultaneous Equation Systems', Ph.D. Thesis, University of Manchester.

SMITH, V. K. (1971) 'A Comparative Tabular Survey of Monte Carlo and Exact Sampling Studies', *Australian Economic Papers*, vol. 10, pp. 196–202.

SMITH, V. K. (1973) *Monte Carlo Methods*, D. C. Heath, Lexington, Mass.

SOWEY, E. R. (1973) 'A Classified Bibliography of Monte Carlo Studies in Econometrics', *Journal of Econometrics*, vol. 1, pp. 377–95.

SUMMERS, R. (1965) 'A Capital Intensive Approach to the Small Sample Properties of Various Simultaneous Equation Estimators', *Econometrics*, vol. 33, pp. 1–41.

ULLAH, A. and NAGAR, A. L (1974) 'The Exact Mean of the Two-Stage Least Squares Estimator of the Structural Parameters in an Equation having Three Endogenous Variables', *Econometrica*, vol. 42, pp. 749–58.

6 FROM THEORY TO PRACTICE: THE CHOICE OF ESTIMATOR

6.1 Handling non-linearity

A reading of Chapters 4 and 5 might suggest that, in the context of KK systems, the problem of choosing an estimator would be reasonably straightforward. The asymptotic results presented in Chapter 4 imply a clear ranking of available estimators, the FISEs being superior, in terms of asymptotic properties, to the LISEs, and these in turn being superior to the SIEs. Furthermore, as we saw in section 5.3, this ranking is not upset when the finite-sample results generated by the available Monte Carlo studies are taken into account. It would seem, then, that in choosing an estimator the KK system-builder should consider only the FISEs or at most the FISEs and the LISEs.

Unfortunately, however, the situation is not quite so simple. For the chosen estimator must not only be attractive in terms of formal statistical properties; it must also be workable in practice. The main purpose of the present chapter is to consider various aspects of 'workability' and to show how the modern KK system-builder strikes a compromise, in the choice of estimator, between theoretical nicety and practicability.

As stressed repeatedly in earlier chapters, modern KK system are invariably non-linear. This being so, applicability to non-linear systems is an important aspect of 'workability' and in the present section we shall consider the available estimators from this point of view.

Notwithstanding that the estimators described in Chapter 4 were devised with linear systems in mind, some of these estimators can be applied nevertheless to non-linear systems. In principle this is true of FIML. As explained in section 4.5, FIML is applicable to any system, linear or otherwise. However, the practical difficulties of handling arbitrary forms of non-linearity are immense. Indeed, the computer software required to handle the FIML estimation of intrinsically non-linear systems has only recently become available (Wymer, 1978) and the associated computational costs are prohibitive other than for very small systems (no larger than twenty to thirty equations). Aside from FIML, the only available estimators which can handle even particular forms of non-linearity without modification are certain of the SIEs, namely OLS,

NLLS, ARMAX and some fixed-point estimators. NLLS, a SIE, can, in principle, be applied seriatum to the stochastic equations of any non-linear system (though, as with FIML, some forms of non-linearity may be troublesome or expensive to deal with from a computational point of view). The same remarks apply to ARMAX. OLS can be applied seriatum to those stochastic equations of a non-linear system which are linear in the parameters. Non-linearity in the variables can be handled by OLS by suitable redefinition of the variables. However, except in a limited set of cases in which the equation concerned is amenable to transformation into the linear in parameters form, OLS cannot cope with equations which are non-linear in the parameters (see Kmenta, 1971, pp. 451–72; Goldberger, 1968, pp. 107–22).

It transpires, then, that only FIML, a very limited group of FISEs (all of which are FP estimators) and certain SIEs (NLLS, ARMAX) can handle any form of non-linear system without modification. In addition, OLS is applicable to those systems in which the only form of non-linearity present is in the variables, as is the case in most working KK systems.

Although 2SLS and 3SLS are applicable only to linear systems, both estimators have recently been generalised for use in non-linear systems. The estimators in question, NL2SLS and NL3SLS, are discussed in Amemiya (1974; 1975; 1977) and Jorgenson and Laffont (1974). Also of interest is Belsley (1979). At present the importance of NL2SLS and NL3SLS for working KK systems lies not so much in their direct applicability as in the fact that certain procedures which are used in practice to deal with non-linearity when the chosen estimator is 2SLS or 3SLS (see below) can be shown to be special cases of NL2SLS or NL3SLS so that their properties can be derived from those which have been established for NL2SLS and NL3SLS. NL2SLS and NL3SLS have been shown by Amemiya (1974; 1977) to have the same asymptotic properties in a non-linear system as do 2SLS and 3SLS in a linear system. Note, however, that this result, and indeed all of the results so far mentioned, apply only to systems in which there are no lagged endogenous variables. No finite-sample analytical results or experimental evidence for NL2SLS and NL3SLS is yet available.

KK system-builders had developed methods of estimating non-linear systems by means of 2SLS or 3SLS long before NL2SLS or NL3SLS appeared. The need for such methods arose principally because ratios and products of variables commonly appear as regressors in the stochastic equations of KK systems, as well as in identities. When such non-linearities occur only in identities, the practice has been to ignore their presence and apply 2SLS in the usual way. What this amounts to is an implicit assumption that an identity which is non-linear in the variables has a good linear approximation.[1] Non-linearities in the variables in the stochastic equations have been dealt with by defining new variables so as to treat a non-linear function of variables as another variable.

To illustrate, suppose the stochastic equation in which the non-linearity appears is:

$$y_{1t} = \alpha_0 + \alpha_1 y_{2t} x_{1t} + \alpha_2 \frac{x_{2t}}{x_{3t}} + u_{1t} \tag{6.1}$$

where, as usual, ys denote the endogenous variables and xs the predetermined variables. The following two identities would be added to the system and used to generate sample observations for the new variables:

$$y_{3t} \equiv y_{2t} x_{1t} \tag{6.2}$$

$$x_{4t} \equiv \frac{x_{2t}}{x_{3t}} \tag{6.3}$$

Because y_3 is a function of variables which involves an endogenous variable, it would itself be regarded as endogenous. However, x_4 is a function of predetermined variables only and accordingly would itself be regarded as predetermined. The structural equation (6.1) can now be written:

$$y_{1t} = \alpha_0 + \alpha_1 y_{3t} + \alpha_2 x_{4t} + u_{1t} \tag{6.4}$$

Estimation using 2SLS or 3SLS would then proceed in the usual way, treating y_3 as endogenous and x_4 as predetermined.

As mentioned earlier, the estimators which result from this treatment have been shown to be special cases of NL2SLS and NL3SLS (Amemiya, 1974; 1977). If these special cases are to achieve the asymptotic properties of the more general estimators, the variables used in the first-stage regressions must be carefully selected. Whereas in the linear case theory is quite prescriptive about these variables, it is at best suggestive in the non-linear case. Kelejian (1971) suggests that low-order polynomials of all predetermined variables (i.e. the variables, their squares and perhaps their cubes) should be used as regressors in the first-stage regressions. As noted in section 5.3, Goldfeld and Quandt (1972) provide some experimental evidence of the finite-sample behaviour of Kelejian's NL2SLS estimator. Although Kelejian's suggestion has received support in the literature, it does not appear to have been followed in practice (see Giles and Morgan, 1977, pp. 57; Nehlawi, 1977, pp. 167–8; McCarthy, 1972, pp. 129–30). One reason for this is the cost in terms of lost degrees of freedom, a point which will be dealt with in detail in section 6.2.

While the generalisations of 2SLS and 3SLS to the non-linear case would appear to broaden the choice of estimators available to KK system-builders, in practice they are very little better off than they would be if restricted to estimators which could handle non-linearity as they stand. The problems are essentially practical and closely related to the matter to be dealt with in the next section.

6.2 The undersized sample problem

In the preceding section we considered the practical problems which arise from the fact that working KK systems are invariably non-linear. The other important feature of working KK systems is that they are *large*. This gives rise to another, more insidious, problem of a practical nature which is called the *undersized sample problem*, or the degrees of freedom problem. Like the problem discussed in the previous section, the undersized sample problem is also related to the applicability of the available estimators.

So far we have not made clear just what is meant by 'large' in this context (how big?). This omission was deliberate because we define a *large system* as one for which the undersized sample problem arises. Hence the meaning of the term 'large' when used to describe a KK system can only be explained by first explaining the undersized sample problem. The undersized sample problem arises if either:

(a) the number of predetermined variables exceeds the number of sample points; or
(b) the number of stochastic equations exceeds the number of sample points.[2]

A typical sample period for a working KK system might be fifteen years of quarterly data, providing around sixty sample points. It is unusual for the sample period of such a system to comprise more than eighty sample points.[3] On the other hand, upwards of 100 stochastic equations is quite typical, while some models run to more than 300 stochastic equations.[4] (Very large systems may have as many as 700 equations in total). Because working KK systems usually include many lagged variables, it is a laborious task to count their predetermined variables. However, it is not uncommon for there to be 200 exogenous variables, some of which may also appear lagged, and at least as many lagged endogenous variables. It is clear, then, that, except in the smallest KK systems, the undersized sample problem will arise in *both* ways.

If the undersized sample problem arises through (a), 2SLS and LIML break down because the rank condition for the first-stage regressions is violated and the OLS estimates of the unrestricted reduced-form coefficients are therefore not defined. In these circumstances 2SLS (and LIML) estimates do not exist. 3SLS will also break down if the undersized sample problem arises through (a) because the existence of 3SLS depends upon the existence of 2SLS.

If the undersized sample problem arises through (b), the FISEs (including FP estimators in this class, such as FIIV) break down because it is not possible to form a non-singular estimate of the covariance matrix $\mathbf{\Omega}$ of the system disturbances at a particular sample point. Since all the FISEs depend on the existence of $\hat{\mathbf{\Omega}}^{-1}$, none of them is defined when the undersized sample problem arises in this way. To illustrate this point, consider again the 3SLS estimation of the structural parameters of SYSTEM III (see section 4.5). SYSTEM III contains two stochastic equations, so the undersized sample problem will arise via (b) if there is just a single sample point ($T = 1$). As was noted in section 4.5 (see equation (4.41)), $\hat{\mathbf{\Omega}}$ takes the form:

$$\hat{\mathbf{\Omega}} = \begin{bmatrix} T^{-1}\Sigma e_{1t}^2 & T^{-1}\Sigma e_{1t}e_{2t} \\ T^{-1}\Sigma e_{1t}\, e_{2t} & T^{-1}\Sigma e_{2t}^2 \end{bmatrix}$$

where e_{1t} and e_{2t} are the 2SLS residuals for the first and second equations respectively. With $T = 1$:

$$\hat{\mathbf{\Omega}} = \begin{bmatrix} e_{11}^2 & e_{11}e_{21} \\ e_{11}e_{21} & e_{21}^2 \end{bmatrix}$$

the determinant of which is:

$$\det(\hat{\mathbf{\Omega}}) = (e_{11}^2)(e_{21}^2) - (e_{11}e_{21})(e_{11}e_{21}) = 0$$

Consequently $\hat{\mathbf{\Omega}}$ is a singular matrix. Its inverse does not exist and 3SLS estimation breaks down.

We have already noted that working KK systems invariably have many more stochastic equations than available sample points. For this reason, although the FISEs are sometimes seen in small models,[5] they are never encountered in working KK systems. Since, as we have also seen, most working KK systems also have many more predetermined variables than sample points, it would also appear that the LISEs (other than FP, for which the undersized sample problem does not arise via (a)) cannot be regarded as feasible in working KK systems. In principle this is the case. In practice, however, methods have been devised to circumvent the undersized sample problem in the case of the LISEs. (Such devices are not possible for the FISEs by virture of the nature of the problem.)

Two main devices have been used to avoid the undersized sample problem in respect of the LISEs in which it arises. The discussion here will be couched in terms of 2SLS but the same remarks apply to LIML. One method is simply to delete predetermined variables thought to be unimportant from the list used in the first-stage regression (see Klein, 1973, pp. 12–14; Giles, 1973, pp. 68–70; Salmon and Eaton, 1975, pp. 326–8). Giles (1973) calls this estimator 'truncated-2SLS'. If the consistency of 2SLS is to carry over to truncated-2SLS, the predetermined variables used in the first-stage regressions must be selected with care. McCarthy (1971; 1972) shows that for any given stochastic equation to be estimated by truncated-2SLS: (a) the same predetermined variables must be used in the first-stage regressions for *every* included right-hand-side endogenous variables, and (b) the predetermined variables which appear in the stochastic equation of immediate interest must all be included in the first-stage regressions. The implication of these rules is that the predetermined variables used in the first-stage regressions will not differ as between stochastic equations. McCarthy (1972) also provides a finite-sample analytical result which shows the bias of truncated-2SLS to be smaller than that of OLS in some circumstances. Various forms of truncated-2SLS have often been used for the estimation of working KK systems.

The other way of circumventing the undersized sample problem as it relates to the LISEs is to replace the predetermined variables in the first-stage regressions with a subset of their *principal components* (see Johnston, 1972, pp. 322–31). In the case of 2SLS the resulting estimator is known as two-stage principal components (2SPC) (see Kloeck and Mennes, 1960). Although the method is open to certain criticisms (see Maddala, 1971) it has been used frequently in working KK systems.

Principal components of a set of variables are just linear combinations of those variables with the weights chosen in such a way that they are pairwise uncorrelated but together account for all the variation in the original variables. For instance, SYSTEM III includes four predetermined variables, x_1, x_2, x_3 and x_4, each of which is observed at the sample points $t = 1, 2, \ldots, T$. From these four variables we can define four principal components, z_1, z_2, z_3 and z_4:

$$\left.\begin{array}{l} z_{1t} = \lambda_{11}x_{1t} + \lambda_{12}x_{2t} + \lambda_{13}x_{3t} + \lambda_{14}x_{4t} \\ z_{2t} = \lambda_{21}x_{1t} + \lambda_{22}x_{2t} + \lambda_{23}x_{3t} + \lambda_{24}x_{4t} \\ z_{3t} = \lambda_{31}x_{1t} + \lambda_{32}x_{2t} + \lambda_{33}x_{3t} + \lambda_{34}x_{4t} \\ z_{4t} = \lambda_{41}x_{1t} + \lambda_{42}x_{2t} + \lambda_{43}x_{3t} + \lambda_{44}x_{4t} \end{array}\right\} (t = 1, 2, \ldots, T)$$

The weight λ_{ij} is the jth element of the characteristic vector corresponding to the ith characteristic root of the matrix $\mathbf{X}'\mathbf{X}$, where $\mathbf{X} = [x_1\ x_2\ x_3\ x_4]$ is the matrix of observations on the four predetermined variables. It is possible to form k principal components from a set of k variables in a similar way.

Replacing the predetermined variables by the full set of their principal components in the 2SLS first-stage regressions will clearly be of no assistance whatever in overcoming the undersized sample problem – the number of principal components is exactly the same as the number of variables from which they are formed. However, if the principal components are arranged in order by the proportion of the total variation of the predetermined variables which they explain, it is typically found that a small number of principal components jointly account for a very high proportion of the total variation. For instance, Evans, Klein and Schink (1968) report that twelve principal components accounted for nearly 98 per cent of the variation in the predetermined variables of a version of the Wharton model. In practice, an appropriate small number of principal components is selected and the *same* set is used in place of the full set of predetermined variables in the first-stage regressions for all stochastic equations.[6] One of the attractions of principal components, additional to the saving in degrees of freedom, is the avoidance of multicollinearity problems, which can be troublesome in the first-stage regressions. Such problems arise because the extent of pairwise correlation between predetermined variables is often high. As was noted above, the principal components are pairwise uncorrelated.

The undersized sample problem does not affect the SIEs or those FP estimators which are LISEs. In the case of the SIEs, the reason is that the remainder of the system is ignored altogether so that satisfaction of the appropriate rank condition for the individual equation of interest is all that is required for their existence.[7] The FP estimators in the LISE class are untroubled by the undersized sample problem because the only estimation involved occurs in individual stochastic equations. The estimated reduced form is called on but the estimates of the reduced-form coefficients are formed from the estimates of the structural parameters. In other words, it is the restricted reduced form (not the unrestricted) which is called upon.

What choice of estimators is available then for use in a KK system in which the undersized sample problem arises? Once again the SIE class survives unscathed but the entire FISE class has been knocked out of contention. The FP estimators from the LISE class are candidates and, although 2SLS no longer remains, its derivatives, truncated-2SLS and 2SPC, go into the list.

6.3 Other practical issues

In the two preceding sections we considered certain practical difficulties that render the LISEs and the FISEs unworkable. In this section we turn to other difficulties of a practical nature which militate against their use in the estimation of KK systems, but this time for a different reason, namely that they undermine the conditions which make the LISEs and the FISEs attractive in the first place.

As we have seen in Chapter 4, the attractive properties of the LISEs and the FISEs exist only when a set of strict assumptions about the form of $\mathbf{\Omega}$, the covariance matrix of the disturbances at a single sample point, are satisfied. In particular, the consistency of the LISEs and both the consistency and the asymptotic efficiency of the FISEs require that the disturbances be identically distributed and independent over sample points. Hence the desirable asymptotic properties of the LISEs and FISEs hinge on the absence of within-equation autocorrelation. Unfortunately, however, the presence of this type of autocorrelation is as much an everyday problem in KK systems as it is in single-equation work. This is particularly so because the stochastic equations of KK systems often include one or more lagged values of the dependent variable among the explanatory variables. When within-equation autocorrelation occurs in a system in which lagged dependent variables appear, the LISEs and FISEs cease to be consistent (see Hendry, 1975).

Good econometric practice demands that the presence of disturbance autocorrelation be taken as a signal of mis-specification (see Johnston, 1972, pp. 243–6; Hendry and Mizon, 1978). Nevertheless it is often easier said than done to eliminate autocorrelation by means of improvements to the specification of the system. There almost always comes a point when the system-builder has to face up to autocorrelation as an estimation problem.

Handling autocorrelation is not a difficult problem when the chosen estimator is a SIE. There are many estimators in this class designed for estimation in the presence of autocorrelation (see Kmenta, 1971, pp. 282–92; Hendry, 1976, pp. 77–85). CO and ARMAX both fall in this group. Variants of all the major LISEs and FISEs are available to handle systems estimation with structural disturbances generated by a vector autoregressive process (see Hendry, 1976, pp. 67–77). However, none of these estimators has so far been put to work in a working KK system.

In practice, three main avenues are followed in the face of autocorrelation in a working KK system. One is to ignore it. The second is to adopt a SIE, like CO or ARMAX, which has desirable properties in the presence of autocorrelation in the single-equation context. This strategy, which is often adopted in working KK systems, is supported by the work of Hendry (1974) and Goldfeld and Quandt (1972), which suggests that it may be no worse to ignore simultaneity by using a SIE than to adopt a LISE or a FISE and ignore the autocorrelation. The third avenue is to treat lagged endogenous variables as if they were current endogenous for the purposes of 2SLS estimation. Such variables then appear as 'dependent' variables in the first-stage regressions, and computed values are used for them in place of the observed values in the second-stage regressions. What this amounts to is doing nothing about the consequences of within-equation autocorrelation as such but severing the link between the presence of lagged endogenous variables and autocorrelation from which the inconsistency of the LISEs and FISEs arises in dynamic systems. This method of treatment of autocorrelation in a KK system has been used in the Wharton Mark III model (McCarthy, 1972) and in the RBNZ model (Giles and Morgan 1977).

More than once before, the interdependence of the processes of specification, estimation and system validation has been noted. In practical terms this has the implication that estimation of a working KK system will frequently be performed using a specification which is not final and which must therefore be regarded as potentially incorrect. (Indeed, since working KK systems are the subject of more or less continuous development, it is arguable that the structure is always mis-specified.) This being the case, the analytical results concerning specification error are of some importance in the choice of estimator.[8] In the single-equation context, the effect of a mis-specification that takes the form of the omission from the relationship of an explanatory variable will be to produce inconsistent parameter estimates, regardless of the estimator used. Other forms of specification error have less serious consequences, loss of efficiency being the main one.

The SIEs do not possess desirable asymptotic properties in the system context. The question which must be asked, therefore, is 'How much worse are the SIEs when the structure of the system is incorrectly specified?' In the nature of the case, analytical results cannot provide us with a general answer to this question. See, however, Hendry (1975) for some illustrative results in a specific three-equation system. Nevertheless, there is something that can be said in respect of the SIEs. Since these estimators ignore all information in the system, outside the equation of immediate interest, the effects of mis-specification on the SIEs are confined to the structural equation in which the error occurs. In this sense use of a SIE 'quarantines' the effects of mis-specification (see Fisher, 1965).

Consistency of the LISEs (other than FP) requires that the equation of interest be correctly specified and that the *list* of predetermined variables for the entire system be correct (see section 4.4). The conditions are stronger for the FP estimators – the entire system must be correctly specified. Except for FP, then, the effects of specification error on the LISEs will also be confined to the equation (or equations) in which it occurs, provided that all predetermined variables have been included and that the variables are correctly classified into the endogenous and predetermined categories. Under these conditions the estimates of the structural parameters in the mis-specified equation will be inconsistent. On the other hand, if a consequence of the specification error is that a variable which is actually endogenous is treated as predetermined (an error which might be expected to be quite common in systems under active development), application of a LISE will produce inconsistent estimates of all structural parameters. This contagion of the effects of the mis-specification arises because the theoretical basis for the first-stage regressions in 2SLS, for instance, rests on the correctness of the classification of the predetermined variables. On the other hand, the seriousness of the inconsistency, or perhaps more to the point the increase in the finite-sample bias, will depend upon the importance of the variable concerned. Omitting an exogenous variable altogether may well be quite serious; omitting a lagged value of a variable which appears with a different lag length may not matter very much.

The FISEs and all FP estimators (including those which are members of the LISE class) require the entire system to be correctly specified for their consistency and asymptotic efficiency. Hence, when estimation is undertaken using a FISE or FP, all structural parameter estimates will be inconsistent if any part of the system is mis-specified. In this sense a specification error which occurs in one structural equation flows throughout the system to affect all parameter estimates.

The experimental evidence discussed in section 5.3 provides further support for the remarks made above concerning the effects of specification error on the LISEs and the FISEs. It was noted there that the main findings of the Monte Carlo studies are that the performance of the FISEs deteriorates markedly in the face of structural mis-specification, while that of 2SLS is not seriously affected.

A final consideration relevant to the choice of estimator for use in a working KK system is the question of computational cost. With modern computing facilities, differences in computational cost are usually trivial when the system is small and linear. However, in large systems, especially those which are non-linear, computational cost becomes an important factor. It is especially important when the structure of the system concerned is the subject of experimentation, as is usually the case during the major developmental stage of KK system-building. The estimation burden is particularly large in this phase because many alternative specifications will usually have to be estimated. Differences in computational cost are consequently magnified dramatically. Although it is difficult to be specific about computational costs because they vary a great deal depending on both computer hardware and software differences, a general indication of the scale of the differences is possible. If the estimation of a particular KK system by OLS costs 1 unit, the same job using 2SLS will be about 2 units, using FP or 3SLS will be 10 units, while using FIML might run to 20 units – all this assuming that the system in question is small and linear. As the size of the system increases, the relativity between OLS and 2SLS is affected very little. On the other hand, the cost differences between OLS and 2SLS and the other estimators increase rapidly with increasing size. Non-linearity is also associated with increasing computational cost. NLLS (a SIE) will typically be two to three times as expensive as a comparable OLS estimation. The cost of the other estimators increases dramatically with non-linearity to the point where FIML estimation of an intrinsically non-linear system, while possible, is prohibitively expensive. To these considerations of computational cost must be added that of the labour cost associated with setting up an estimation. Here again OLS and 2SLS are relatively straightforward and therefore inexpensive; 3SLS is a little more expensive in terms of labour time; FIML and FP, on the other hand, make quite heavy demands.

6.4 The choice of estimator

A clear ranking of system estimators on the basis of analytical asymptotic results was established in Chapter 4. OLS and the other SIEs are at the bottom of the pile, outranked by the LISEs, with the FISEs at the top. In Chapter 5 we saw that such finite-sample analytical results as are available do nothing to disturb this ranking. It also survives untouched by the experimental evidence in so far as this relates to a small, linear system free of complications. On the other hand, some damage is done when certain departures from textbook assumptions are considered experimentally. The general impression given by the experimental evidence is that the superiority of the LISEs and FISEs over OLS is much less marked when such departures occur. However, the experimental evidence (although scant) is more dramatic when questions of special relevance to working KK systems are considered. In highly sparse systems OLS ranks equal with 2SLS. In large systems such evidence as there is gives OLS the edge.

The analytical and experimental evidence is not easy to interpret. Principally, the reason is that the range of potential values of system attributes (size, number of variables, degree of non-linearity, sparseness, etc.) has not been explored sufficiently systematically or intensively for any clear picture to emerge. It does nevertheless provide us with some guidance.

A much clearer picture emerges when the practical issues of estimation in working KK systems are considered. The undersized sample problem effectively knocks out of contention all of the FISEs. Of the LISEs, we are left with FP and derivatives of 2SLS, truncated-2SLS and 2SPC. (IV could be included in this list but will not be in view of its inferiority to 2SLS and the fact that it is effectively indistinguishable from truncated-2SLS.) The SIEs are unaffected by the undersized sample problem. The problem of handling non-linearity, in the form which is typical in KK systems, leaves the list of candidates untouched. Autocorrelation, on the other hand, is much more easily handled using a SIE than by an of the LISEs still in the list.

Had the FISEs still been in contention, they would have been deleted when considered in the light of their poor performance when mis-specification of the structure occurs. For the same reason, the FP estimators are ruled out. The SIEs and the 2SLS derivatives, by contrast, are adequately robust in the face of structural mis-specification.

The final consideration is that of computational and labour cost. Here OLS is a clear leader, but the other SIEs and the 2SLS derivatives are not sufficiently more costly for them to be ruled out.

On practical grounds, then, the list of estimators from which the choice must be made for use in a working KK system is narrowed down to OLS, SIEs like CO, ARMAX and NLLS, truncated-2SLS and 2SPC. Given the virtual necessity to undertake the developmental work on a system with SIEs, given the ease with which OLS can be applied and its familiarity, OLS is overwhelmingly favoured in practice as the principal estimator in working KK systems.[9] It is usually backed up with other SIEs (CO, ARMAX and NLLS in particular) to cope with within-equation autocorrelation and non-linearity in the parameters. The only other estimator which is seen more than very occasionally in working KK systems is 2SPC.

Notes

1. This will usually be the case. For instance, the identity $Z_t \equiv S_t/Y_t$ can be approximated very well by the linear identity $Z_t \equiv aS_t + bY_t + c$, where $a = (\bar{Y})^{-1}$, $b = -\bar{S}/\bar{Y}^2$ and $c = \bar{S}/\bar{Y}$, the over bar denoting the sample mean of the variable concerned. See Challen and Hagger (1979).
2. System estimation is feasible by any method only if the product of the number of stochastic equations and the number of sample points exceeds the number of parameters. In this context the number of parameters includes the distinct elements of the covariance matrix $\boldsymbol{\Omega}$ of the system disturbances at a particular point when the estimator is a FISE. See Klein (1973).
3. Intriligator (1978, pp. 454–6) provides a useful survey of the attributes of models of the US economy. Most of the recent KK models use quarterly data from the mid–1950s to the mid–1970s. The longest sample period is that for the Data

Resources (1976) model, which consists of 82 sample points. The picture for models from other countries is similar. The Bank of England model of the UK (Latter, 1979) uses about 60 sample points, the Canadian model RDX2 (Maxwell, 1978) about 60, the Australian model NIF (Department of the Treasury, 1981) about 56, the Japanese EPA model (Yoshitomi *et al.*, 1980) about 48.

4. The DRI model of the US economy has nearly 400 stochastic equations, the Bank of England UK model nearly 300, RDX2 about 160, NIF 80 and EPA about 60.
5. Perhaps the largest systems in which FISEs are used are those in the PB class such as the Australian RBII model (Jonson, Moses and Wymer, 1977), the UK model of Knight and Wymer (1976) and the New Zealand model of Bailey, Hall and Phillips (1979). RBII, for instance, has about 20 structural equations (depending on the version) and uses about 65 sample points. Because these models are highly non-linear and call on many restrictions on the parameters both within and across equations, it is not clear precisely when the undersized sample problem arises (see Brown, 1981). All PB systems have to date been estimated using FIML.
6. There are other variations on this theme. See Salmon and Eaton (1975, pp. 329–30), Kloeck and Mennes (1960) and Giles (1973, pp. 70–3).
7. For instance, the existence of OLS requires that the rank of the observations matrix on the regressors (the matrix $\mathbf{X}_i$ in (4.18)) be smaller than the number of sample points.
8. See Kmenta (1971, pp. 391–405) for a general account of specification error.
9. An illustration of the supremacy of OLS is that, of the fourteen models of Project LINK as it stood in 1976 (Waelbroeck, 1976), only two used any other estimator.

References and further reading

AMEMIYA, T. (1966) 'Specification Analysis in the Estimation of Parameters of a Simultaneous Equation Model with Autoregressive Residuals', *Econometrica*, vol. 34, pp. 283–306.

AMEMIYA, T. (1974) 'The Nonlinear Two-Stage Least-Squares Estimator', *Journal of Econometrics*, vol. 2, pp. 105–10.

AMEMIYA, T. (1975) 'The Nonlinear Limited-Information Maximum-Likelihood Estimator, and the Modified Nonlinear Two-Stage Least-Squares Estimator', *Journal of Econometrics*, vol. 3, pp. 375–86.

AMEMIYA, T. (1977) 'The Maximum Likelihood and the Nonlinear Three-Stage Least Squares Estimator in the General Nonlinear Simultaneous Equation Model', *Econometrica*, vol. 45, pp. 955–68.

BAILEY, R.E., HALL, V.E. and PHILLIPS, P.C.B. (1979) 'A Model of Output, Employment and Inflation in an Open Economy', paper to the 49th ANZAAS Congress, Auckland.

BELSLEY, D.A. (1979) 'On the Computational Competitiveness of Full-Information Maximum-Likelihood and Three-Stage Least-Squares in the Estimation of Nonlinear, Simultaneous-Equations Models', *Journal of Econometrics*, vol. 9, pp. 315–42.

BROWN, B.W. (1981) 'Sample Size Requirements in Full Information Maximum Likelihood Estimation', *International Economic Review*, vol. 22, pp. 443–59.

CHALLEN, D.W. and HAGGER, A.J. (1979) *Modelling the Australian Economy*, Longman-Cheshire, Melbourne.

Data Resources (1976) *The Data Resources National Economic Information System*, North-Holland, Amsterdam.

Department of the Treasury (1981) *The NIF–10 Model of the Australian Economy,* Australian Government Publishing Service, Canberra.

Evans, M.K., Klein, L.R. and Schink, G.R. (1968) *The Wharton Econometric Model,* 2nd edn., Studies in Quantitative Economics No 2, University of Pennsylvania.

Fair, R.C. (1970) 'The Estimation of Simultaneous Equation Models with Lagged Endogenous Variables and First Order Correlated Errors', *Econometrica*, vol. 38, pp. 507–16.

Fisher, F.M. (1965) 'Dynamic Structure and Estimation in Economy-Wide Econometric Models', in J. S. Duesenberry *et al.*, *The Brookings Quarterly Econometric Model of the United States,* Rand McNally, Chicago.

Giles, D.E.A. (1973) *Essays on Econometric Topics: From Theory to Practice,* Research Paper No. 10, Reserve Bank of New Zealand, Wellington.

Giles, D.E.A. and Morgan, G.H.T. (1977) 'Alternative Estimates of a Large New Zealand Econometric Model', *New Zealand Economic Papers,* vol. 11, pp. 52–67.

Goldberger, A.S. (1968) *Topics in Regression Analysis,* Macmillan, New York.

Goldfeld, S.M. and Quandt, R.E. (1972) *Nonlinear Methods in Econometrics,* North-Holland, Amsterdam.

Hendry, D.F. (1974) 'Stochastic Specification in an Aggregate Demand Model of the United Kingdom', *Econometrica*, vol. 42, pp. 559–78.

Hendry, D.F. (1975) 'The Consequences of Mis-Specification of Dynamic Structure, Autocorrelation, and Simultaneity, in a Simple Model with an Application to the Demand for Imports', in G. A. Renton (ed.), *Modelling the Economy*, Heinemann, London.

Hendry, D.F. (1976) 'The Structure of Simultaneous Equations Estimators', *Journal of Econometrics*, vol. 4, pp. 51–88.

Hendry, D.F. and Mizon, G.E. (1978) 'Serial Correlation as a Convenient Simplification, Not a Nuisance: A Comment on a Study of the Demand for Money by the Bank of England', *Economic Journal,* vol. 88, pp. 549–63.

Intriligator, M.D. (1978) *Econometric Models, Techniques and Applications,* Prentice-Hall, Englewood Cliffs, N.J.

Johnston, J. (1972) *Econometric Methods*, 2nd edn., McGraw-Hill, New York.

Jonson, P.D., Moses, E.R. and Wymer, C.R. (1977) 'The RBA76 Model of the Australian Economy', in W. E. Norton (ed.), *Conference in Applied Economic Research,* Reserve Bank of Australia, Sydney.

Jorgenson, D. and Laffont, J. (1974) 'Efficient Estimation of Non-Linear Simultaneous Equations with Additive Disturbances', *Annals of Economic and Social Measurement*, vol. 3, pp. 615–40.

Kelejian, H.H. (1971) 'Two-Stage Least Squares and Econometric Systems Linear in Parameters but Non-linear in the Endogenous Variables', *Journal of the American Statistical Association,* vol. 66, pp. 373–4.

Klein, L.R. (1973) 'The Treatment of Undersized Samples in Econometrics', in A. A. Powell and R. A. Williams (eds), *Econometric Studies of Macro and Monetary Relations*, North-Holland, Amsterdam.

Kloeck, T. and Mennes, L.B.M. (1960) 'Simultaneous Equations Based on Principal Components of Predetermined Variables', *Econometrica,* vol. 28, pp. 45–61.

Kmenta, J. (1971) *Elements of Econometrics,* Macmillan, New York.

KNIGHT, M.D. and WYMER, C.R. (1976) 'A Monetary Model of an Open Economy with Particular Reference to the United Kingdom', in M. J. Artis and A. R. Nobay (eds), *Essays in Economic Analysis*, Cambridge University Press, Cambridge.

LATTER, A.R. (1979) *Bank of England Model of the UK Economy*, Bank of England Discussion Paper No. 5, London.

MADDALA, G.S. (1971) 'Simultaneous Estimation Methods for Large- and Medium-Size Econometric Models', *Review of Economic Studies,* vol. 38, pp. 435–45.

McCARTHY, M.D. (1971) 'Notes on the Selection of Instruments for Two Stage Least Squares and k-Class Type Estimators of Large Models', *Southern Economic Journal,* vol. 37, pp. 251–9.

McCARTHY, M.D. (1972) *The Wharton Quarterly Econometric Forecasting Model Mark III*, Studies in Quantitative Economics No. 6, University of Pennsylvania.

MAXWELL, T. (1978) 'A Primer on RDX2', *Bank of Canada Review,* January, pp. 3–10.

NEHLAWI, J.E. (1977) 'Consistent Estimation of Real Econometric Models with Undersized Samples: A Study of the TRACE (Mk IIIR) Econometric Model of the Canadian Economy', *International Economic Review,* vol. 18, pp. 163–79.

SALMON, M.H. and EATON, J.R. (1975) 'Estimation Problems in Large Econometric Models: An Application of Various Estimation Techniques to the London Business School Model', in G. A. Renton (ed.), *Modelling the Economy*, Heinemann, London.

SARGAN, J.D. (1961) 'The Maximum Likelihood Estimation of Economic Relationships with Autoregressive Residuals', *Econometrica,* vol. 29, pp. 414–26.

WAELBROECK, J.L. (1976) *The Models of Project LINK*, North-Holland, Amsterdam.

WYMER, C.R. (1978) 'Continuous Time Models in Macroeconomics: Specification and Estimation', in A. Swoboda, M. Mussa and C. R. Wymer (eds), *Macroeconomic Policy and Adjustment in Open Economies,* Proceedings of SSRC Conference, Ware, England.

YOSHITOMI, M., KATO, H., SAKUMA, T., MASUMOTO, H. and ARAI, K. (1980) *Japan: Econometric Model for Short-Term Prediction*, EPA World Econometric Model, Discussion Paper No. 1, Economic Research Institute, Economic Planning Agency, Tokyo.

Part III Validation

7 MULTIPLIER ANALYSIS IN KK SYSTEMS

7.1 Linear multiplier analysis

This part of the book is concerned with the procedures which are nowadays used in the validation of KK systems. These procedures form the subject-matter of Chapter 8. The aim of the present chapter is to consider various techniques which are basic to these procedures and which must be explained before they can be properly presented. Essentially these techniques, known collectively as *multiplier analysis*, are concerned with finding out what a KK system has to say about the effects on the endogenous variables of specified changes in the exogenous variables. The techniques which are used for obtaining this information differ fundamentally as between linear and non-linear systems. Since all working KK systems are non-linear, it is non-linear multiplier techniques which are of key interest. However, the best way to approach these non-linear techniques is via the more straightforward linear techniques. This is the approach that will be adopted here. The present section will be devoted to a discussion of the linear multiplier techniques and section 7.2 to a discussion of the non-linear techniques.

Our starting-point is a special case of the general KK system, first introduced in section 2.2. The particular special case is a system in which the maximum lag on any endogenous variable is unity (i.e. $p = 1$) and the maximum lag on any exogenous variable is zero (i.e. $q = 0$). Thus attention will be focused initially on the system:

$$\mathbf{A}\mathbf{y}_t = \mathbf{B}_0\mathbf{x}_t + \mathbf{C}_1\mathbf{y}_{t-1} + \mathbf{e}_t \qquad (7.1)$$

where $\mathbf{y}_t$ is the n x 1 vector of endogenous variables, $\mathbf{y}_{t-1}$ is this vector lagged one period, $\mathbf{x}_t$ is the k x 1 vector of exogenous variables and $\mathbf{e}_t$ is the n x 1 vector of residuals; $\mathbf{A}$, $\mathbf{B}_0$ and $\mathbf{C}_1$ are numerical matrics of order n x n, n x k and n x n, respectively.

In section 2.2 the solution to (7.1) was shown to be:

$$\mathbf{y}_t = \mathbf{\Pi}_{10}\mathbf{x}_t + \mathbf{\Pi}_{21}\mathbf{y}_{t-1} + \mathbf{e}'_t \qquad (7.2)$$

where $\mathbf{\Pi}_{10} = \mathbf{A}^{-1}\mathbf{B}_0$, $\mathbf{\Pi}_{21} = \mathbf{A}^{-1}\mathbf{C}_1$ and $\mathbf{e}_t = \mathbf{A}^{-1}\mathbf{e}_t$. As mentioned there, this solution is often referred to as the *reduced form*. The reduced form expresses the solution value of each endogenous variable at sample point t (in period t) in terms of predetermined variables and residuals at that sample point. Some of the predetermined variables, however, are lagged endogenous variables. Under certain conditions it is possible, by a process of substitution and manipulation, to eliminate these lagged endogenous variables and arrive at a set of solution expressions in which the endogenous variables are expressed in terms only of their *ultimate* determinants, the exogenous variables. The set of solution expressions obtained in this way is called the *final form* of the system.

To obtain the final form of the system represented by (7.1), we first lag (7.2) by one period, giving:

$$\mathbf{y}_{t-1} = \mathbf{\Pi}_{10}\mathbf{x}_{t-1} + \mathbf{\Pi}_{21}\mathbf{y}_{t-2} + \mathbf{e}'_{t-1} \tag{7.3}$$

Substituting (7.3) into (7.2), we obtain:

$$\mathbf{y}_t = \mathbf{\Pi}_{10}\mathbf{x}_t + \mathbf{\Pi}_{21}[\mathbf{\Pi}_{10}\mathbf{x}_{t-1} + \mathbf{\Pi}_{21}\mathbf{y}_{t-2} + \mathbf{e}'_{t-1}] + \mathbf{e}'_t$$

i.e.

$$\mathbf{y}_t = \mathbf{\Pi}_{10}\mathbf{x}_t + \mathbf{\Pi}_{21}\mathbf{\Pi}_{10}\mathbf{x}_{t-1} + \mathbf{\Pi}^2_{21}\mathbf{y}_{t-2} + \mathbf{e}'_t + \mathbf{\Pi}_{21}\mathbf{e}'_{t-1} \tag{7.4}$$

Lagging (7.3) by one period and substituting the result into (7.4) gives:

$$\mathbf{y}_t = \mathbf{\Pi}_{10}\mathbf{x}_t + \mathbf{\Pi}_{21}\mathbf{\Pi}_{10}\mathbf{x}_{t-1} + \mathbf{\Pi}^2_{21}[\mathbf{\Pi}_{10}\mathbf{x}_{t-2} + \mathbf{\Pi}_{21}\mathbf{y}_{t-3} + \mathbf{e}'_{t-2}] + \mathbf{e}'_t + \mathbf{\Pi}_{21}\mathbf{e}'_{t-1}$$

i.e.

$$\mathbf{y}_t = \mathbf{\Pi}_{10}\mathbf{x}_t + \mathbf{\Pi}_{21}\mathbf{\Pi}_{10}\mathbf{x}_{t-1} + \mathbf{\Pi}^2_{21}\mathbf{\Pi}_{10}\mathbf{x}_{t-2} + \mathbf{\Pi}^3_{21}\mathbf{y}_{t-3} + \mathbf{e}'_t + \mathbf{\Pi}_{21}\mathbf{e}'_{t-1} + \mathbf{\Pi}^2_{21}\mathbf{e}'_{t-2} \tag{7.5}$$

Continuing in this way, we obtain, after $t - 1$ substitutions:

$$\begin{aligned}\mathbf{y}_t = {} & \mathbf{\Pi}_{10}\mathbf{x}_t + \mathbf{\Pi}_{21}\mathbf{\Pi}_{10}\mathbf{x}_{t-1} + \mathbf{\Pi}^2_{21}\mathbf{\Pi}_{10}\mathbf{x}_{t-2} + \mathbf{\Pi}^3_{21}\mathbf{\Pi}_{10}\mathbf{x}_{t-3} + \dots \\ & + \mathbf{\Pi}^{t-1}_{21}\mathbf{\Pi}_{10}\mathbf{x}_1 + \mathbf{\Pi}^t_{21}\mathbf{y}_0 + \mathbf{e}'_t + \mathbf{\Pi}_{21}\mathbf{e}'_{t-1} + \mathbf{\Pi}^2_{21}\mathbf{e}'_{t-2} + \mathbf{\Pi}^3_{21}\mathbf{e}'_{t-3} + \dots \\ & + \mathbf{\Pi}^{t-1}_{21}\mathbf{e}'_1\end{aligned} \tag{7.6}$$

The expression (7.6) constitutes the *final form*[1] of the linear KK system (7.1). It comprises n solution expressions, each of which gives an endogenous variable as a particular linear combination of all exogenous variables in periods 1, 2, ..., t plus a particular linear combination of all equation residuals in periods 1, 2, ..., t, plus a particular multiple of the period 0 values of the endogenous variables.

Replacing t by $t + r$ everywhere in (7.6) we obtain:

$$\mathbf{y}_{t+r} = \boldsymbol{\Pi}_{10}\mathbf{x}_{t+r} + \boldsymbol{\Pi}_{21}\boldsymbol{\Pi}_{10}\mathbf{x}_{t+r-1} + \boldsymbol{\Pi}_{21}^{2}\boldsymbol{\Pi}_{10}\mathbf{x}_{t+r-2} + \dots + \boldsymbol{\Pi}_{21}^{r}\boldsymbol{\Pi}_{10}\mathbf{x}_{t} + \dots + \boldsymbol{\Pi}_{21}^{t+r-1}\boldsymbol{\Pi}_{10}\mathbf{x}_{1} + \boldsymbol{\Pi}_{21}^{t+r}\mathbf{y}_{0} + \mathbf{e}'_{t+r} + \boldsymbol{\Pi}_{21}\mathbf{e}'_{t+r-1} + \boldsymbol{\Pi}_{21}^{2}\mathbf{e}'_{t+r-2} + \dots + \boldsymbol{\Pi}_{21}^{t+r-1}\mathbf{e}'_{1} \quad (7.7)$$

Four types of multipliers can now be defined and (7.6) or (7.7) used to obtain expressions for each of them for the linear KK system (7.1). The multipliers in question are (a) impact multipliers, (b) delay multipliers, (c) intermediate-run multipliers, and (d) long-run multipliers.[2]

All four types of multipliers are defined in terms of particular partial derivatives of an endogenous variable with respect to an exogenous variable. The *impact multiplier* of the ith endogenous variable with respect to the jth endogenous variable is defined as $\partial y_t^i/\partial x_t^j$, where y_t^i denotes the ith element of $\mathbf{y}_t$ and x_t^j the jth element of $\mathbf{x}_t$. This multiplier measures the change in the period t value of the ith endogenous variable per unit increase in the period t value of the jth exogenous variable, with all other determinants of y_t^i held fixed. Equivalently, the impact multiplier gives the immediate effect on the endogenous variable in question of a unit increase in the specified exogenous variable. From the ith row of (7.6) (i.e. the ith of the n expressions in the set (7.6)), it can be seen that the i,jth impact multiplier can be evaluated from:

$$\frac{\partial y_t^i}{\partial x_t^j} = \Pi_{10}^{ij}$$

where Π_{10}^{ij} denotes the element in row i, column j of the matrix $\boldsymbol{\Pi}_{10}$.

The *delay multiplier* of the ith endogenous variable with respect to the jth exogenous variable for a delay of r periods is defined as $\partial y_{t+r}^i/\partial x_t^j$. It measures the change in the period $t + r$ value of the ith endogenous variable per unit increase in the period t value of the jth exogenous variable, with all other determinants of y_{t+r}^i held fixed. Equivalently, this delay multiplier gives the effect after r periods on the particular endogenous variable of a unit *maintained* increase in the specified exogenous variable.

From (7.7) we see that the 'r period delay i,jth delay' multiplier can be evaluated from:

$$\frac{\partial y^i_{t+r}}{\partial x^j_t} = (\Pi^r_{21}\Pi_{10})^{ij}$$

where the expression on the right-hand side denotes the element in row i, column j of the matrix in the parentheses.

We turn next to the *intermediate-run multiplier*. The intermediate-run multiplier of the ith endogenous variable with respect to the jth exogenous variable for a run of s periods is defined as:

$$\frac{\partial y^i_t}{\partial x^j_t} + \frac{\partial y^i_{t+1}}{\partial x^j_t} + \ldots + \frac{\partial y^i_{t+s-1}}{\partial x^j_t}$$

for any positive integer s. This intermediate-run multiplier measures the *cumulated* change in the value of the ith endogenous variable over the run of s periods t to $t + s - 1$, per unit maintained increase in the period t value of the jth exogenous variable, with all other determinants of $y^i_t, \ldots, y^i_{t+s-1}$ held fixed. It gives us the total effect over s periods on the endogenous variable of interest of a unit maintained increase in the specified exogenous variable.

The 's period run i,jth intermediate run' multiplier can be evaluated, using (7.7), from:

$$\frac{\partial y^i_t}{\partial x^j_t} + \frac{\partial y^i_{t+1}}{\partial x^j_t} + \ldots + \frac{\partial y^i_{t+s-1}}{\partial x^j_t} = (\Pi_{10} + \Pi_{21}\Pi_{10} + \ldots + \Pi^{s-1}_{21}\Pi_{10})^{ij}$$

Finally, we come to the *long-run multiplier* of the ith endogenous variable with respect to the jth exogenous variable. This is defined as the limit as s tends to infinity of the corresponding intermediate-run multiplier, *provided* that limit exists. Thus the long-run multiplier measures the *total* change in the value of the ith endogenous variable per unit maintained increase in the period t value of the jth exogenous variable.

The i,jth long-run multiplier can be evaluated as the element in row i, column j of the matrix:

$$\lim_{s\to\infty} [\Pi_{10} + \Pi_{21}\Pi_{10} + \ldots + \Pi^{s-1}_{21}\Pi_{10}]$$

provided that limit exists.

The conditions under which the required limit exists can be established in the following way. Let **K** denote the $(n \times k)$ matrix of intermediate-run multipliers. That is:

$$\mathbf{K} = \mathbf{\Pi}_{10} + \mathbf{\Pi}_{21}\mathbf{\Pi}_{10} + \ldots + \mathbf{\Pi}_{21}^{s-1}\mathbf{\Pi}_{10} \tag{7.8}$$

Then:

$$\mathbf{\Pi}_{21}\mathbf{K} = \mathbf{\Pi}_{21}\mathbf{\Pi}_{10} + \mathbf{\Pi}_{21}^{2}\mathbf{\Pi}_{10} + \ldots + \mathbf{\Pi}_{21}^{s}\mathbf{\Pi}_{10} \tag{7.9}$$

It follows from (7.8) and (7.9) that:

$$\mathbf{K} - \mathbf{\Pi}_{21}\mathbf{K} = \mathbf{\Pi}_{10} - \mathbf{\Pi}_{21}^{s}\mathbf{\Pi}_{10}$$

That is

$$(\mathbf{I} - \mathbf{\Pi}_{21})\mathbf{K} = (\mathbf{I} - \mathbf{\Pi}_{21}^{s})\mathbf{\Pi}_{10}$$

Hence:

$$\mathbf{K} = (\mathbf{I} - \mathbf{\Pi}_{21})^{-1}(\mathbf{I} - \mathbf{\Pi}_{21}^{s}]\mathbf{\Pi}_{10} \tag{7.10}$$

Let **L** denote the $(n \times k)$ matrix of long-run multipliers. Then, from the definition of these multipliers:

$$\mathbf{L} = \lim_{s \to \infty} \mathbf{K}$$

provided that limit exists. From (7.10):

$$\mathbf{L} = \lim_{s \to \infty} (\mathbf{I} - \mathbf{\Pi}_{21})^{-1}(\mathbf{I} - \mathbf{\Pi}_{21}^{s})\mathbf{\Pi}_{10} \tag{7.11}$$

If the characteristic roots of $\mathbf{\Pi}_{21}$ are less than unity in absolute value, then $\mathbf{\Pi}_{21}^{s}$ will tend to a null matrix as s tends to infinity, the limit in (7.11) will exist and the matrix of long-run multipliers will be given by:

$$\mathbf{L} = (\mathbf{I} - \mathbf{\Pi}_{21})^{-1}\mathbf{\Pi}_{10} \tag{7.12}$$

On the other hand, if the characteristic roots of $\mathbf{\Pi}_{21}$ are not all less than unity in absolute value, $\mathbf{\Pi}_{21}^{s}$ will not tend to a null matrix as s tends to infinity. Rather, the elements of $\mathbf{\Pi}_{21}^{s}$ will increase without limit. In this circumstance, the limit in (7.11), and the long-run multipliers, will not exist. Hence a necessary and sufficient condition for the existence of the long-run multipliers is that all of the characteristic roots of $\mathbf{\Pi}_{21}$ be less than unity in absolute value.

If all characteristic roots of $\mathbf{\Pi}_{21}$ are less than unity in absolute value, i.e. if the long-run multipliers exist, the system is said to be *stable*.

Up to this point the discussion of the final form and of the associated multipliers has been for the special case of the linear KK system in which $p = 1$ and $q = 0$. We turn now to consider the general case in which p and q can take any integer values. The general form of the linear KK system, introduced in section 2.2, is:

$$\mathbf{A}\mathbf{y}_t = \mathbf{B}_0\mathbf{x}_t + \mathbf{B}_1\mathbf{x}_{t-1} + \ldots + \mathbf{B}_q\mathbf{x}_{t-q} + \mathbf{C}_1\mathbf{y}_{t-1} + \mathbf{C}_2\mathbf{y}_{t-2} + \ldots + \mathbf{C}_p\mathbf{y}_{t-p} + \mathbf{e}_t \quad (7.13)$$

and the associated reduced form is:

$$\mathbf{y}_t = \mathbf{\Pi}_{10}\mathbf{x}_t + \mathbf{\Pi}_{11}\mathbf{x}_{t-1} + \ldots + \mathbf{\Pi}_{1q}\mathbf{x}_{t-q} + \mathbf{\Pi}_{21}\mathbf{y}_{t-1} + \mathbf{\Pi}_{22}\mathbf{y}_{t-2} + \ldots + \mathbf{\Pi}_{2p}\mathbf{y}_{t-p} + \mathbf{e}'_t \quad (7.14)$$

where $\mathbf{\Pi}_{10} = \mathbf{A}^{-1}\mathbf{B}_0$, $\mathbf{\Pi}_{11} = \mathbf{A}^{-1}\mathbf{B}_1, \ldots, \mathbf{\Pi}_{1q} = \mathbf{A}^{-1}\mathbf{B}_q$, $\mathbf{\Pi}_{21} = \mathbf{A}^{-1}\mathbf{C}_1, \ldots, \mathbf{\Pi}_{2p} = \mathbf{A}^{-1}\mathbf{C}_p$ and $\mathbf{e}'_t = \mathbf{A}^{-1}\mathbf{e}_t$.

In principle, the final form can be obtained from (7.14) by the same process of substitution as used above for the $p = 1$, $q = 0$ case. The required manipulations would, however, be impossibly complicated. Fortunately, a shortcut, based on a device known as *stacking*, is available. The idea behind this device is to put (7.14) in the same form as (7.2), the reduced form for the case $p = 1$, $q = 0$. This having been done, all the results which hold for this case can be extended without difficulty.

To begin with, a new vector, denoted by $\mathbf{y}^*_t$, is formed in the following way:

$$\mathbf{y}^*_t = \begin{bmatrix} \mathbf{y}_t \\ \mathbf{y}_{t-1} \\ \vdots \\ \mathbf{y}_{t-(p-1)} \end{bmatrix}$$

$\mathbf{y}_t^*$ is of order $pn \times 1$. The vector $\mathbf{y}_{t-1}^*$, of the same dimensions, will take the form:

$$\mathbf{y}_{t-1}^* = \begin{bmatrix} \mathbf{y}_{t-1} \\ \mathbf{y}_{t-2} \\ \vdots \\ \mathbf{y}_{t-p} \end{bmatrix}$$

We also form the $(q + 1)k \times 1$ vector $\mathbf{x}_t^*$:

$$\mathbf{x}_t^* = \begin{bmatrix} \mathbf{x}_t \\ \mathbf{x}_{t-1} \\ \vdots \\ \mathbf{x}_{t-q} \end{bmatrix}$$

and the $pn \times 1$ vector $\mathbf{e}_t'^*$:

$$\mathbf{e}_t'^* = \begin{bmatrix} \mathbf{e}_t' \\ \mathbf{0} \\ \mathbf{0} \\ \vdots \\ \mathbf{0} \end{bmatrix}$$

where $\mathbf{0}$ denotes an $n \times 1$ null vector. Finally, we form two new numerical coefficient matrices using the elements of the $\mathbf{\Pi}$s in (7.14), namely:

$$\Pi^*_{10} = \begin{bmatrix} \Pi_{10} & \Pi_{11} & \dots & \Pi_{1q} \\ 0 & 0 & \dots & 0 \\ 0 & 0 & \dots & 0 \\ \vdots & \vdots & & \vdots \\ 0 & 0 & \dots & 0 \end{bmatrix} \quad \Pi^*_{21} = \begin{bmatrix} \Pi_{21} & \Pi_{22} & \dots & \Pi_{2,p-1} & \Pi_{2p} \\ I & 0 & \dots & 0 & 0 \\ 0 & I & \dots & 0 & 0 \\ \vdots & \vdots & & \vdots & \vdots \\ 0 & 0 & \dots & I & 0 \end{bmatrix}$$

Here **0** denotes an $n \times k$ null matrix in Π^*_{10} and an $n \times n$ null matrix in Π^*_{21}, while **I** denotes an $n \times n$ identity matrix. The dimensions of Π^*_{10} are $pn \times (q + 1)k$ while those of Π^*_{21} are $pn \times pn$.

Consider the matrix equation:

$$y^*_t = \Pi^*_{10} x^*_t + \Pi^*_{21} y^*_{t-1} + e'^*_t \tag{7.15}$$

In full, this reads:

$$\begin{bmatrix} y_t \\ y_{t-1} \\ \vdots \\ y_{t-(p-1)} \end{bmatrix} = \begin{bmatrix} \Pi_{10} & \Pi_{11} & \Pi_{12} & \dots & \Pi_{1q} \\ 0 & 0 & 0 & \dots & 0 \\ \vdots & & & & \\ 0 & 0 & 0 & \dots & 0 \end{bmatrix} \begin{bmatrix} x_t \\ x_{t-1} \\ \vdots \\ x_{t-q} \end{bmatrix}$$

$$+ \begin{bmatrix} \Pi_{21} & \Pi_{22} & \dots & \Pi_{2,p-1} & \Pi_{2p} \\ I & 0 & \dots & 0 & 0 \\ \vdots & & & & \\ 0 & 0 & \dots & I & 0 \end{bmatrix} \begin{bmatrix} y_{t-1} \\ y_{t-2} \\ \vdots \\ y_{t-p} \end{bmatrix} + \begin{bmatrix} e'_t \\ 0 \\ \vdots \\ 0 \end{bmatrix} \tag{7.16}$$

which is just a short way of stating the following set of matrix equalities:

$$\mathbf{y}_t = \Pi_{10}\mathbf{x}_t + \Pi_{11}\mathbf{x}_{t-1} + \ldots + \Pi_{1q}\mathbf{x}_{t-q} + \Pi_{21}\mathbf{y}_{t-1} + \Pi_{22}\mathbf{y}_{t-2} + \ldots + \Pi_{2p}\mathbf{y}_{t-p} + \mathbf{e}'_t$$

$$\mathbf{y}_{t-1} = \mathbf{y}_{t-1}$$

$$\mathbf{y}_{t-2} = \mathbf{y}_{t-2}$$

$$\vdots$$

$$\mathbf{y}_{t-(p-1)} = \mathbf{y}_{t-(p-1)}$$

The first of these equalities is just (7.14), the reduced form of the general linear KK system (7.13). Consequently, (7.15) represents a legitimate way of writing (7.14). However, (7.15) has exactly the same *form* as (7.2), the reduced form for the $p = 1$, $q = 0$ case. (It is certainly *not* the same matrix equation, however, because $\mathbf{y}_t^* \neq \mathbf{y}_t$, $\Pi_{10}^* \neq \Pi_{10}$, and so on.)

Since (7.15) has the same form as (7.2), it must be possible to apply the same manipulations to (7.15) as were applied to (7.2) to obtain (7.6). It follows that the *final form* corresponding to the general linear KK system (7.13) is:

$$\mathbf{y}_t^* = \Pi_{10}^*\mathbf{x}_t^* + \Pi_{21}^*\mathbf{x}_{t-1}^* + \ldots + (\Pi_{21}^*)^{t-1}\Pi_{10}^*\mathbf{x}_1^* + (\Pi_{21}^*)^t\mathbf{y}^*_0 + \mathbf{e}'^*_t + \Pi_{21}^*\mathbf{e}'^*_{t-1} + \ldots + (\Pi_{21}^*)^{t-1}\mathbf{e}'^*_1 \tag{7.17}$$

The definitions of the various mulitipliers given above were perfectly general and do not require any modification for the general case. However, a new set of expressions for evaluating the multipliers is required since those given earlier apply only to the $p + 1$, $q = 0$ case. In the general case, the *impact multiplier* of the *i*th endogenous variable with respect to the *j*th exogenous variable can be evaluated from:

$$\frac{\partial y_t^i}{\partial x_t^j} = (\Pi_{10}^*)^{ij}$$

where $(\Pi_{10}^*)^{ij}$ denotes the element in row i, column j of Π_{10}^*. That this is the case follows from the fact that y_t^i is the ith element in $\mathbf{y}_t^*$ (as it was in $\mathbf{y}_t$) and that x_t^j is the jth element in $\mathbf{x}_t^*$ (as it was in $\mathbf{x}_t$). (Reference to (7.16) shows that $(\Pi_{10}^*)^{ij} = \Pi_{10}^{ij}$, as required.)

The *delay multiplier of the* ith endogenous variable with respect to the jth exogenous variable for a delay of r periods can be evaluated from:

$$\frac{\partial y_{t+r}^i}{\partial x_t^j} = (\{\Pi_{21}^*\}^r\ \Pi_{10}^*)^{ij}$$

Similarly, the *intermediate-run multiplier* of the ith endogenous variable with respect to the jth exogenous variable for a run of s periods can be evaluated as the element in row i, column j of the matrix:

$$\mathbf{K}^* = \mathbf{\Pi}^*_{10} + \mathbf{\Pi}^*_{21}\mathbf{\Pi}^*_{10} + \ldots + (\mathbf{\Pi}^*_{21})^{s-1}\mathbf{\Pi}^*_{10}$$

Finally, the *long-run multiplier* of the ith endogenous variable with respect to the jth exogenous variable can be evaluated as the element in row i, column j of the matrix:

$$\mathbf{L}^* = \lim_{s \to \infty} [\mathbf{\Pi}^*_{10} + \mathbf{\Pi}^*_{21}\mathbf{\Pi}^*_{10} + \ldots + (\mathbf{\Pi}^*_{21})^{s-1}\mathbf{\Pi}^*_{10}]$$

provided that limit exists. Analogously with the $p = 1$, $q = 0$ case, the matrix of long-run multipliers will exist if and only if all of the characteristic roots of $\mathbf{\Pi}^*_{21}$ are less than unity in absolute value. In these circumstances the system (7.13) is stable and the matrix of long-run multipliers can be obtained from the sub-matrix formed by taking the elements in the first n rows and the first k columns of the matrix:

$$\mathbf{L}^* = (\mathbf{I} - \mathbf{\Pi}^*_{21})^{-1}\mathbf{\Pi}^*_{10}$$

It transpires, then, that in the general case all four types of multipliers are evaluated in the same way as in the special case $p = 1$, $q = 0$ except that $\mathbf{\Pi}^*_{10}$ replaces $\mathbf{\Pi}_{10}$ everywhere and $\mathbf{\Pi}^*_{21}$ replaces $\mathbf{\Pi}_{21}$.

7.2 Non-linear multiplier analysis

In the previous section four types of multipliers were defined and techniques were developed for their evaluation. These multipliers provide us with information about the response of a particular endogenous variable of a *linear* KK system to a shock in the form of a unit maintained increase in a specified exogenous variable. The response of interest may be the immediate response, the response after a specified delay, the cumulated response over a particular run of periods or the long-run response after all dynamic effects have been fully worked out. Should we be interested in the response of an endogenous variable to a unit impulse increase in an exogenous variable, it is a simple matter to extend the results of the previous section to obtain expressions for the relevant multipliers.[3] Furthermore, there is no difficulty in determining the response of an endogenous variable to simultaneous increases in two or more exogenous variables. Since the system is linear, the combined response of any endogenous variable is just the sum of the responses to the increases in the individual exogenous variables.

Information about the way in which the endogenous variables respond to changes in the exogenous variables is also of interest in the case of non-linear systems. However in the non-linear case it is not possible to provide this information by means of the four multipliers because in the non-linear case the reduced form from which the multipliers are evaluated in the linear case does not exist. The alternative is to make use of an appropriately designed *simulation experiment.*

Before discussing the details of a simulation experiment it is necessary to consider briefly the general features of the technique of *system simulation*. Broadly speaking, system simulation comprises two sequences (or 'runs') of solutions over the same time period, known as the *simulation period*. (Methods of system solution were discussed in section 2.3.) The first of these sequences of system solutions is called the *control run*, the second the *shocked run*.[4] The difference between the shocked run and the control run is that in the case of the shocked run some form of shock is introduced into the system. The shock often takes the form of a change in the time path of one or more exogenous variables. However, it may also take the form of a change in one or more parameters of the system or even involve replacing one of the equations of the system by another. This point will be clarified further below. By comparing the solution values of the endogenous variables which are generated in the shocked run with those which are generated in the control run, one can obtain information on the response of the system to the postulated shock.

The account of system simulation given in the preceding paragraph draws attention to the main features of the technique. There are, however, a number of important matters of detail to be dealt with. The first concerns the sense in which the control and shocked runs consist of two sequences of system solutions over the simulation period. The simulation period is a sequence of time periods which is contained within the sample period used in the estimation of the system; it may coincide with that period, though this is unusual. In the control run the system is solved for each of the sequence of periods comprising the simulation period. It is solved again for the same sequence of periods in the shocked run. If historical values of the lagged endogenous variables are used in the successive solutions the system simulation is described as *static*. Most often, however, a *dynamic* simulation is performed. In this case the values used in the period t solution for the lagged endogenous variables subscripted $t-1, t-2, \ldots$, are the solution values obtained for the corresponding endogenous variables in the period $t-1$, period $t-2$, ... solution of the system, whenever these solution values are available.

A second matter of detail concerns the treatment of the *residuals* in system simulation. Here again there are two possibilities. The simpler of the two, and that which is adopted in the overwhelming majority of system simulations, is to set all residuals to zero. The system simulation is then described as *deterministic*. The alternative is *stochastic* simulation in which artificial time series are generated for each residual in much the same way as the values are generated for the random disturbances in a Monte Carlo experiment (see section 5.2). Stochastic simulations are comparatively rare and will not figure prominently in the rest of this book. The interested reader may consult Sowey (1973).

We turn next to the choice of time paths for the exogenous variables in the control run of a system simulation. The usual practice is to adopt the historical time paths – those actually observed over the relevant time period. By doing so, we ensure (as far as is possible) that the simulation is conducted in a relevant context, namely the state of the system which prevailed during the simulation period. It is important to note, however, that the results obtained from system simulation are not independent of the time paths chosen for the exogenous variables. This means that if historical time paths are used, the results will not be independent of the choice of simulation period.

It might be wondered why, if historical time paths are used for the exogenous variables, there is any need to bother with the control run at all. Why not use the *historical* time paths of the *endogenous* variables as the benchmark for comparison with the shocked run instead of going to the effort and expense of generating time paths for the endogenous variables in the control run? This question is a very important one, and is right at the heart of simulation technique. The point here is that any KK system is no more than a representation of the true system – the system which is actually generating the observed values of the variables. As such, the KK system is subject to errors and to inadequacies of one form or another. In measuring the response of the KK system to a postulated shock, it is necessary to abstract from these inadequacies. We do not want to burden our simulation results with them, if only because it would be impossible for us to tell how they affect the results. For these reasons, we set aside the historical time paths of the endogenous variables and use as our control (or benchmark) the time paths for the endogenous variables which would have occurred had the true system been exactly as portrayed by the KK system.

The preceding discussion of the system simulation technique can be illustrated with the aid of SYSTEM II, the illustrative system introduced in section 2.3. The endogenous variables of this simple non-linear KK system are C_t, X_t, Y_t, T_t and R_t. The predetermined variables are I_t and G_t, both exogenous, and the lagged endogenous variable C_{t-1}. Historical time paths of these variables are shown in Table 7.1. Table 7.2 provides the control run (solution) time paths for the endogenous variables, for both static and

Table 7.1 Historical time paths for the variables of SYSTEM II*

t	C_t	X_t	Y_t	T_t	R_t	I_t	G_t
0	2,147	2,369	2,895	526	0.182		454
1	2,375	2,539	3,009	470	0.156	534	472
2	2,486	2,690	3,198	508	0.159	478	552
3	2,577	2,778	3,362	584	0.174	561	666
4	2,715	2,968	3,612	644	0.178	716	804
5	2,609	2,977	3,489	515	0.147	820	915
6	2,540	2,948	3,596	648	0.180	332	859
7	2,753	3,133	4,011	878	0.219	649	814
8	3,025	3,398	4,354	956	0.220	820	875
9	3,103	3,565	4,505	940	0.209	747	931
10	3,123	3,587	4,665	1,078	0.231	719	911
11	3,324	3,706	4,912	1,206	0.246	808	947
12	3,440	3,850	5,112	1,262	0.247	789	1,023
13	3,713	4,109	5,494	1,385	0.252	901	1,078
14	3,752	4,204	5,607	1,403	0.250	1,039	1,111

* Units are $ million in all cases except R, which is a proportion.

dynamic simulations. It is left to the reader to verify the calculations. In doing so, one should recall that the historical value of the lagged endogenous variable C_{t-1} is used in every period in the static simulation. For the purposes of the dynamic simulation, the period 1 solution value is used for C_{t-1} in period 2, the period 2 solution value in period 3, and so on. Since no solution value is available for C_{t-1} in period 1 (period 1 being the first of the simulation period), the historical value is used in this one period.

In Figure 7.1 one of the control-run time paths, that for Y_t, is depicted for both static and dynamic simulation modes. For purposes of comparison, the historical time path for Y_t is also shown.

It remains to illustrate the shocked run and the interpretation of the simulation results. Before doing so, let us return to the main theme of the section – the means by which multiplier-type information can be obtained when the KK system is non-linear. At the outset it was noted that this information is obtained with the aid of a particular form of simulation experiment. The precise details of the experiment will of course depend on the type of information required, but the general principles are now apparent. Suppose that the requirement is for information of the kind represented by the impact and intermediate-run multipliers in the linear case. These multipliers are designed to tell us how the KK system responds immediately, after a run of 1 period, 2 periods, etc, to a unit maintained increase in a specified exogenous variable. In principle, the same

Table 7.2 SYSTEM II simulation – control-run time paths*

t	C_t	X_t	Y_t	T_t	R_t
Static simulation mode					
1	1,901	2,453	2,907	454	0.156
2	1,832	2,420	2,862	442	0.154
3	1,957	2,651	3,184	533	0.167
4	2,203	3,020	3,723	703	0.189
5	2,419	3,298	4,154	857	0.206
6	2,133	2,749	3,325	575	0.173
7	2,224	2,996	3,687	691	0.187
8	2,402	3,262	4,097	835	0.204
9	2,449	3,280	4,127	846	0.205
10	2,434	3,241	4,064	823	0.203
11	2,505	3,364	4,260	896	0.210
12	2,561	3,433	4,373	940	0.215
13	2,672	3,600	4,651	1,051	0.226
14	2,796	3,770	4,946	1,176	0.238
Dynamic simulation mode					
1	1,901	2,453	2,907	454	0.156
2	2,000	2,541	3,030	488	0.161
3	2,182	2,808	3,409	601	0.176
4	2,407	3,153	3,927	774	0.197
5	2,583	3,399	4,318	918	0.213
6	2,198	2,794	3,389	595	0.176
7	2,359	3,085	3,822	737	0.193
8	2,571	3,367	4,266	899	0.210
9	2,647	3,404	4,325	921	0.213
10	2,644	3,372	4,274	902	0.211
11	2,722	3,496	4,477	981	0.219
12	2,817	3,587	4,629	1,042	0.225
13	2,941	3,755	4,920	1,165	0.237
14	3,108	3,942	5,258	1,316	0.250

* Units are $ million in all cases except R, which is a proportion.

information can be obtained for a non-linear system from the following simulation experiment. First, a control run is performed in which all exogenous variables take their historical values. The simulation mode is dynamic and deterministic. Next, a shocked run is performed in which all exogenous variables but one take their historical values. The one remaining exogenous variable is given a time path which is the historical value plus one unit in every period. Comparison of the difference between the shocked-run and control-run solution values (the *deviation from control*) for any particular endogenous variable in the period in which the shock was introduced (implicity assumed to be period 1 of the simulation

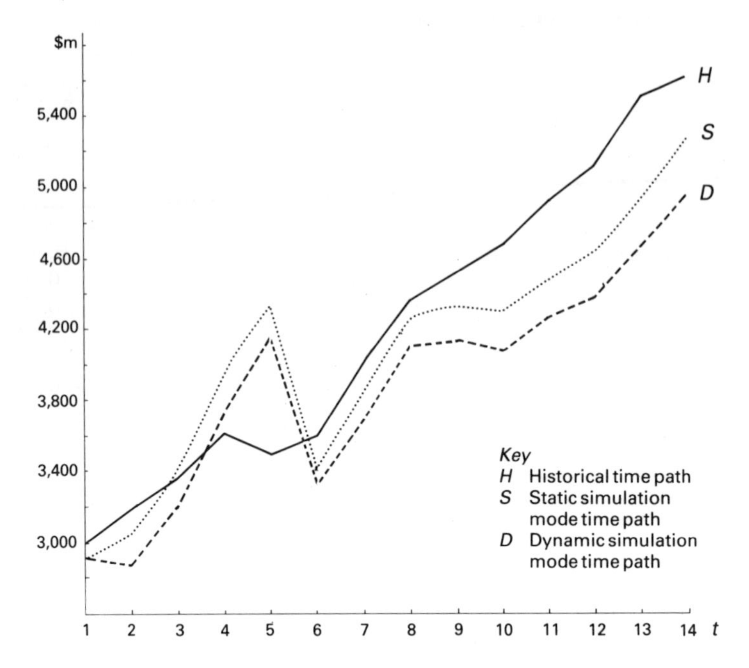

Figure 7.1 Historical and SYSTEM II simulation control-run time paths for *Y*

period) provides a measure of the impact multiplier of the given endogenous variable with respect to the shocked exogenous variable. The corresponding one-period intermediate-run multiplier is measured by the deviation from control in the shocked run for the given endogenous variable in the period after the shock was introduced (period 2), and so on.

In principle, then, it is a fairly straightforward matter to design a simulation experiment to obtain multiplier-type information from a non-linear system. There are, nevertheless, some practical difficulties to which attention should be drawn. The first is that to avoid rounding error and to make the numbers easy to manage, the 'unit increase' is more likely to be 100 than unity. The size of the shock is optional but is typically an increase of the order of 10 per cent of the simulation-period mean historical value of the exogenous variable in question. Multipliers are then calculated as the result of dividing the difference between the appropriate shocked-run and control-run solution values by the shock size. While this procedure is quite straightforward, it must not be forgotten that, the system being non-linear, the values obtained for the multipliers are not independent of the shock size. Furthermore, there is nothing that can be said, in general, about the way in which multiplier values will change with increasing shock size.

A second practical issue concerns the type of shock imposed. In the discussion above it was envisaged that the shock would be a unit maintained increase. However, since the control-run time path of the shocked exogenous variable is the historical time path, it will fluctuate over the simulation period and may well be subject to a trend. The consequence is that the shock will represent a varying proportion of the control-run value of the exogenous variable in different periods of the simulation. Where the exogenous variable exhibits an upward trend, the shock will represent a declining proportion of the control-run value. This matters because the system is non-linear. Many investigators avoid the problem entirely by concentrating their attention on the response of the system to *impulse* changes in the exogenous variables, not maintained changes. Alternatively, the shock can be made a constant percentage of the control-run value of the exogenous variable. The percentage deviations of the shocked-run from the control-run solution values in each period then represent *elasticities*, analogous to the impact and intermediate-run multipliers.

These points can be illustrated with the aid of SYSTEM II. The shock to be considered is an impulse increase in period 1 of \$100m in G. The control-run and shocked-run time paths for this exogenous variable will therefore be as follows:

	Period				
	1	2	3	4	...
Control G_t	472	552	666	804	...
Shocked G_t	572	552	666	804	...

In every other respect, the shocked run is identical with the control run. The solution time paths for the shocked run of this experiment are shown in Table 7.3, while Figure 7.2 depicts the deviation of the shocked-run time path of Y from the control-run time path. This (or percentage deviations from control) is the usual form in which system simulation results are presented.

It is clear that the greatest effect on Y of the impulse change in G is the impact effect. This impact effect is to increase Y by \$176m or by about 6 per cent, implying an impact multiplier of about 1.8. Figure 7.2 also shows that the intermediate-run multipliers of Y with respect to G are positive, though declining, for runs of one to six periods. However, seven periods

Table 7.3 SYSTEM II simulation – $100m impulse increase in G in period 1: shocked-run time paths*

t	C_t	X_t	Y_t	T_t	R_t
1	1,977	2,580	3,083	504	0.163
2	1,859	2,440	2,889	450	0.156
3	1,967	2,658	3,194	536	0.168
4	2,207	3,022	3,727	705	0.189
5	2,420	3,298	4,155	857	0.206
6	2,134	2,750	3,325	575	0.173
7	2,224	2,996	3,687	691	0.187
8	2,402	3,262	4,097	835	0.204
9	2,449	3,280	4,127	846	0.205
10	2,434	3,241	4,064	823	0.203
11	2,505	3,364	4,260	896	0.210
12	2,561	3,433	4,373	940	0.215
13	2,672	3,600	4,651	1,051	0.226
14	2,796	3,770	4,946	1,176	0.238

* Units are $ million in all cases except R, which is a proportion.

after the shock occurred, the effects have disappeared for all practical purposes, having worked their way fully through the system. The fact that the effects of an impulse change in an exogenous variable disappear after a few periods suggests that SYSTEM II is stable. In practice, this is the means by which the stability of non-linear KK systems is established.

Note that the intermediate-run multipliers referred to in the previous paragraph relate to an impulse change, not a maintained change in G. Thus they correspond to the linear intermediate-run multipliers of note 3 (see p. 159) which are defined in terms of an impulse change in the relevant exogenous variable, not to those of section 7.1, which are defined in terms of a maintained change.

As will be seen in subsequent chapters, the technique of system simulation is both very versatile and quite powerful. The key to the design of a simulation experiment is the shocked run. In the present section only one type of experiment has been considered, that in which the shocked run is based on a change, relative to control, in the time path of an exogenous variable. Other examples of this kind of simulation experiment will be considered in sections 10.2 and 10.3. Another form of simulation experiment bases the shocked run on a change in a particular parameter of the system. Simulations of this kind are sometimes described as *sensitivity analysis*. A third form of simulation experiment calls for the replacement in the shocked run of an entire equation of the system with some alternative equation. An example of this variety of simulation is discussed in section 10.4. Finally, it should be noted that the three forms of simulation

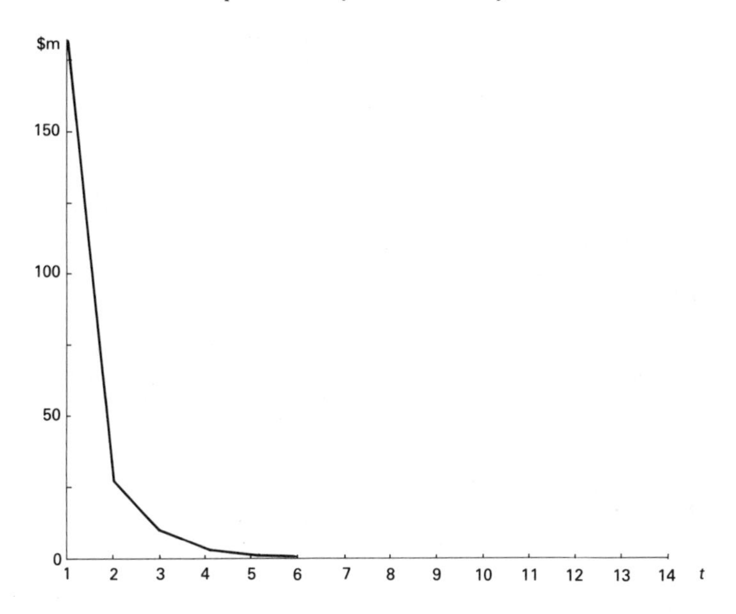

Figure 7.2 SYSTEM II simulation — $100m impulse increase in *G* in period 1: deviation of shocked-run time path of *Y* from the control-run time path

experiment need not be mutually exclusive. All sorts of combinations are possible,[5] a feature which makes system simulation a very powerful technique.

Notes

1. The originators of the final form, Theil and Boot (1962), applied the term to a limiting form of (7.6) in which the process of substitution is continued indefinitely. Aside from the fact that the sequences in $\mathbf{x}_t$, $\mathbf{x}_{t-1}$, ..., and in $\mathbf{e}'_t$,$\mathbf{e}'_{t-1}$, ..., continue indefinitely, the term in $\mathbf{y}_0$ disappears provided that the system is stable, the condition for this being that the characteristic roots of $\mathbf{\Pi}_{21}$ are less than unity in absolute value. See later in the chapter for further discussion of this point.
2. The terminology used for the various multipliers is not completely uniform. Delay multipliers are sometimes described as *interim* multipliers, intermediate-run multipliers as *dynamic* or *cumulative-interim* multipliers, and long-run multipliers as *total*, *long-term* or *final-form* multipliers.
3. Expressions for the impulse-change multipliers can be obtained by treating the unit impulse increase as a maintained unit increase followed by a maintained unit decrease with a lag of one period, and simply adding up the corresponding multipliers. The legitimacy of this device follows from the linearity of the system. It is left to the reader to verify that, in the $p = 1$, $q = 0$ case (or in the

general case with the coefficient matrices replaced by their 'asterisked' counterparts), the matrix of impact impulse multipliers is $\mathbf{\Pi}_{10}$, the matrix of delay impulse multipliers for a delay of r periods ($r = 1, 2, \ldots$) is $\mathbf{\Pi}_{10}\mathbf{\Pi}_{21}^{r-1}(\mathbf{\Pi}_{21} - \mathbf{I})$, the matrix of intermediate-run impulse multipliers over a run of s periods is $\mathbf{\Pi}_{10}\mathbf{\Pi}_{21}^{s}$, while the matrix of long-run impulse multipliers is a null matrix provided the system is stable.

4. As we shall see in Chapter 8, one special form of system simulation does not require a shocked run. In all other cases, however, both a control and a shocked run are required.
5. Combinations are indeed essential in some instances. We noted earlier that, in the *linear* case, the (combined) effects on the endogenous variables of simultaneous changes in two (or more) exogenous variables can be determined simply by adding up the appropriate multipliers. In a non-linear system, adding the deviations from control obtained in individual experiments will not work. It is essential to undertake an experiment in which all exogenous variables are shocked simultaneously.

References and further reading

SOWEY, E. R. (1973) 'Stochastic Simulation of Macroeconometric Models: Methodology and Interpretation', in A. A. Powell and R. A. Williams (eds), *Econometric Studies of Macro and Monetary Relations,* North-Holland, Amsterdam.

THEIL, H. and BOOT, J. C. G. (1962) 'The Final Form of Econometric Equation Systems', *Review of the International Statistical Institute*, vol. 30, pp. 136–52.

8 EVALUATION PROCEDURES

8.1 Individual-equation procedures

Before being put to work, a KK system is normally subjected to a number of tests which are collectively described as *evaluation procedures*. The objective of this testing is to *validate* the system – to determine whether the system reaches an acceptable standard of performance. The evaluation procedures in current use fall into two main groups:

(a) procedures which are applied to individual equations; and
(b) procedures which are applied to the system as a whole.

Typically, the procedures which fall in the first group are performed concurrently with the development of the individual stochastic equations and are as much a part of the search for the most appropriate specification as they are of system validation. Group (b) procedures, on the other hand, are normally applied only when the specification of the system as a whole, or at least of a complete 'block' of related equations, is available. These whole-system evaluation procedures are also called on at later stages of the evolution of the system when the specification of one or more individual equations is revised, the objective being to assess the effects on the whole-system performance of the specification changes in question.

Group (a) procedures will be considered in this section. Since the reader will be familiar with them already from his background in econometrics and since some have been touched on in Chapter 3, the individual-equation procedures will be given only a very brief treatment. The whole-system procedures which comprise group (b), being less familiar, will be discussed in detail in sections 8.2 and 8.3.

Perhaps the most widely used individual-equation test is that for disturbance autocorrelation based on the residuals which emerge after preliminary estimation. When, as is most frequently the case, the equation in question has been estimated by OLS (even when a FISE or LISE is used to estimate the complete system, preliminary estimation of individual equations is most often undertaken by OLS), a formal test for autocorrelation can be employed. The Durbin–Watson and Durbin–*h* tests provide a test for first-order autocorrelation when the lagged dependent variable is respectively absent and present in the equation under scrutiny (see Johnston, 1972, pp. 250–4, 312–13). Wallis (1972) provides a test for a simple kind of fourth-order autocorrelation. When testing for more general forms of autocorrelation is called for, or where an estimator other than OLS has provided the residuals, a less formal test may be used. This might consist only of a direct examination of the residual time series. Alternatively, it might centre upon the correlogram of the residuals (Nelson, 1973, p. 27). The residuals correlogram represents an estimate of the autocorrelation function (ACF) of the random disturbances. The ACF is the set of (true) correlations between disturbances one sample point apart, two sample points apart, and so on, regarded as a function of their separation (the 'lag'). If, as postulated, the random disturbance is free of autocorrelation, the ACF will be zero at every lag. Under the null hypothesis that the residuals represent drawings from a random disturbance with the classical properties (including absence of autocorrelation), the kth element of the residuals correlogram is normally distributed with zero mean and standard error of approximately $1/\sqrt{T}$, where T is the number of sample points.[1] With the help of this result it is a straightforward matter to test the hypothesis that any given element of the ACF is zero. The residuals correlogram is also called on in a χ^2 test, due to Box and Pierce (1970), that the entire sequence of elements of the ACF is zero.

The system-builder has two options available when confronted with evidence of disturbance autocorrelation. In the first instance, and particularly during the developmental stages of the system, the presence of disturbance autocorrelation will be taken as a signal that the equation in question has been mis-specified. The response will therefore be to search for an alternative specification. This might involve a change in the list of explanatory variables, the adoption of a different lag structure or an alternative mathematical form. However, it sometimes happens that autocorrelation remains after all reasonable attempts to improve the specification have been explored. In these circumstances the system-builder will usually take the second option, which is to live with the autocorrelation, and turn to an estimation procedure which is known to exhibit satisfactory properties in the presence of disturbance autocorrelation. Examples of estimators of this type were discussed in section 4.3.

Once the autocorrelation issue has been settled, the equation concerned is typically scrutinised from three points of view. First, the goodness of fit to the sample data will be examined, normally using $\bar{R}^2$ or a similar goodness-of-fit statistic. The system-builder will be looking for an $\bar{R}^2$ value which is acceptable in the light of the form in which the dependent variable is expressed. When the dependent variable is a level, the equation should show an $\bar{R}^2$ not far short of unity. If, however, the dependent variable is a difference or a rate of change, a somewhat lower $\bar{R}^2$ would be judged acceptable. In looking at a goodness-of-fit statistic such as $\bar{R}^2$, the system-builder is seeking reassurance that each equation, standing alone, adequately tracks the within-sample historical time path of its dependent variable. As will be shown below, this is one of a number of types of tracking performance that are scrutinised in the evaluation of a KK system.

Each equation will next be checked from the point of view of sign and size of its parameter estimates. All parameter estimates should conform with the relevant prior information as regards sign and, where appropriate, as regards size. In addition, the system-builder will wish to see that all parameter estimates have values which can be accepted as plausible. For example, the estimate of a parameter in a consumption equation which can be interpreted as a short-run marginal propensity to consume would be expected, on the basis of prior information, to lie between zero and one. However, a value of 0.2, say, which implied a long-run marginal propensity to consume of something like 0.3 would be rejected as implausible, since the main body of empirical evidence suggests that such long-run propensities lie quite close to unity. Similarly, the negative estimate of a parameter which can be interpreted as a damping factor in the Koyck-lag equation would be unacceptable in the light of prior information. A positive estimate, smaller than unity, conforming with prior information but implying that the variable in question will take ninety years to adjust fully to a change in one of the other explanatory variables, would likewise be unacceptable on the grounds of implausibility.

Finally, each equation will be examined from the standpoint of the relevance of the explanatory variables. Here the system-builder will call on the appropriate tests of hypotheses, and will wish to be able to accept the hypothesis that each of the parameters is non-zero at an appropriate significance level, to confirm that each of the included explanatory variables is indeed relevant. What this amounts to, of course, is that the system-builder will be looking for '*t*-ratios' in excess of 2.0 in absolute value. (Only when OLS has been used are the *t*-ratios, the ratio of a structural parameter estimate to its standard error, *t*-distributed. In the case of 2SLS, IV, 3SLS and FIML, these ratios have asymptotically the standard normal distribution – see Dhrymes, 1978, p. 301 and Giles, 1977.) In addition, when OLS has been used, the system-builder will employ the standard *F*-tests to check that the hypothesis that all parameters are zero can be rejected and, where appropriate, the hypothesis that all members of groups of related parameters are zero can also be rejected. (For a discussion of these tests consult Intriligator, 1978, pp. 129–34 – see also Dhrymes *et al.*, 1972; Morgan and Vandaele, 1974.)

Should the equation under scrutiny prove to be unsatisfactory from any one of these three standpoints, the system-builder will re-specify the equation in the search for an alternative which is free of autocorrelation and acceptable in terms of goodness of fit, and in terms of sign, size and significance of parameter estimates.

Good practice also demands that each equation be examined to check that it is acceptable on the grounds of intertemporal stability. As a minimum, this will involve checking that the parameter estimates are insensitive to small changes in the sample period used in estimation. When the estimator is OLS, more powerful procedures may also be employed. The Chow (1960) *F*-test can be called on to verify that the parameter vectors do not differ significantly between identifiable historical episodes within the sample period. Alternatively, the Brown–Durbin–Evans (1975) procedure can be used to test for a more subtle form of intertemporal instability in which the parameters of the equation change gradually over time, as can the Cooley–Prescott (1973a; 1973b; 1976) procedure (for a comparison of these two procedures see Garbade, 1977).

8.2 Whole-system procedures – tracking performance

The second group of evalution procedures used in the validation of a KK system are those which are applied to the system as a whole. With this group of procedures, two main sub-groups can be identified. The first sub-group aims to assess the tracking performance of the whole system, while the second sub-group assesses the plausibility of the dynamic properties of the system.

We turn first to the assessment of the *tracking performance* of the whole system. Most system-builders would regard the ability of the system to track the historical time paths of its endogenous variables, the system's *within-sample* tracking performance, as the most important of all the evaluation procedures. It is possible that every stochastic equation of the system performs adequately on the basis of the individual-equation evaluation procedures but that the system as a whole gives a poor representation of the real economy in which the historical time paths of the endogenous variables were generated. Until such time as an assessment of the within-sample tracking performance of the whole system is made, the system-builder has no way of knowing how the system will perform – notwithstanding a high degree of confidence in the quality of its individual equations.

The mechanics of the evaluation of within-sample tracking performance are relatively straightforward. The centrepiece is the set of control-run solutions of the endogenous variables generated by a dynamic simulation of the system,[2] with the simulation period coinciding, as far as is possible, with the sample period used in the estimation of the system.[3] The sequence of solution values obtained from this control run for a particular endogenous variable are the values which *would have been* observed for that variable in the simulation period if the system had given an exact representation of the real economy. The historical time paths of the endogenous variables are the values which *actually were* observed during the period in question. Should the solution and historical time paths coincide for every endogenous variable, the system would be tracking perfectly. Although perfect tracking is virtually inconceivable in practice, a comparison of the dynamic system simulation control-run solution time paths with the corresponding historical time paths provides a basis for the evaluation of the within-sample tracking performance of the system.

It then remains to decide precisely how this comparison is to be made. Perhaps the simplest way is to calculate the *simulation errors,* defined as the difference for each endogenous variable in each period between the historical value and the control-run solution value, and to summarise them into a single measure of tracking performance, much like a goodness-of-fit statistic. The simulation error for the ith endogenous variable in time period t, r_{it}, is given by:

$$r_{it} = y_{it} - \tilde{y}_{it}$$

y_{it} being the observed value of endogenous variable i in period t, and $\tilde{y}_{it}$ the corresponding control-run solution value. Several summary measures of tracking performance based on the simulation errors are in current use and none is necessarily any better than the rest. One such measure is the root mean squared error (RMSE), which is defined by:

$$\text{RMSE} = \sqrt{\frac{\sum_{t=1}^{\tau} r_{it}^2}{\tau}}$$

where the simulation period is $t = 1, 2, \ldots, \tau$. As will be clear from the above, RMSE is calculated for each endogenous variable.

RMSE is expressed in the same units as the endogenous variable concerned. In many instances a unit-free measure will be preferable. Such a measure is the root mean squared percentage error (RMSPE), which is defined by:

$$\text{RMSPE} = 100 \sqrt{\frac{1}{\tau} \sum_{t=1}^{\tau} \frac{r_{it}^2}{y_{it}^2}}$$

Both RMSE and RMSPE have a lower limit of zero, corresponding to perfect tracking for the endogenous variable concerned – zero simulation errors in every period of the simulation period. What the system-builder will require, therefore, is that the value of RMSE or RMSPE, as the case may be, be close to zero for all endogenous variables.

Some care must be exercised in the choice of summary measure on which to base the assessment of tracking performances. Generally, RMSPE will be preferred to RMSE for the simple reason that a unit-free measure is easier to interpret. However, if the observed values of the endogenous variable are typically very small, as in the case of a rate of change such as the inflation rate, or if the observed values switch frequently between positive and negative values, as in the case of variables obtained as residuals such as the balance of trade, the use of RMSPE is not recommended. In these instances a modest error can be associated with a very large value of RMSPE, simply because the observed value on which the percentage error is calculated is very close to zero. RMSE is preferable in such cases, notwithstanding the fact that it is a little more difficult to interpret.

Another difficulty which arises in connection with the evaluation of tracking performance using summary measures like RMSE or RMSPE is knowing how 'close to zero' is acceptable. No problem arises when these measures are used to make comparisons between competing systems. In this situation it is sufficient to note which system exhibits the smallest RMSE, say, and conclude that its tracking performance is superior for the endogenous variable concerned. Most frequently, however, the objective is not to make comparisons between systems but to evaluate the tracking performance of a KK system in isolation. How, then, does the system-builder decide what represents an acceptable value for RMSE and RMSPE? Clearly, some kind of benchmark is required. The simplest benchmark, and that most frequently called upon, is formed from the system-builder's own experience. From his knowledge of other systems' performance and from previous attempts to explain particular variables, the builder will have in mind values of RMSE and RMSPE that are regarded as achievable for various classes of endogenous variables. For instance, for real aggregates like private consumption expenditure or national product an RMSPE of 1 to 2 per cent should be possible; for nominal aggregates from the monetary and financial sectors of the system, an RMSPE of 6 to 8 per cent might be the best the system-builder could expect to achieve. An RMSPE of under 1 per cent might be considered acceptable for a price level, while an RMSE of 1 to 2 percentage points may be the benchmark for a rate of price increase.

A more formal means of establishing benchmarks is to call on so-called *naive models*. The system-builder would then regard the tracking performance of the system as acceptable if, for each endogenous variable, the RMSE of the system is smaller than that of the naive model. The simplest naive model is one which predicts that the value of the endogenous variable concerned in period t will be the same as its actual value in period $t - 1$. A slightly less naive model is one which predicts that the change in the endogenous variable between periods $t - 1$ and t will be the same as the actual change between periods $t - 2$ and $t - 1$. Both of these models are frequently used in the evaluation of tracking performance. Another naive model gaining in popularity is the one which predicts that the value of the endogenous variable in period t will be the figure generated by a Box–Jenkins forecast equation (see Nelson, 1973; Box and Jenkins, 1970).

Up to this point we have concentrated on the assessment of within-sample whole-system tracking performance by means of summary measures based on the simulation errors. While such measures are simple to calculate and straightforward to use, they are inclined to obscure much useful information concerning system tracking performance. For this reason, more direct inspection of the solution and historical time paths is often profitable. One very important basis for the evaluation of system tracking performance which falls under this head is the ability of the system to predict correctly *turning-points* in the historical time paths of the endogenous variables. Although a little tedious, it is a straightforward matter to count the number of turning-points in the historical time paths of each endogenous variable which do not appear in the corresponding control-run solution time path. Similarly, the number of turning-points *falsely predicted* can be counted for each variable. Another basis for the evaluation of tracking performance is the ratio of the number of positive simulation errors (underpredictions) to the number of negative simulation errors (overpredictions) for a given endogenous variable. A value of unity for this ratio shows that there is no tendency for the endogenous variable in question to be systematically over- or underpredicted. Yet another useful measure is the correlation between the period-by-period changes in the historical time path and those in the control-run solution time path of each endogenous variable. Once again, some of the measures of tracking performance just described are most easily interpreted in relation to benchmarks. As before, these benchmarks can be drawn from the system-builder's experience or can be formed from the prediction sof a naive model.

Suppose that the evaluation of the within-sample whole-system tracking performance of a KK system reveals unacceptably large simulation errors in respect of one or more endogenous variables. The KK system-builder will almost certainly wish to investigate the possibilities of respecification to improve the system's in-sample tracking performance. Before doing so, however, the major sources of the large simulation errors must be identified. Since the system is dynamic, non-linear and simultaneous, it may well be the case that the problem lies outside the equation for an endogenous variable which the system tracks poorly, or can be traced to problems in earlier time periods than those in which the errors become noticeably large. To help the system-builder identify and hence rectify failings in system tracking performance, a decomposition of the simulation errors into their components is often of assistance. To this end, consider the following representation of a non-linear KK system in which $p = 1$ and $q = 0$. (The generalisation to any p and q is obvious.)

$$\left.\begin{array}{lll} y_{1t} & = & f_1(y_{2t}, y_{3t}, \ldots, y_{nt}, y_{1,t-1}, \ldots, y_{n,t-1}, x_{1t}, \ldots, x_{kt}) + e_{1t} \\ y_{2t} & = & f_2(y_{1t}, y_{3t}, \ldots, y_{nt}, y_{1,t-1}, \ldots, y_{n,t-1}, x_{1t}, \ldots, x_{kt}) + e_{2t} \\ \vdots & & \vdots \\ y_{nt} & = & f_n(y_{1t}, y_{2t}, \ldots, y_{n-1,t}, y_{1,t-1}, \ldots, y_{n,t-1}, x_{1t}, \ldots, x_{kt}) + e_{nt} \end{array}\right\} \quad (t = 1, 2, \ldots, T) \quad (8.1)$$

As usual y_{it} denotes endogenous variable i in period t, and x_{it} exogenous variable i in period t; e_{it} is the estimation residual for the ith equation in period t; $f_1, f_2, \ldots, f_n$ stand for specified numerical forms, values for the parameters of which have been obtained in the estimation of the system.

Consider the set of solution values $\hat{y}^c_{it}$ obtained from the system in the following way:

$$\left.\begin{array}{lll} \hat{y}^c_{1t} & = & f_1(y_{2t}, y_{3t}, \ldots, y_{nt}, y_{1,t-1}, \ldots, y_{n,t-1}, x_{1t}, \ldots, x_{kt}) \\ \hat{y}^c_{2t} & = & f_2(y_{1t}, y_{3t}, \ldots, y_{nt}, y_{1,t-1}, \ldots, y_{n,t-1}, x_{1t}, \ldots, x_{kt}) \\ \vdots & & \vdots \\ \hat{y}^c_{nt} & = & f_n(y_{1t}, y_{2t}, \ldots, y_{n-1,t}, y_{1,t-1}, \ldots, y_{n,t-1}, x_{1t}, \ldots, x_{kt}) \end{array}\right\} \quad (t = 1, 2, \ldots, \tau) \quad (8.2)$$

Note that the estimation residuals have been suppressed and that *observed* values have been used on the right-hand side for *all* variables. Thus no account has been taken of either simultaneity or of system dynamics. Clearly the values obtained for the $\hat{y}^c_{it}$ will coincide with the individual-equation computed values for the endogenous variables, and the errors, defined by:

$$e_{it} = y_{it} - \hat{y}^c_{it} \quad (8.3)$$

will coincide exactly with the estimation residuals. The generation of the $\hat{y}^c_{it}$ according to (8.2) can be thought of as a kind of simulation run, and is known as a *residuals run*. Since it can be used to generate the estimation residuals, a residuals run is used to provide a check, prior to undertaking any simulations, on the accuracy of the coding of the system in the computer simulation program.

The static-simulation (control-run) solution values $\tilde{y}^s_{it}$ are given by:

$$\left.\begin{array}{lllll}
\tilde{y}^s_{1t} = f_1(\tilde{y}^s_{2t}, \tilde{y}^s_{3t}, \ldots, & \tilde{y}^s_{nt}, y_{1,t-1}, \ldots, & y_{n,t-1}, x_{1t}, \ldots, & x_{kt}) \\
\tilde{y}^s_{2t} = f_2(\tilde{y}^s_{1t}, \tilde{y}^s_{3t}, \ldots, & \tilde{y}^s_{nt}, y_{1,t-1}, \ldots, & y_{n,t-1}, x_{1t}, \ldots, & x_{kt}) \\
\vdots \qquad \vdots & \vdots & \vdots & \vdots \\
\tilde{y}^s_{nt} = f_n(\tilde{y}^s_{1t}, \tilde{y}^s_{2t}, \ldots, & \tilde{y}^s_{n-1,t}, y_{1,t-1}, \ldots, & y_{n,t-1}, x_{1t}, \ldots, & x_{kt})
\end{array}\right\}$$

$$(t = 1, 2, \ldots, \tau) \quad (8.4)$$

Once again the residuals are suppressed and observed values are used for all *predetermined* variables. In this case, however, the simultaneity of the system is brought into the picture because all values for the (current-period) endogenous variables are solution values.

Finally, the now familiar dynamic-simulation (control-run) solution values $\tilde{y}^D_{it}$ are given by:

$$\left.\begin{array}{llll}
\tilde{y}^D_{1t} = f_1(\tilde{y}^D_{2t}, \tilde{y}^D_{3t}, \ldots, \tilde{y}^D_{nt}, & \tilde{y}^D_{1,t-1}, \ldots, & \tilde{y}^D_{n,t-1}, x_{1t}, \ldots, x_{kt}) \\
\tilde{y}^D_{2t} = f_2(\tilde{y}^D_{1t}, \tilde{y}^D_{3t}, \ldots, \tilde{y}^D_{nt}, & \tilde{y}^D_{1,t-1}, \ldots, & \tilde{y}^D_{n,t-1}, x_{1t}, \ldots, x_{kt}) \\
\vdots \qquad \vdots & \vdots & \vdots \qquad \vdots \\
\tilde{y}^D_{nt} = f_n(\tilde{y}^D_{1t}, \tilde{y}^D_{2t}, \ldots, \tilde{y}^D_{n-1},t, & \tilde{y}_{Dt-1}, \ldots, & \tilde{y}^D_{1,t-1}, x_{1t}, \ldots, x_{kt})
\end{array}\right\}$$

$$(t = 1, 2, \ldots, \tau) \quad (8.5)$$

These solution values differ from those of the static simulation (8.4) only in that the solution values from earlier periods are now used for the lagged endogenous variables, instead of the historically observed values. In this way both the dynamic character of the system and its simultaneity are taken into account.

Recall that the simulation errors for the ith endogenous variable are given by:

$$r_{it} = y_{it} - \tilde{y}^D_{it} \tag{8.6}$$

(The D superscript was omitted in the earlier discussion.) This error can be decomposed in the following way:

$$\begin{aligned} r_{it} &= (y_{it} - \hat{y}^C_{it}) + (\hat{y}^C_{it} - \tilde{y}^S_{it}) + (\tilde{y}^S_{it} - \tilde{y}^D_{it}) \\ &= e_{it} + r^S_{it} + r^D_{it} \end{aligned} \tag{8.7}$$

where $e_{it} = y_{it} - \hat{y}^C_{it}$, $r^S_{it} = \hat{y}^C_{it} - \tilde{y}^S_{it}$ and $r^D_{it} = \tilde{y}^S_{it} - \tilde{y}^D_{it}$.

The first of the three components of the simulation error for endogenous variable i in period t, e_{it}, is simply the *estimation residual* – the error which arises because the equation in question does not provide a perfect explanation, given the *observed* values of the explanatory variables, of the endogenous variable in every period. The second error component, r^S_{it}, is described as the *simultaneity error.* It is the error which arises because the solution values which the system generates, given the *observed* values of the predetermined variables, do not coincide exactly with the values predicted by each estimated equation for the given endogenous variable. That this error is aptly named can be seen by noting that, in the absence of any simultaneity (i.e. if no current endogenous variable appears more than once in the system), $\hat{y}^C_{it}$ and $\tilde{y}^S_{it}$ will coincide for every i and for all t, in which case the error component r^S_{it} disappears. The final component of the simulation error, r^D_{it}, arises because the solution values from earlier periods used for the lagged endogenous variables do not coincide exactly with their historical observed values, and in consequence the dynamic-simulation solution values do not coincide exactly with their static-simulation counterparts. Accordingly, this component of the simulation error is called the *dynamic error*. Clearly, the dynamic error will not be present for those endogenous variables for which the corresponding equation of the system does not include any lagged endogenous variable.

With the decomposition of the simulation error at hand, the KK system-builder has a means of identifying the most important sources of large simulation errors in the cases of those endogenous variables for which the whole-system within-sample tracking performance is judged to be inadequate. When the estimation residuals dominate, the KK system-builder will put additional effort into improvement of the specification of the equation for the endogenous variable in question. If it is the dynamic errors which are most important, attention will be focused on the lag structures of the equations for the endogenous variable in question and for those endogenous variables which appear with a lag in this equation. Simultaneity error is the most troublesome of the three sources of simulation error to deal with, signalling a non-specific problem with the system as a whole. Although the discovery that simultaneity errors dominate does not signal any obvious avenue of corrective action, it is nevertheless important and perhaps helpful for the system-builder to know that simultaneity error, and not another, is the source of the problem.

To this point we have dealt exclusively with the evaluation of the whole system from the point of view of its ability to track the historical time paths of the endogenous variables over a simulation period which corresponds exactly or very nearly to the sample period used for the estimation of the system. This we have described as the assessment of *within-sample* tracking performance. A stiffer test of the tracking performance of the whole system is its ability to track the historical time paths of the endogenous variables over a period which lies entirely outside the estimation sample period. We describe the evaluation of the system from this point of view as the assessment of *outside-sample* tracking performance. (This form of evaluation is also frequently referred to as *ex post* forecasting.)[4] In practice, the period over which outside-sample tracking performance is evaluated is invariably the period immediately subsequent to the estimation sample period. This need not be the case, however. The technique might profitably be applied to other periods, removed a number of periods in time from the sample period or perhaps earlier in time than the sample period.

The key to the assessment of outside-sample tracking performance is the availability of the necessary data. What is required is the full set of historically observed time paths for all variables, including the endogenous variables. For the exercise to be worth while, these time paths must be of reasonable length, about ten sample points as a minimum. It is common for KK system-builders to be confronted with a general shortage of sample points for use in estimation (not in the chronic sense that estimation breaks down but rather that for some equations, especially those with long and complex lag structures, the system-builder has fewer degrees of freedom available than is regarded as being comfortable). Accordingly, it is often the case that the system-builder has no sample points in reserve to call on for an evaluation of the system from the point of view of outside-sample tracking performance. With the passage of time, of course, new sample points become available, and such an evaluation may therefore be possible in due course, provided that such data are not immediately 'consumed' by re-estimation of the system. Sometimes the system-builder attempts to get around this shortage-of-data problem by re-estimating the system after shortening the sample period and then using the sample points which thereby become available for the purposes of an evaluation of outside-sample tracking performance. Although better than nothing, it is important to realise that this device provides a less than pure test of the system's outside-sample tracking performance. The reason is that the data on which this evaluation rests will have influenced the specification of the system. As such the test does not really call on the system to track the endogenous variables over an entirely 'unseen' period, as intended.

The mechanics of the evaluation of the whole system from the point of view of outside-sample tracking performance are identical to those of within-sample tracking performance. As with the assessment of within-sample tracking performance, the main steps are the calculation of the dynamic-simulation control-run solution time paths for the endogenous, variables, calculation of the outside-sample simulation errors and summary statistics such as RMSE and RMSPE, formation of benchmarks from experience or with the aid of one or more naive models and comparison of the solution and historical time paths to determine the quality of tracking performance in the light of turning-points missed, wrongly predicted, and so on. The decomposition of simulation errors also carries over to the outside-sample case with the one modification that the e_{it} must now be described as individual-equation forecast errors rather than estimation residuals.

8.3 Whole-system procedures – dynamic properties

Having dealt with the evaluation of a KK system in terms of its tracking performance, we now turn to consider procedures which are designed to assess the plausibility of the dynamic properties of the system. Although potentially very powerful, these procedures are relatively straightforward in conception. The procedures used to uncover the dynamic properties of a KK system are quite standard applications of the methods of multiplier analysis in non-linear systems which were discussed in section 7.2. The basic idea is to undertake a series of dynamic simulations to determine the way in which the system responds to a particular shock. The results of these dynamic simulations are typically in the form of sequences of percentage deviations from control over the simulation period for each endogenous variable. A careful inspection of each of the 'percentage deviations from control' sequences is undertaken by the system-builder with a view to isolating any response which appears unacceptable on plausibility or other prior grounds. In particular, the system-builder will be looking for responses which are either exceptionally rapid or slow, any response which is explosive or otherwise suggestive of system instability, any pairs of responses which imply an implausible long-run relationship between the variables concerned, and so on. Needless to say, the KK system will be regarded as passing its evaluation test from this viewpoint if no implausible responses emerge. What system-builders regard as implausible or otherwise unacceptable on prior grounds depends to some extent, of course, on their background, experience and on the schools of thought to which they subscribe. Nevertheless, there is a surprising degree of unanimity among KK system-builders about the forms of responses to various types of shock which can be regarded as plausible (though it may be the case that this unanimity does no more than reflect the fact that the economists who are interested in building and using KK systems all come from one school of thought!).

The shocks which are chosen for an evaluation of the plausibility of the system's dynamic properties will vary from one system to another and also between system-builders. Nevertheless, there are some generally accepted principles which govern the choice of the shocks. Almost invariably the shocks will include a real shock, usually an increase in an appropriate form of government expenditure, a monetary shock and an external shock. The monetary shock may take the form of an increase in an exogenous component of the money supply or, where one operates, a change in the reserve requirements applicable to the banking system. Another candidate is an increase in one or more regulated interest rates. Yet another is a change in the rate of open-market sales (or purchases) of bonds by the central bank. An increase in exogenous exports or a terms-of-trade change are examples of commonly used external shocks. Other examples are a change in the exchange rate where this is exogenous or a change in an exogenous item in the capital account of the balance of payments. See FitzGerald and Higgins (1977), Helliwell and Higgins (1976). De Bever *et al.* (1979), Ball, Burns and Miller (1975), Evans and Riley (1975) and Christ (1975) for concrete examples.

Should an examination of the system's dynamic properties throw up one or more responses which are regarded as implausible, the system-builder will wish to re-specify to improve this aspect of the system's performance. Once again, however, it may well be far from obvious what avenues of respecification are likely to be profitable. A technique known as *response dissection analysis* has been developed to assist in the diagnosis of the causes of implausible dynamic properties. Like multiplier analysis generally, response dissection analysis is also useful as a means of enriching our understanding of the characteristics and behaviour of a particular KK system. Only a very brief discussion of response dissection analysis will be given here, principally because the technique is very much dependent on the features of the particular system under study. Further details can be obtained from Helliwell and Higgins (1976), FitzGerald and Higgins (1977), Modigliani (1975) and Spencer (1980).

The first step in response dissection analysis is no different from that of any examination of the dynamic properties of a system. A dynamic-simulation control run is performed, followed by a shocked run incorporating the shock of interest. As usual the percentage deviations from control of the shocked-run solution time paths are obtained for endogenous variables of interest. A series of alternate responses to the postulated shock are then computed (by repeating the shocked run) but in each member of the series the system is modified in such a way that particular *channels* of dynamic response are suppressed. By comparing the unmodified response of the system to the shock with one of the series of modified responses, the effect of the corresponding suppressed channel of influence can be determined. Examination of this effect might then reveal the cause of the implausible dynamic response.

Two matters require further elaboration. The first concerns the nature of channels of dynamic response, a matter which can be explained only by example. Suppose that it is the response of real output to a maintained increase in real government expenditure that is under scrutiny. The system-builder might identify a number of channels in the system through which a change in real government expenditure influences real output, including perhaps:

(a) a change in firms' production decisions following a change in inventory holdings;
(b) a change in the money supply and consequential changes in consumption and investment following the funding of the increased government budget deficit;
(c) an increase in interest rates and consequential changes in consumption, investment and the composition of asset portfolios following a change in interest rates, itself a consequence of bond sales to fund the government budget deficit.

Many other channels of influence are possible, depending on the structural details of the system.

The other matter to be dealt with is the method by which particular channels of influence are suppressed. Once again an example will serve to illustrate. Suppose that the objective is to examine the effect of the first of the illustrative channels set out above: namely, that which operates through a change in inventory holdings. To suppress this channel, the shocked run is undertaken with the system modified in such a way that the inventory-holdings (endogenous) variable is held equal to its control solution value in every period. (To achieve this, the equation for inventory holdings is temporarily deleted from the system. This variable is then moved into the exogenous category and assigned the control-run solution time path.) Note that the effects of the channel are determined by comparing the deviations of shocked-run solution values from control in the modified and unmodified system.

Finally, it is worth while referring once again to the interdependence of the specification, estimation and validation stages of KK system-building. Throughout this chapter the objective has been to shed light on deficiencies of one kind or another in the performance of the estimated KK system. Quite clearly, however, the discovery of such a deficiency is not the end of the matter. Rather, it sets in train, once again, the process of (re-)specification, estimation and further validation. As a consequence of this more or less continual cycle, working KK systems are forever in an evolutionary state, undergoing refinements and improvement all the time – sometimes in response to routine validation procedures and sometimes as the result of a weakness showing up for the first time after the incorporation of a new release of data.

Notes

1. This approximation can be unreliable for small values of k in certain circumstances and must therefore be used with care. See Box and Pierce (1970).
2. This is the one form of simulation in which no shocked run is required. See note 4 of Chapter 7.
3. Frequently, the KK system-builder is forced by availability of data and the need to provide for lagged variables, while using as many sample points as possible, to use different sample points in the estimation of the stochastic equations. When this is the case the simulation period chosen for the evaluation of the system within-sample tracking performance will be longer than the estimation sample period of some equations.
4. *Ex post* refers to the fact that the forecasting exercise is undertaken when the variables being forecast are actually known, the point of the exercise being system evaluation rather then genuine forecasting. Forecasting in the true sense, from a point in time which actually precedes the period for which the forecast is made, is then described as *ex ante* forecasting. This form of system *application* is dealt with in Chapter 9.

References and further reading

BALL, R. J., BURNS, T. and MILLER, G. W. (1975) 'Preliminary Simulations with the London Business School Macro-Economic Model', in G. A. Renton (ed.), *Modelling the Economy*. Heinemann, London.

BOX, G. E. P. and JENKINS, G. M. (1970) *Time Series Analysis: Forecasting and Control*, Holden-Day, San Francisco.

BOX, G. E. P. and PIERCE, D. A. (1970) 'Distribution of Residual Autocorrelations in Autoregressive–Integrated Moving Average Time Series Models', *Journal of the American Statistical Association*, vol. 65, pp. 1509–26.

BROWN, R. L., DURBIN, J. and EVANS, J. M. (1975) 'Techniques for Testing the Constancy of Regression Relationships over Time', *Journal of the Royal Statistical Society*, vol. 37, pp. 149–63.

CHOW, G. (1960) 'Tests of the Equality Between Two Sets of Coefficients in Two Linear Regressions', *Econometrica*, vol. 28, pp. 591–605.

CHRIST, C. F. (1975) 'Judging the Performance of Econometric Models of the US Economy', *International Economic Review*, vol. 16, pp. 54–74.

COOLEY, T. F. and PRESCOTT, E. C. (1973a) 'Tests of the Adaptive Regression Model', *Review of Economics and Statistics*, vol. 55, pp. 248–56.

COOLEY, T. F. and PRESCOTT, E. C. (1973b) 'An Adaptive Regression Model', *International Economic Review*, vol. 14, pp. 364–71.

COOLEY, T. F. and PRESCOTT E. C. (1976) 'Estimation in the Presence of Stochastic Parameter Variation', *Econometrica*, vol. 44, pp. 167–84.

DE BEVER, L. *et al.* (1979) 'Dynamic Models: A Collaborative Research Project', *Canadian Journal of Economics*, vol. 12, pp. 133–9.

DHRYMES, P.J. (1978) *Introductory Econometrics,* Springer-Verlag, New York.

DHRYMES, P. J. *et al.* (1972) 'Criteria for Evaluation of Econometric Models', *Annals of Economic and Social Measurement*, vol. 1, pp. 291–324.

EVANS, H.P. and RILEY, C.J. (1975) 'Simulations with the Treasury Model', in G.A. Renton (ed.), *Modelling the Economy,* Heinemann, London.

FITZGERALD, V. W. and HIGGINS, C. I. (1977) 'Inside RBA76', in W. E. Norton (ed.), *Conference in Applied Economic Research*, Reserve Bank of Australia, Sydney.

GARBADE, K. (1977) 'Two Methods for Examining the Stability of Regression Coefficients', *Journal of the American Statistical Association*, vol. 72, pp. 54–63.

GILES, D. E. A. (1977) 'Statistical Inference and the RBA76 Project', in W. E. Norton (ed.), *Conference in Applied Economic Research*, Reserve Bank of Australia, Sydney.

HELLIWELL, J. F. and HIGGINS, C. I. (1976) 'Macroeconomic Adjustment Processes', *European Economic Review*, vol. 7, pp. 221–38.

INTRILIGATOR, M. D. (1978) *Econometric Models, Techniques and Applications,* Prentice-Hall, Englewood Cliffs, N.J.

JOHNSTON, J. (1972) *Econometric Methods*, 2nd edn, McGraw-Hill, New York.

MODIGLIANI, F. (1975) 'The Channels of Monetary Policy in the Federal Reserve–MIT–University of Pennsylvania Econometric Model of the United States', in G. A. Renton (ed.), *Modelling the Economy*, Heinemann, London.

MORGAN, A. and VANDAELE, W. (1974) 'On Testing Hypotheses in Simultaneous Equation Models', *Journal of Econometrics*, vol. 2, pp. 55–65.

NELSON, C. R. (1973) *Applied Time Series Analysis for Managerial Forecasting*, Holden-Day, San Francisco.

SPENCER, G. H. (1980) 'Macroeconomic Adjustment Processes and the Core Model', in G. H. Spencer (ed.), *Experiments with a Core Model of the New Zealand Economy*, Research Paper No. 29, Reserve Bank of New Zealand, Wellington.

WALLIS, K.F. (1972) 'Testing for Fourth Order Autocorrelation in Quarterly Regression Equations', *Econometrica*, vol. 40, pp. 617–36.

Part IV Applications

9 FORECASTING

9.1 Arithmetical KK forecasting

Forecasting has been one of the main applications of KK systems since they first made their appearance in the early post-war years. Two types of KK forecasting may be distinguished: (i) arithmetical forecasting; and (ii) judgemental forecasting. The first type will be discussed in this section and the next and the second type in section 9.3. In this section the procedure used in arithmetical KK forecasting will be described, while section 9.2 will be concerned with the main problem which is involved in KK forecasting of this type.

Suppose that, standing at the end of quarter T, an arithmetical KK forecast of one of the endogenous variables (call it y_i) of a KK system for the next quarter, quarter $T + 1$ is required. The forecast will be made in the following way: (i) form forecasts of the values of the predetermined variables of the system for quarter $T + 1$; and (ii) solve the system for y_i using the forecast values for the predetermined variables. The solution value represents the arithmetical KK forecast of y_i for quarter $T + 1$. If the requirement is for a forecast of y_i for quarter $T + 2$ as at the end of quarter T, the procedure is to forecast the values of the predetermined variables of the system for quarter $T + 2$ and then solve the system for y_i using these forecast values for the predetermined variables. In general, to forecast y_i for quarter $T + j$ ($j = 1, 2, 3, \ldots$), as at the end of quarter T, the steps are to forecast the values of the predetermined variables for quarter $T + j$ and then solve the system for y_i using the forecast values for the predetermined variables. The solution value represents the arithmetical KK forecast of y_i for quarter $T + j$.

So far, the problem considered has been that of forecasting a *single* endogenous variable y_i. A more likely situation is that, standing at the end of quarter T, arithmetical KK forecasts of *several* of the endogenous variables of the system in quarter $T + j$ are called for. In this case the procedure, as before, is to forecast the values of the predetermined variables for quarter $T + j$. The system is then solved for each of the endogenous variables concerned, using the forecast values for the predetermined variables. The set of solution values constitutes the arithmetical KK forecasts for the endogenous variables concerned for quarter $T + j$.

In section 2.2. it was shown that the solution of a linear KK system can be found for any endogenous variable for any specified set of values of the predetermined variables simply by substituting this specified set of values in the reduced-form expression for the endogenous variable concerned. Thus to make an arithmetical KK forecast of y_i from a linear KK system, it is necessary only to substitute in the reduced-form expression for y_i the relevant forecast values for the predetermined variables. In the non-linear case, on the other hand, it is not possible to find a set of 'solution expressions' – the reduced-form expressions have no counterpart in the non-linear case. Hence in the non-linear case an arithmetical KK forecast of y_i cannot be generated merely by substitution. Instead some computational routine like the Gauss–Seidel algorithm is required to solve the system for y_i on the basis of the relevant forecast values for the predetermined variables. This means, of course, that the arithmetic involved in making arithmetical KK forecasts is of a much more elaborate and difficult kind in the case of non-linear KK systems than it is in the case of linear systems.

9.2 Forecasting the predetermined variables

It will be clear from the previous section that, computation aside, the main problem associated with making an arithmetical KK forecast from a KK system is the problem of forecasting the predetermined variables. This problem will be dealt with in the present section. Initially, it will be assumed that we wish to forecast *one quarter ahead*. To be specific, suppose that we are standing at the end of quarter T and that an arithmetic KK forecast of the endogenous variable y_i for quarter $T + 1$ is required. The problem of forecasting the predetermined variables for this case can be broken down into two sub-problems: (i) the problem of forecasting the lagged endogenous variables for quarter $T + 1$; and (ii) the problem of forecasting the exogenous variables (lagged and unlagged) for quarter $T + 1$. Each of these sub-problems will now be considered in turn.

Lagged endogenous variables

Consider those of the set of lagged endogenous variables which are lagged one quarter. Their value for quarter $T + 1$ is the value actually recorded in quarter T; similarly, the value for quarter $T + 1$ of those lagged endogenous variables which are lagged two quarters is the value recorded in quarter $T - 1$; and so on. Thus any one of the set of lagged endogenous values can be forecast for quarter $T + 1$ simply by noting the value actually recorded for the variable concerned, either in quarter T or in some earlier quarter. Since, by hypothesis, we are standing at the *end* of quarter T, it would seem to follow that this simple forecasting procedure will be available, and hence that, as far as the lagged endogenous variables are concerned, no forecasting problem will arise.

In practice, however, things will not be quite so simple. While it is certainly true that the values of all lagged endogenous variables for quarter $T + 1$ will be 'history' from the standpoint of the end of quarter T, some of these figures will not yet be 'recorded history', i.e. the required figure will still be in the course of compilation at the end of quarter T, in some cases, and in the course of publication in others. This applies particularly to those variables which are lagged only one quarter, but it may well be also true of some variables with even longer lags. All depends on the amount of work involved in the compilation and publication of the figure in question and on the priority given to this work by the relevant statistical agency.

To sum up, while the values of all lagged endogenous variables for quarter $T + 1$ will be history at the end of quarter T, it will be a matter of recorded history in some cases and unrecorded history in others. In the former cases, the forecasts of the lagged endogenous variables can be obtained directly from the historical record. In the latter cases, however, this will not be possible and a real forecasting problem will have to be faced.

Suppose, for example, that one of the lagged endogenous variables of the system is GDP lagged one quarter. To make an arithmetical KK forecast of the endogenous variable y_i for quarter $T + 1$ we would need a forecast of this variable for quarter $T + 1$, i.e. we would need to know its historical value for quarter T. Suppose, further, that the forecast of y_i is being made at the end of quarter T and that, at this time, the historical value of GDP for quarter T is as yet unrecorded. Since GDP for quarter T is unavailable, a forecasting problem arises which is no different in principle from that of forecasting y_i for quarter $T + 1$. The problem is handled by using values for the predetermined variables for quarter T to solve the system for the endogenous variables, including GDP_T. Of course, the quarter T value of the predetermined variable GDP lagged one quarter will be required to make this possible. This is the historical value of GDP for quarter $T - 1$. If, as at quarter T, the quarter $T - 1$ value of GDP is available (i.e. is recorded history), no further problems arise in this connection. The historical record provides sufficient information to obtain a forecast of GDP for quarter T, by solving the system for that quarter. On the other hand, if the quarter $T - 1$ value of GDP is also as yet unrecorded, as it may well be, it will be necessary to solve the system for quarter $T - 1$, using the predetermined variables for that quarter, to form a forecast of GDP for quarter $T - 1$. Once again, the predetermined variables will include GDP lagged one quarter – in this case the historical value of GDP for quarter $T - 2$. If this value is available, it will be used in the quarter $T - 1$ solution, which will yield a forecast of GDP for quarter

$T - 1$. This value can be fed into the quarter T solution to provide a forecast of GDP in quarter T as required at the outset. If, however, GDP for quarter $T - 2$ is not recorded, it will be necessary to go back yet another quarter.

The problem of forecasting the lagged endogenous variables can always be handled in this way. It is simply a matter of going back far enough to find a period for which all lagged endogenous variables appearing among the predetermined variables are recorded history. The system is then solved. The solution values of the endogenous variables are used as forecasts of these variables in the next period in those cases where the historical value of the variable is as yet unrecorded. Where the historical value is known, it is used instead. The system is solved again and the process repeated for as many periods as necessary.

Exogenous variables

The exogenous variables of a modern KK system consist of: (i) unlagged; and (ii) lagged. We shall begin by considering the problem of forecasting the unlagged exogenous variables of the system for period $T + 1$ as at the end of period T. For this purpose it will be convenient to divide the variables concerned into three groups: (i) dummy variables; (ii) policy variables; (iii) other miscellaneous unlagged exogenous variables.

The first group can be disposed of without much difficulty. In most cases there will be no problem in forecasting the values of unlagged exogenous variables of this type. Consider, for example, the variable t, denoting time measured in quarters from some arbitrary origin. This variable is a member of group (i) in virtually all modern KK systems. To place a value on t for quarter $T + 1$ one will merely have to count the number of quarters between quarter $T + 1$ and quarter zero – the arbitrary time origin. As a second example, take seasonal dummies – also typical of the unlagged exogenous variables which fall in group (i). To forecast these variables for quarter $T + 1$ it will be necessary to do no more than decide whether quarter $T + 1$ is the first, second or third quarter of the year. As these two examples make clear, the problem of forecasting the unlagged exogenous variables of group (i) is trivial – in most cases their values for quarter $T + 1$ can be determined at the end of quarter T in a purely mechanical way.

Examples of the unlagged exogenous variables in group (ii) are fiscal policy instruments – in particular, government expenditures, tax variables and transfer-payment variables – and monetary and external policy instruments. A large number of unlagged exogenous variables of these types are to be found in virtually all modern KK systems, their precise nature varying from system to system depending on the institutional framework of the economy concerned.

To make the necessary forecasts of the group (ii) variables for period $T + 1$, the KK forecaster usually relies heavily on announcements which the government and other policy-making authorities make from time to time as to their plans and intentions in the economic field. This applies particularly to forecasts of government expenditure. Most modern governments make very detailed announcements of their expenditure intentions at budget time and, in some cases and for some classes of expenditure, in between budgets as well. Of course, these announcements are in no way binding, and frequently the expenditure actually undertaken is found to differ significantly from that planned. Nevertheless, several studies (see, for example, Stekler, 1967; Brown and Taubman, 1962) have shown that the announced expenditure intentions of governments constitute a reasonably firm basis for forecasting the expenditure that will, in due course, be undertaken; and in practice they are invariably used by KK forecasters, not uncommonly through the medium of a formal forecasting equation, as the main tool for forecasting government expenditure variables for quarter $T + 1$.

In the case of some of the exogenous variables in group (ii), changes are always made by the relevant policy-making authorities without warning because otherwise there would be undesirable opportunities for private profit. For example, changes to the exchange rate are never announed in advance, nor are changes to rates of sales tax and excise duty. To forecast policy variables of this type the forecaster usually proceeds on the basis of 'no change'. Typically this assumption is also used as a basis for forecasting certain other policy variables, like rates of income tax and interest rates. Usually the authorities give reasonable notice of their intention to change variables such as these, and if no change has been announced the assumption will be that none is intended.

We turn now to those unlagged exogenous variables which fall in group (iii). In most of the KK systems that have been built in recent years group (iii) is quite large and covers a wide range of variables whose main common element is that they can, to a large extent, be forecast independently of the rest of the system. Typically, demographic variables feature prominently, and where they occur they are usually forecast by means of the standard and well-tried forecasting procedures which demographers have developed. Other group (iii) variables are forecast in a variety of *ad hoc* ways, sometimes informal and sometimes formal. One formal *ad hoc* forecasting device which is frequently employed is a forecasting equation which 'explains' the variable to be forecast largely, if not entirely, in terms of a simple trend variable. Another is a forecasting equation in which the variable to be forecast is explained exclusively in terms of its own history. Nowadays Box–Jenkins procedures are commonly employed to develop forecasting equations of this latter type.

So far we have been concentrating on the problem of forecasting the *unlagged* exogenous variables for quarter $T + 1$, as at the end of quarter T.

We turn now to those exogenous variables which are lagged.

We noted earlier that the values of the lagged *endogenous* variables for quarter $T + 1$ are history from the standpoint of the end of quarter T. The same is true, of course, of the values of the lagged exogenous variables. This being so, the lagged exogenous variables fall into two groups, as far as the problem of making forecasts for quarter $T + 1$ is concerned; (i) those whose values are *recorded* history at the end of quarter T; and (ii) the rest. As far as the first group are concerned, there will be no forecasting problem; to make the required forecasts for quarter $T + 1$ it will be a matter, in each case, simply of taking the appropriate figure from the historical record. As for the second group, a distinction can be made between those lagged exogenous variables which have an unlagged counterpart and those which do not. In the former case, the procedure which has been devised to make the required forecasts of the unlagged variable will usually be applied to the lagged variable as well. Where there is no unlagged counterpart the forecasting problem will have to be tackled from scratch and will normally be approached along the lines already discussed for the unlagged case. In particular, the nature of forecasting procedure used will depend very much on whether the variable concerned is a policy variable or not.

We began this section by assuming that, standing at the end of quarter T, we wish to make an arithmetical KK forecast of the endogenous variable y_i for *quarter* $T + 1$, i.e. that the problem is to forecast one quarter ahead. In practice a more likely situation is that, as at the end of quarter T, we wish to forecast y_i for a succession of future quarters beginning with quarter $T +$ 1 and ending with quarter $T + j$, where $j \geqslant 2$. In this case, forecasts of all predetermined variables for each of the quarters $T + 1$ to $T + j$ will be required. As far as the *unlagged exogenous* variables are concerned, this raises no fresh problem. Some forecasting procedure is required for each of these variables even in the one-quarter-ahead case, and in the case now under discussion it will be a matter simply of applying this procedure to each of the succesion of quarters in turn. The same cannot be said of the other two sub-groups of the predetermined-variables group, i.e. the lagged exogenous variables and the lagged endogenous variables. In both cases, the need for forecasts for each quarter from quarter $T + 1$ through quarter $T + j$ will cause fresh problems.

Take the lagged exogenous variables first. As we have seen, in the one-quarter-ahead situation, it will be possible to derive the required forecasts for most (possibly all) of these variables simply by plucking the appropriate figure from the historical record. In the more complicated situation now under discussion, this will no longer be the case. While some of the lagged exogenous variables which appear in the typical KK system may have quite long lags, most will enter with lags of, say, four quarters or less, and for many of these an explicit forecasting procedure (unnecessary in the one-quarter-ahead situation) will have to be devised. For example, the value of a variable which appears with a lag of two quarters will be history as at the end of quarter T for quarters $T + 1$ and $T + 2$ but not for quarters $T + 3$, $T + 4$, $T + 5$ and $T + 6$. Hence if j is 3 or more, an explicit forecasting procedure will have to be devised for all lagged exogenous variables which enter with a lag of two quarters.

The same difficulty will arise in the case of the lagged endogenous variables. Here again it will be necessary to devise an explicit forecasting procedure for many variables which in the one-quarter-ahead case could be forecast straight from the historical record. For example, a forecasting procedure will be required for all lagged endogenous variables which appear with a lag of one quarter if y_i is to be forecast beyond quarter $T + 2$, for all variables which appear with a lag of two quarters if y_i is to be forecast beyond quarter $T + 3$, and so on. In the case of the lagged endogenous variables, however, the required forecasting procedure already exists in the shape of the KK system itself.

Suppose, for example, that at the end of quarter T we wish to make an arithmetical KK forecast of the endogenous variable y_i for quarter $T + 2$. We then require, among other things, forecasts for quarter $T + 2$ of all lagged endogenous variables which enter the system with a lag of one quarter because the values of these variables for quarter $T + 2$, though history at the end of quarter $T + 1$ will not be history, let alone recorded history, at the end of quarter T. To make the required forecasts we would use the system, in the way already described, to make a *one*-quarter-ahead forecast for all the (lagged) endogenous variables concerned. Similarly, if we wish to make a forecast of the endogenous variable y_i for quarter $T + 3$ we shall use the system to make a *two*-quarter-ahead forecast for all endogenous variables which enter the system with a lag of one quarter and a one-quarter-ahead forecast for all those which enter with a lag of two quarters.

In short, if we wish to make a sequence of arithmetical forecasts of some endogenous variable y_i we need to make, in addition, a sequence of such forecasts (beginning one quarter later) for all those endogenous variables which enter the system with a lag of one quarter, a sequence (beginning two quarters later) for all those which enter with a lag of two quarters, and so on.

9.3 Judgemental KK forecasting

We turn now to the second of the two types of KK forecasting distinguished at the outset, namely judgemental KK forecasting. Our discussion will be unavoidably brief, concentrating on the central issues.

The reader who wishes a more detailed treatment of particular issues will find the references listed at the end of the chapter of some help.

Judgemental forecasting is best regarded as a modified form of arithmetical forecasting. Indeed, it is for this reason that we have dealt with arithmetical forecasting as some length in the two previous sections. Arithmetical KK forecasting was the rule in the early days of KK systems. Nowadays, however, it is rarely used and would not warrant detailed treatment were it not for the fact that it constitutes the starting-point for KK forecasting of the judgemental type.

In discussing judgemental KK forecasting we shall assume that the forecasting operation is on-going, not once for all, and that it is multi quarter ahead, not one quarter ahead. Thus we shall suppose that the forecasting operation begins at the end of quarter T, at which point forecasts are made for one or more endogenous variables of the system for a sequence of quarters beginning with quarter $T + 1$ and ending with quarter $T + j$, where $j \geqslant 2$. At the end of quarter $T + 1$ fresh forecasts are made for the endogenous variables concerned for a sequence of quarters beginning with quarter $T + 2$ and ending with quarter $T + j + 1$. And so on.

Given this situation, the steps in judgemental KK forecasting, each of which will be explained below, are:

1. Arithmetical KK forecasting with constant-term adjustment is used to forecast the endogenous variables of interest for each of the j quarters in the relevant sequence $T + 1$ through $T + j$, $T + 2$ through $T + j + 1$, etc., as the case may be.
2. The forecasts of the endogenous variables are checked for consistency with the forecasts of the predetermined variables and the relationships between endogenous variables are checked over the forecast quarters for possible distortion. In the event of inconsistency and/or distortion the constant-term adjustments are revised and step 1 is repeated. The new forecasts are checked for consistency and distortion in the same way as the original forecasts and, in the event of either still appearing, step 1 is repeated a second time. This process continues until consistency is achieved and no distortion in endogenous-variable relationships is apparent.
3. Comments on the forecasts are sought from outside experts with specialised knowledge of particular sectors of the economy and, if necessary, the forecasts are revised in the light of what they say.

We shall now discuss each of these three steps in turn.

Step 1

We begin by explaining how ‘arithmetical KK forecasting with constant-term adjustment' is carried out. The simplest way to do this is to explain how it differs from the ordinary arithmetical KK forecasting discussed in the two preceeding sections.

The KK system from which the forecasts are generated will contain both stochastic relationships and definitional relationships. The typical stochastic relationship may be written as:

$$y_{it} = f_i(y_{1t}, \ldots, y_{(i-1)t}, y_{(i+1)t}, \ldots, y_{nt}, x_{1t}, x_{2t}, \ldots, x_{mt}) + e_{it} \qquad (9.1)$$

where $y_{1t}, \ldots, y_{it}, \ldots, y_{nt}$ are the endogenous variables of the system, $x_{1t}, x_{2t}, \ldots, x_{mt}$ are the predetermined variables and f_i is some numerical function; e_{it} is the 'residual' in the equation – that is, e_{it} is given by:

$$e_{it} = y_{it} - \hat{y}_{it} \qquad (9.2)$$

where $\hat{y}_{it}$ is the estimate of y_{it} given by substituting the historical values of *all* variables in the right-hand side of (9.1) together with zero for the residual.

In arithmetical KK forecasting of the ordinary kind, $x_{1t}, \ldots, x_{mt}$ are replaced throughout the system (in both stochastic and definitional relationships) by the values which have been forecast for these variables for the forecast quarter concerned ($t = T + j$) and all residuals are put at zero. The system is then solved for some or all of $y_{1t}, \ldots, y_{it}, \ldots, y_{nt}$. Arithmetical KK forecasting with constant-term adjustment proceeds in exactly the same way except that, instead of putting all residuals at zero, some or all residuals are entered with non-zero values for some or all of the sequence of forecast quarters.

The residual, e_{it}, is known in KK forecasting circles as the 'constant-term adjustment' or 'the con-adjustment' because in the case of a *linear* stochastic relationship, entering a non-zero value for e_{it} can be thought of as an adjustment to the estimate of the intercept (constant term) of the relationship. We shall refer to it, for short, as the CA.

In sum, in arithmetical KK forecasting of the ordinary kind we require for each quarter in the sequence of j for which forecasts are being generated a forecast value for each predetermined variable. In arithmetical KK forecasting with constant-term adjustment we require, as well, a figure (possibily zero) for each CA.

Two questions arise quite naturally from this discusssion. The first is: (i) Why are the CAs introduced into the forecasting process in the manner just described? (ii) How are the values of the CAs for a particular quarter in the sequence of j forecast quarters fixed? Each of these questions will now be discussed in turn.

The CAs are introduced into the forecasting process for two main reasons. The first is to provide a means of keeping the KK system being used to generate the forecasts on track. The second is to provide a means for accommodating such future shocks as are not readily captured by the system as currently specified. Both require further discusssion.

As regards the first, there will normally be some lapse of time between the estimation of the relevant KK system and the commencement of the forecasting operation. Suppose that the interval is one year. Thus when forecasting begins the parameter estimates of the relevant KK system will be out of date to the extent of four quarters – there will be four data points which could have been but were not used in estimation. By the time the forecasting has been in operation for one year the parameter estimates will be out of date, in this sense, to the extent of eight quarters, after two years of forecasting by the extent of twelve quarters, and so on. In view of this one must expect that the (outside-sample) tracking performance of the KK system on which the forecasts are based will deteriorate steadily as the forecasting proceeds. Eventually this will be remedied by re-estimation. In the meantime, however, the system must be kept roughly on track in the interests of forecast accuracy. The first reason for introducing the CAs is to enable this to be done in a simple way.

As for the second reason, it is clear that some of the shocks which at the forecast point seem likely to occur in one or other of the sequence of forecast quarters can be captured by the predetermined variables of the system. Suppose, for example, that at the end of quarter T an increase in government expenditure seems likely to occur in quarter $T + 2$. Assuming that government expenditure is among the exogenous variables of the system, this particular shock can be accommodated by seeing that the forecast value of government expenditure for quarter $T + 2$ exceeds that for quarter $T + 1$ by the appropriate amount.

In many cases, however, this simple solution will not be available. Suppose, for example, that as at the end of quarter T it is known that some revolutionary new private motor-vehicle will be put on the market for the first time in quarter $T + 3$. It will not be possible to allow for this particular shock via the predetermined variables because, presumably, expenditure on private motor-vehicles will be endogenous, not predetermined. On the other hand, it may well be possible to take care of the shock in question via one of the CAs. The effect of the shock will be to make expenditure on new private motor-vehicles higher than normal in quarter $T + 3$. In other words, the value of the dependent variable in the stochastic equation which explains this class of expenditure will be higher in quarter $T + 3$, for given values of the explanatory variables, than the estimated relationship would suggest. To accommodate the shock, therefore, it would be a matter of allotting the appropriate positive value to the CA which enters the stochastic equation concerned when making the forecast for quarter $T + 3$.

As another example, suppose that at the end of quarter T it is known that an entirely new policy instrument is to be introduced in quarter $T + 2$ and given some non-zero setting in this and the following quarter. This will represent a shock from the standpoint of these quarters. It will not be one, however, which can be accommodated *via* the predetermined variables of the relevant KK system since, presumably, the specification of this system will reflect only those policy instruments which operated during the sample period. Once again the CAs might well provide the way out. If, for instance, the new instrument happened to be a set of physical import controls, the shock could be taken care of by allotting appropriate values to the CA appearing in the imports equation when making the forecasts for quarters $T + 2$ and $T + 3$. The values so allotted would have to be negative since the purpose of the controls would be to make the dependent variable in the imports equation lower in quarters $T + 2$ and $T + 3$, for given values of the explanatory variables, than the estimated function would suggest.

So much for the question of why the CAs are introduced. We turn now to the question of how their values are determined for a particular quarter in the sequence of j quarters for which the forecasts are being made.

The task of fixing the value of a particular CA for a particular forecast quarter may be thought of as proceeding in two stages, corresponding to the two reasons for introducing CAs just discussed. The first involves fixing the value that will serve to keep the relationship in question on track in the forecast quarter in the absence of significant shocks of a kind that cannot be accommodated by the system as specified. The second involves modifying this value if necessary to take care of any such shocks which seem likely to occur.

The CA value that will serve to keep a particular relationship on track in the forecast quarter concerned is usually determined from an examination of a run of past residuals for that relationship. (Recall that the CA for a particular relationship for a particular period is just e_{it} – its residual, as defined in (9.2), for the period.) The usual practice is to use (9.2) to compute a run of, say, ten or fifteen residuals for a succession of quarters up to and including the quarter in which the sequence for forecasts is being made, e.g. up to and including quarter T for the first round of forecasts, up to and including quarter $T + 1$ for the second, etc., and to allow this run of residuals to suggest a figure for the relevant CA for each of the quarters in the sequence of j quarters for which the forecasts are being made.

In this connection there are four main possibilites. Examination of the residuals may suggest: (i) that they are behaving in a roughly random fashion around an approximately zero mean; (ii) that they are behaving in a roughly random fashion around a non-zero mean; (iii) that they are subject to an upward trend; and (iv) that they are controlled by a first-order autoregressive process. In the first case it would be usual to put the CA in question at zero for each of the succession of j quarters and in the second case at the non-zero mean, whatever that may be. Where the residuals show an identifiable upward trend, the CA would be made to rise from one quarter to the next by the trend increment. Finally, in the autoregressive case the CA figure fixed for each quarter would be some fraction of the figure fixed for the preceding quarter.

The CA figures that will serve to keep the relationship in question on track in each of the forecast quarters having been fixed along the above lines, it will then be a matter of deciding whether one or more of these figures require adjustment to accommodate specific shocks that are likely or certain to occur. Should adjustment be called for it will normally be made in each case solely on the basis of judgement.

Step 2

The endogenous variables of interest having been forecast for each of the j forecast quarters by means of arithmetical forecasting with constant-term adjustment, the next step in judgemental KK forecasting is to check that there is no serious inconsistency between the forecasts of the endogenous variables and the forecasts of the predetermined variables and that the relationships between endogenous variables have not become distorted in the sequence of forecast quarters by the process of constant-term adjustment.

The type of inconsistency that may exist between the forecasts of the endogenous variables and those of the predetermined variables is suggested by the following hypothetical examples: (i) the forecasts used for certain exogenous fiscal and monetary instruments may imply virtually no change in these instruments over the sequence of forecast quarters, whereas the forecasts generated for the endogenous variables may imply a rapid deterioration in output and employment; (ii) the forecasts used for certain exogenous price variables may imply a rate of price increase of 5 per cent per annum over the sequence of forecast quarters, whereas the forecasts generated for the endogenous variables may imply an overall rate of price increase of 1 per cent per annum; (iii) the forecasts of the predetermined variables may imply a fixed (exogenous) exchange rate over the forecast quarters whereas the forecasts of the endogenous variables may indicate a sharp decline in the level of official reserve assets; (iv) the forecasts used for (exogenous) labour productivity may imply a steady upward movement in output per man-hour and the forecasts of the endogenous variables a sharp decline in employment. Examples of the type of distortion in endogenous-variable relationships that may be introduced by the process of constant-term adjustment are: (i) a saving–income ratio in the forecast quarters which is out of line with the historical ratio; (ii) an unemployment percentage which is too high in the forecast quarters in relation to the vacancy percentage; (iii) a counter-cyclical relationship between output and man-hours over the forecast quarters.

Should inconsistencies and/or distortions of these types be revealed, the forecasts of the predetermined variables and/or the figures used for the CAs will be revised and a fresh set of forecasts of the endogenous variables produced by arithmetical forecasting with constant-term adjustment. The checks for inconsistency and/or distortion will then be applied once again, and so on until no serious inconsistency and/or distortion is apparent.

Step 3

Typically the last step in judgemental KK forecasting is to submit the final forecast sequence, together with the forecasts of the predetermined variables and the values of the CAs on which it is based, to the critical scrutiny of a group of outsiders. Each member of this group will have been chosen because he or she has specialised knowledge of some key area of the economy, e.g. durable consumer goods, residential construction, foreign trade, government, private finance, and so is well equipped to comment on the appropriateness of the predetermined-variable forecasts and CA values and on the plausibility of the endogenous-variable forecasts to which they have provided the inputs. In most cases the comments of this group of outside experts will lead to some revision both of the forecasts of the predetermined variables and the CA values and, in turn, to the preparation of a new set of forecasts of the endogenous variables.

Judgemental KK forecasting derives its name from the fact that judgement is added to arithmetic at several key points. What these key points are will be clear from the preceding discussion. Judgement comes into play in step 1 when values are being fixed to the CAs. It is also heavily involved in step 2 when the forecasts of the endogenous variables are checked against the forecasts of the predetermined variables in a bid to detect inconsistency and against each other in a bid to detect distortion of endogenous-variable relationships via the values used for the CAs. Finally, it is dominant in step 3. How far to go in accepting criticisms made by the outside experts and how to make use of those criticisms which are accepted are both entirely questions of judgement.

9.4 How accurate is KK forecasting?

Since KK forecasting is an expensive business, it is not surprisng that, once it became a going concern, the question as to whether KK forecasts are more accurate than forecasts made by simpler and hence cheaper means should have been regarded as an important one. By and large the numerous studies (mainly American) which attempted to grapple with this question in the late 1960s and early 1970s were somewhat indecisive. See, for example, Stekler (1968), Fair (1974), Evans, Klein and Saito (1972),

Evans, Haitovsky and Treyz (1972), McNees (1973; 1974), Sims (1967), Howrey, Klein and McCarthy (1974) and Moore (1969). This was due partly to the fact that the record was (still is) too scanty to provide the basis for a definitive answer. A more important reason, however, is that the question itself is by no means straightforward.

One obvious complication is suggested by the phrase 'KK forecasts'. KK forecasts are far from homogeneous. For a start arithmetical KK forecasts are very different from judgemental and KK forecasts of either type made with one KK system are very different from those made with another. Thus the question whether KK forecasts are more accurate than forecasts made by simpler means is too imprecise to be answered in a definitive way.

This complication can, of course, be avoided by narrowing the question so that it relates not to KK forecasts in general but to those generated by a specific KK system. But this raises difficulties of its own. One is that the question may now be so narrow that it is no longer of much interest. Another arises from the fact that most modern KK systems – certainly those which are regularly used in a forecasting role – are subject to more or less continual revision. This means that any comparative evaluation of the forecast accuracy of a specific KK system is bound to be inconclusive. For one cannot assume that conclusions reached in relation, say to the mark V version of some KK system will apply also to the (possibly very different) mark VI version. A third difficulty arises from the fact that where the forecasting is judgemental the accuracy of the forecasts generated by a particular KK system will depend very much on the membership of the forecasting team and hence may either improve or deteriorate when this changes. This is yet another source of inconclusiveness.

The above is by no means a complete catalogue. It serves to show, however, that the question whether KK forecasts are more accurate than those made by less sophisticated methods is a very tricky one indeed.

In any event interest in the question now seems to be on the wane. For this there are two main reasons. In the first place, it has become clear that KK forecasting possesses certain distinct advantages over its less sophisticated and cheaper rivals – advantages which might well be sufficient to justify its continued use regardless of whether it is ahead or behind in terms of accuracy. Foremost among these advantages is its flexibility. With KK forecasting it is no more difficult to produce forecasts of, say, one hundred endogenous variables for a sequence of ten future quarters than it is to produce a forecast of one endogenous variable one quarter ahead. No other forecasting method has anything like this flexibility. Another advantage of KK forecasting is that it guarantees the consistency of arithmetic forecasts of the endogenous variables and provides a mechanism for achieving consistency in the case of judgemental forecasts. Other forecasting methods have a tendency to produce forecasts which are individually plausible but which are inconsistent one with another. For instance, forecasts may not satisfy the basic output–expenditure identity.

A second reason for loss of interest in the question which heads this section is that KK forecasting is obviously here to stay so that the question no longer has a great deal of point. KK forecasting is here to stay because KK systems are here to stay. This, in turn, can be ascribed to their ability to give numerical answers to a wide range of questions which have fundamental significance for economic policy. The nature of these questions will become clear in the next chapter.

References and further reading

Brown, M. and Taubman, P. (1962) 'A Forecasting Model of Federal Purchases of Goods and Services', *Journal of the American Statistical Association*, vol. 57, pp. 633–47.

Evans, M. K., Haitovsky, Y. and Treyz, G. I. (1972) 'An Analysis of the Forecasting Properties of US Econometric Models', in B. G. Hickman (ed.), *Econometric Models of Cyclical Behavior*, National Bureau of Economic Research, New York.

Evans, M. K., Klein, L. R. and Saito, M. (1972) 'Short-Run Prediction and Long-Run Simulation of the Wharton Model', in B. G. Hickman (ed.), *Econometric Models of Cyclical Behavior*, National Bureau of Economic Research, New York.

Fair, R. C. (1974) 'An Evaluation of a Short-Run Forecasting Model', *International Economic Review*, vol. 15, pp. 285–303.

Fair, R. C. (1979) 'An Analysis of the Accuracy of Four Macroeconometric Models', *Journal of Political Economy*, vol. 87, pp. 701–18.

Haitovsky, Y. and Treyz, G (1972) 'Forecasts with Quarterly Macroeconometric Models, Equation Adjustments, and Benchmark Predictions: The US Experience', *Review of Economics and Statistics*, vol. 54, pp. 317–25.

Howrey, E. P., Klein, L. R. and McCarthy, M. D. (1974) 'Notes on Testing the Predictive Performance of Econometric Models', *International Economic Review*, vol. 15, pp. 366–83.

Klein L. R. (1971) *An Essay on the Theory of Economic Prediction*, Markham, Chicago.

Klein, L. R. and Young, R. M. (1980) *An Introduction to Econometric Forecasting and Forecasting Models*, D. C. Heath, Lexington, Mass.

Kmenta, J. and Ramsey, J. B. (1981) *Large-Scale Macro-Econometric Models*, North-Holland, Amsterdam.

McNees, S. K. (1973) 'The Predictive Accuracy of Econometric Forecasts', *New England Economic Review*, September–October, pp. 3–27.

McNees, S. K. (1974) 'How Accurate Are Economic Forecasts?', *New England Economic Review*, November–December, pp. 2–19.

Moore, G. H. (1969) 'Forecasting Short-Term Economic Change', *Journal of the American Statistical Association*, vol. 64, pp. 1–22.

Sims, C. A. (1967) 'Evaluating Short-Term Macro-Economic Forecasts: The Dutch Performance', *Review of Economics and Statistics*, vol. 49, pp. 225–36.

Stekler, H. O (1967) 'Federal Budget as a Short-Term Forecasting Tool', *Journal of Business*, vol. 40, pp. 280–5.
Stekler, H. O. (1968) 'Forecasting with Econometric Models: An Evaluation', *Econometrica*, vol. 36, pp. 437–63.

10 COUNTER-FACTUAL ANALYSIS

10.1 Counter-factual analysis in outline

Perhaps the most interesting and productive use of estimated KK systems is in 'counter-factual' analysis. Counter-factual analysis deals with questions of the 'what if' variety. In KK counter-factual analysis the 'what if' questions addressed are usually of three broad types. The first are questions of the form: What if the macro economy were to be subjected to a particular pattern of exogenous change at some specific point of time, or over some specific interval of time in the future? Examples of questions which could be cast in this form are the following: How would the macro economy respond if a 5 per cent tax surcharge were to be imposed in three months' time? What would happen to output, employment and the inflation rate if the price of imported oil were to rise by 25 per cent over the next twelve months? When called on to examine questions of this type, counter-factual analysis is often referred to as *conditional forecasting* to convey the idea that in this area of counter-factual analysis we are concerned with the implications for the future of a *purely hypothetical* pattern of exogenous change.

The second type of question addressed in KK counter-factual analysis are questions of the form: What if the pattern of exogenous change had been different in some past period from that actually observed? Examples of questions which could be cast in this form are: What would the macro economy look like now if the currency had been devalued three years ago? Would employment have been higher or lower in 1978 if the rate of increase of money wages had been two percentage points less in 1974? In applications of this type, counter-factual analysis is often called *causal analysis* because the main aim is usually (though not invariably) to throw light on the causes of present or past macroeconomic behaviour.

Finally, we have questions of the form: What if a particular institutional change were to be engineered? For example, what would be the macroeconomic consequences of a change in the arrangements which surround the determination of the exchange rate? How would the rate of inflation respond to the introduction of prices and incomes policy? Would the introduction of wage indexation lower the inflation rate, and if so would this be at the cost of an increase in the unemployment rate? When applied to 'what if' questions of this third type counter-factual analysis is commonly called *analysis of alternative regimes*.

When KK systems are used for conditional forecasting the basic technique is *system solution*; in this respect conditional KK forecasting is no different from the ordinary KK forecasting discussed in the previous chapter. When KK systems are used for causal analysis and analysis of alternative regimes, however, the essential technique is *system simulation*. System simulation was fully discussed in Chapter 7. The reader will recall that in any application of this techique the following four steps are involved: (i) the *simulation period* – a sequence of quarters included in (perhaps coinciding with) the sample period – is chosen; (ii) a *control run* is undertaken for the simulation period; (iii) a series of *shocked runs* are undertaken for the simulation period; (iv) the values of the relevant endogenous variables generated in the control run are compared with the values generated in the series of shocked runs.

Discussion of the three forms of counter-factual analysis just introduced is best continued in terms of specific examples. Accordingly, an example of conditional forecasting will be presented in the next section and an example of causal analysis and analysis of alternative regimes in sections 10.3 and 10.4, respectively. All three examples have been drawn from the published literature.

10.2 A US example of conditional forecasting

As our example of conditional forecasting we have chosen a study by Klein (1974). The main object of this study was to examine the following question: How will the US economy fare in 1974 if it is subjected to an oil shortage of approximately 2 million barrels per day during the first half of the year because of a curtailment of oil imports consequent on an 'embargo' by Middle East producers on oil exports? This question is concerned with the implications for the US economy during a specific future time period (the year 1974) of a hypothetical pattern of exogenous change (an oil shortage of a specified magnitude in the first half of the year) and is therefore typical of the 'what if' questions examined in the conditional-forecasting area of counter-factual analysis.

The system which Klein used to address the oil-shortage question was the *Wharton Annual Model* (WAM). WAM is a hybrid system in which an annual KK system of a fairly conventional kind is combined with the conventional input–output system (see Preston, 1975). A brief discussion of the input–output system has been given in section 1.5 (pp. 20–2) and the reader should return to that discussion before proceeding.

As just remarked, WAM is a hybrid system – one which combines a KK system with the input–output system of (1.24). Moreover, the systems are interdependent in the sense that neither can be solved independently of the other. As will be clear from (1.24), solution of the input–output component requires the **f** (final demand) vector. This is supplied by the KK component. At the same time solution of the KK component requires the **q** (output) vector and this is supplied by the input–output component. Thus it is not possible to solve one component system and then the other; the two components must be solved jointly.

With this brief discussion of WAM at our disposal we can now explain how it was used by Klein to answer the oil-shortage question posed at the outset.

The main technical problem which he faced was to find a way of imposing the relevant hypothetical pattern of exogenous change on WAM. Once this problem had been solved it remained only to solve WAM for the year 1974. Thus the rest of the job was relatively straightforward.

A problem of this type arises whenever conditional KK forecasting is undertaken, and broadly speaking there are three possible ways in which it can be handled. The relevant hypothetical pattern of exogenous change can be imposed: (i) by making appropriate adjustments to the estimated relationships of the system which is being used to address the 'what if' question concerned; (ii) by allotting appropriate values to the predetermined variables of the estimated system; and (iii) by doing both (i) and (ii).

In the Klein study the first of these three approaches was adopted. It will be recalled that, in this instance, the hypothetical pattern of exogenous change was an oil shortage of some 2 million barrels per day throughout the first six-months of 1974 –a shortage induced by an embargo on exports of oil from the Middle East and the consequent curtailment of US oil imports. To impose this scenario on WAM, Klein made a number of adjustments to the estimated relationships of the system. These were of two types: (i) adjustments to the estimated relationships of the input–output component of WAM; and (ii) adjustments to the estimated KK component. We shall consider each type in turn.

The adjustments made to the estimated input–output component were concentrated in three of the relationships of that component, as represented by (1.24). They were the relationships for crude petroleum products and refined petroleum products on the one hand, and the relationship for coal on the other. Let us take them in turn.

To explain the adjustments made to the crude petroleum and refined petroleum relationships we must first digress briefly to deal with a relevant point in input–output accounting. In input–output accounting imports of intermediate commodities are divided into: (i) non-competing; (ii) competing. Non-competing imports relate to intermediate commodities for which there are no domestic substitutes, while competing imports relate to intermediate commodities which are produced domestically as well as being imported. Non-competing imports of intermediate commodites, together with imports of final goods, are allocated directly along one of the rows of the input–output table to the using industries, or to the appropriate final demand categories, as the case may be. On the other hand, competing imports of intermediate commodities are allocated in the first instance to the corresponding domestic industries. They are then allocated by those industries, as part of their own input, to the using industries.

For the USA imports of both crude and refined petroleum products are 'competitive' since both commodities are produced at home as well as being imported. Hence any exogenous reduction in the output of crude and/or refined petroleum products such as that envisaged in the 'what if' question under examination is tantamount, in input–output terms, to an exogenous reduction of an equivalent amount in the output ceiling of the corresponding domestic industries – the crude petroleum industry and the petroleum-refining industry.

On this basis it was argued that imposition of the relevant hypothetical pattern of exogenous change on WAM called for a negative adjustment to both the estimated crude petroleum relationship and the estimated refined petroleum relationship. The adjustment of the former would need to be such that the WAM solution for crude petroleum output fell within the new output ceiling and similarly for the latter.

To determine the required adjustments in numerical terms, Klein proceeded as follows. First, he translated the hypothetical physical shortage of 2 million barrels per day into dollar-value output ceilings for crude petroleum products and refined petroleum products respectively. Next he noted that the original (unadjusted) versions of the two relationships in question (regarded as the ith and the jth) were of the form:

$$q_i = \sum_{w=1}^{n} \alpha_{iw} f_w \qquad q_j = \sum_{w=1}^{n} \alpha_{jw} f_w \tag{10.1}$$

where the α_{iw} and the α_{jw} are the numbers appearing in the ith and jth rows of $(\mathbf{I} - \mathbf{A})^{-1}$, respectively (see (1.24)). Given unadjusted versions of the form of (10.1) the adjusted versions would be of the form:

$$q_i = \sum_{w=1}^{n} \alpha_{iw} f_w + \delta_i \qquad q_j = \sum_{w=1}^{n} \alpha_{jw} f_w + \delta_j \tag{10.2}$$

where δ_i and δ_j are two negative numbers. He next generated a succession of WAM solutions for q_i and q_j each corresponding to a particular pair of negative values for δ_i and δ_j. The same values for the predetermined variables were, of course, used throughout. Finally, from the various pairs of values for δ_i and δ_j which were tried, one which gave solution values for q_i and q_j within their new (dollar-value) output ceilings was chosen.

We turn now to the relationship for coal. The argument here was that the reduction in the output of crude and refined petroleum products would be offset in part by an increase in the output of coal. To allow for this consideration the relationship for coal was adjusted to:

$$q_k = \sum_{w=1}^{n} \alpha_{kw} f_w + \delta_k \qquad (10.3)$$

where δ_k is some positive number. The number selected for δ_k was based on information supplied by the mining industry.

The above adjustments to the estimated relationships of the input–output component served to impose the 'supply-side' effects of hypothetical patterns of exogenous change. Further adjustments were made to the estimated relationships of the KK component to impose the 'demand-side' effects. These consisted of con-adjustments, of the type discussed in section 9.3, to several of the estimated relationships of this component. For example, a negative con-adjustment was added to the appropriate consumption function to reflect the efforts of the authorities to persuade people to consume less petrol for motoring and less oil for residential heating than they would otherwise have done.

All the adjustments to estimated relationships described above were, of course, appropriately scaled to reflect the hypothesis that the oil shortage would operate only during the first half of 1974.

Having thus imposed the hypothetical pattern of exogenous change on WAM, the final step in Klein's conditional-forecasting exercise was to solve WAM using the appropriately adjusted estimated version of the system and a plausible set of values for the predetermined variables. The solution values generated for q_i and q_j were checked to ensure that they still fell within the new output ceiling implied by the hypothetical curtailment of imports.

The answer which this WAM solution gave to the oil-shortage question posed at the outset was that the US economy would fare rather badly in 1974 if subjected to an oil shortage of the magnitude envisaged. The growth rate of the economy would be only 0.6 per cent, the inflation rate would be just over 7 per cent per annum and the unemployment rate about 5.5 per cent. In all three respects the outcome would be noticeably worse than that which could be reasonably expected in the absence of an oil shortage.

10.3 A US example of causal analysis

To illustrate causal analysis we shall take the US study of Cooper and Fischer (1972). Many economists (most notably Milton Friedman) advocate that the monetary authorities should be constrained by a very simple rule, namely:

maintain a constant rate of growth in the money supply.

In the study in question Cooper–Fischer (CF) consider whether it is possible to improve on this rule. Various alternative rules are examined and a specified alternative is regarded as improving on the constant rate of growth rule if it leads to a significant reduction, relative to that rule, in the variability of two key macro variables – the inflation rate and the unemployment rate.

CF's approach was to ask the following question in relation to each of their alternative rules: What would the variability of the US inflation rate and the US unemployment rate have been in the 1950s and 1960s if the alternative rule under consideration had been followed, compared with their variability under the constant rate of growth rule? In essence, this is a question of the form: What if the pattern of exogenous change had been different in some past period? Thus, effectively, CF's approach to the task was to undertake a piece of counter-factual analysis of the 'causal-analysis' type.

The system which CF used for their counter-factual analysis was a US system known as MPS. MPS is a medium-sized quarterly KK system constructed jointly by the University of Pennsylvania, the Federal Reserve Board and the Massachusetts Institute of Technology (see Table 1.2).

The first step in the study was to formulate the alternative rules. To this end the following rule-generating formula was laid down:

$$\frac{M_t - M_{t-1}}{M_{t-1}} = a_1 - a_2\left(\frac{P_{t-1} - P_{t-2}}{P_{t-2}} - a_3\right) + a_4(U_{t-1} - a_5)$$
$$- a_6\left(\frac{P_{t-1} - P_{t-2}}{P_{t-2}} - \frac{P_{t-2} - P_{t-3}}{P_{t-3}}\right) + a_7(U_{t-1} - U_{t-2}) \qquad (10.4)$$

where M denotes the money supply, P the price level, U the unemployment rate and the as a set of non-negative constants. The alternative rules were then generated by allotting different values to the as. For example, one of the rules was formed by setting $a_1 = 0.01$, $a_2 = 1$, $a_3 =$

0.0062 and all other *a*s at zero. Given these values of the *a*s, (10.4) implies the following rule:

> *maintain a constant rate of growth of 1 per cent per quarter (about 4 per cent per annum) in the money supply subject to the proviso that the growth rate is to be reduced below (increased above) this figure in any quarter by 1 percentage point for every one point by which last quarter's inflation rate exceeded (fell short of) the 'target' rate of 0.62 per cent per quarter.*

Another rule was formed by setting $a_1 = 0.01$, $a_4 = 0.40$, $a_5 = 0.0466$ and all other *a*s at zero. With these values of the *a*s, the rule generated by (10.4) is:

> *maintain a constant rate of growth of 1 per cent per quarter in the money supply subject to the proviso that the growth rate is to be reduced below (increased above) this figure in any quarter by 1 percentage point by which last quarter's unemployment rate fell short of (exceeded) the target rate of 4.66 per cent.*

Altogether nineteen alternative rules were formulated in the manner just described. Rules corresponding to non-zero values of a_2 and/or a_4 were described as 'proportional' and those corresponding to non-negative values of a_6 and/or a_7 as 'derivative', using terms first proposed by Phillips (1954; 1957). All the rules examined were either proportional, derivative or some mixture of the two.

Having formulated the alternatives to the constant rate of growth rule, CF then applied the deterministic form of the technique of system simulation. For the simulation period they chose the fifty-two quarters beginning with the first quarter 1956 and ending with the fourth quarter 1968. They then undertook a control run for this sequence of quarters. For this purpose they transferred *M* from the endogenous category to the exogenous category and transferred one of the other MPS monetary variables in the reverse direction to maintain equality between the number of endogenous variables and the number of equations. They then solved MPS for the inflation rate and the unemployment rate (two of its endogenous variables) for each of the fifty-two quarters covered by the simulation period on the basis of a constant rate of growth of 1 per cent per quarter in *M* and historical values of all other exogenous variables.

It should be noted that CF's control run differs slightly from the usual concept. As ordinarily understod, 'control run' implies solution on the basis of historical values of *all* exogenous variables (see section 7.2). In CF's control run, however, solution was based on historical time paths for all exogenous variables apart from M and a *hypothetical* time path (constant growth rate of 1 per cent per quarter) for M. This particular departure from the usual control-run concept was required in the CF study because the object was to compare the alternative rules not with 'history' but with the constant rate of growth rule.

The next step was to perform a set of nineteen shocked runs – one for each of the nineteen alternative rules. In each of these shocked runs MPS was solved for the inflation rate and the unemployment rate for each quarter of the simulation period on the basis of historical values for all exogenous variables other than M. For M the time path used for solution purposes was a hypothetical path generated by the appropriate rule formula. Where the rule formula involved non-zero values of a_3 and/or a_5, the values used were, respectively, the mean inflation rate and the mean unemployment rate generated in the control run.

The final step was to compare the variability of the inflation rate and the unemployment rate in each of the shocked runs with their variability in the control run. For the inflation rate, variability was measured by means of the standard deviation of the fifty-two values of the inflation rate generated in the shocked run concerned or in the control run, as the case may be, and similarly for the unemployment rate.

In the control run the standard deviations of the inflation rate and the unemployment rate were 0.0026 and 0.00719, respectively. In those shocked runs which employed a 'proportional' rule, broadly similar figures were obtained. On the other hand, in some of the shocked runs in which the rule employed was a mixed proportional–derivative rule, one or both standard deviations was significantly lower than those characterising the control run. For example, in one such shocked run the standard deviations were 0.0021 and 0.00593 respectively, in another 0.0021 and 0.00550 and in another 0.0020 and 0.00516.

It would appear from the CF study, then, that there is scope for improving on the constant rate of growth rule, in particular via a mixed proportional–derivative modification.

10.4 An Australian example of analysis of alternative regimes

We come finally to the third main type of counter-factual analysis – analysis of alternative regimes. This will be illustrated by the Australian study of Caton (1977).

As is well known, a feature of the progressive taxation of nominal personal incomes which is nowadays practically universal is that a taxpayer's after-tax *real* income may well fall simply because of inflation. Suppose, for example, that a taxpayer's nominal income *before* tax rises in proportion to the price level and that as a consequence, is subject to a higher rate of tax. Then the individual's tax payment will rise more than in proportion to the price level. Hence nominal income *after* tax will rise less than in proportion to the price level, i.e. *real* income after tax will fall.

This feature of progressive taxation is generally thought to be unjust. Moreover, it may well be self-intensifying in the sense that it may exacerbate the inflation from which it springs. For example, it may (almost certainly will) cause wage-earners to press for higher increases in money wages than they otherwise would. For given this feature of progressive taxation nominal wages before tax will have to rise faster than the price level to guard against the possibility of a fall in real wages after tax, whereas otherwise they would have to rise only at the same rate as the price level to remove this possibility.

One suggestion for dealing with the problem which has been put forward is that tax rates should be revised at regular intervals (say annually) in such a way that an individual whose nominal income before tax rises in line with prices is taxed at the same rate as before, i.e. in such a way that a taxpayer's real income *after* tax remains the same from year to year so long as the individual's real income before tax remains the same. This proposal is known as *tax indexation*.

Tax indexation has been widely endorsed. Nevertheless, governments have hesitated to put it into effect for fear that it will change for the worse the way in which the macro economy responds to exogenous shocks. The main object of the study to be discussed in this section was to throw some light on this matter. The specific question asked was: How will the Australian economy respond to a once-for-all increase in the volume of exports with and without tax indexation? This question is concerned with the macroeconomic implication of engineering a particular institutional change and so is typical of the 'what if' questions addressed in the area of counter-factual analysis covered by the label: analysis of alternative regimes.

The system which Caton used to address his tax-indexation question was an early version of NIF, the Australian quarterly KK system referred to in Chapter 3 (see also Table 1.2). As is invariably the case when a KK system is applied in the area of analysis of alternative regimes, the technique which he used was the deterministic form of system simulation.

In more detail Caton first chose a simulation period. The period chosen was a sub-period of the estimation period consisting of the sequence of thirty-two quarters from 1966(III) to 1974(II). Next, he undertook a control run for this sequence of quarters. Two shocked runs were then undertaken for the simulation period. In both cases the shock was an increase of $A50m in exports in each of the four quarters preceding the simulation period. In the first shocked run tax indexation was imposed on the system, whereas in the second the normal tax arrangements (those which applied in the control run) were assumed to be in force.

We shall not enter into the details of the procedure used to impose tax indexation on the system for the purposes of the first shocked run. Suffice it to say that it was imposed via one of the exogenous variables of the system, the rate of personal income tax, and consisted of using for this variable its historical time path for all quarters except for the eight September quarters included in the simulation period. For these the value used was obtained by reducing the historical value by a percentage determined, in a specific way, by the elasticity of tax payable with respect to income and the four-quarter percentage increase in the implicit deflator of personal consumption expenditure.

The position may thus be summed by saying that for the purposes of the control run all exogenous variables were given their historical values for all quarters in the simulation period. For the purposes of the first shocked run all but two (the rate of personal income tax and exports) were given their historical values. Finally, for the purposes of the second shocked run historical values applied for all but one of the exogenous variables, namely exports.

To answer the 'what if' question posed at the outset, Caton compared the results of each of the two shocked runs, in turn, with those of the control run. It turned out that for all the key endogenous variables, deviation from control was practically the same in the first shocked run as it was in the second. Thus the answer to the question which the system simulation suggested was that the Australian economy will respond to exogenous shocks in much the same way under the alternative (tax-indexation) regime as under the original regime.

10.5 A criticism of causal analysis

To conclude this chapter we shall briefly discuss a criticism levelled at causal analysis (the most widely used form of counter-factual analysis) by Lucas (1976) which has attracted a good deal of attention. As we have seen, in causal analysis an estimated KK system is used to determine what the past would have looked like if the pattern of exogenous change had been different from that which actually occurred. Lucas regards this particular way of using a KK system as unacceptable. His argument runs as follows.

The parameters of any KK system reflect the optimal decision rules of economic agents. Among the variables which constitute the arguments of these decision rules are agents' expectations about the future time paths of the variables which form the exogenous group of the KK system concerned. If these expectations change, the true structure of the system will change too, and so, presumably, will the estimated structure. But these expectations are bound to change when their historical time paths change. It follows that the use to which an estimated KK system is put in causal analysis is unacceptable. For if the pattern of exogenous change had been different, the estimated structure would also have been different. Causal analysis ignores this fact, and its conclusions are therefore, bound to be misleading.

While the validity of the above criticism has been generally acknowledged, it appears to have had very little practical effect – the use of estimated KK systems in causal analysis is still as widespread as ever. There are, we suspect, two main reasons. The first is that nothing is yet known about the *quantitative* significance of Lucas's point – about whether the results of causal analysis in its traditional form are so misleading as to be practically useless or whether they mislead in a comparatively insignificant and harmless way. Second, even if the practical significance of the point be accepted, it is by no means clear how traditional causal-analysis procedures should be amended to meet it – though the work of Cooley and Prescott (1973a; 1973b; 1976) would appear to form a good starting-point. Most users of KK systems would argue that it is far too early to abandon or even limit the use of causal analysis. The time for that will have arrived once it has been established that Lucas's point matters and that nothing effective can be done to meet it. This we regard as a perfectly reasonable standpoint.

References and further reading

CATON, C. N. (1977) 'Some Macro-Economic Implications of Indexation of Personal Income Taxes', *Economic Record*, vol. 53, pp. 137–48.

COOLEY, T. F. and PRESCOTT, E. C. (1973a) 'Tests of the Adaptive Regression Model', *Review of Economics and Statistics*, vol. 55, pp. 248–56.

COOLEY, T. F. and PRESCOTT. E. C. (1973b)'An Adaptive Regression Model', *International Economic Review*, vol. 14, pp. 364–71.

COOLEY, T. F. and PRESCOTT, E. C. (1976) 'Estimation in the Presence of Stochastic Parameter Variation', *Econometrica*, vol. 44, pp. 167–84.

COOPER, J. and FISCHER, S. (1972) 'Simulation of Monetary Rules in the FRB–MIT–Penn Model', *Journal of Money, Credit and Banking*, vol. 4, pp. 384–96.

LUCAS, ROBERT E. JR. (1976) 'Econometric Policy Evaluation: A Critique', in K. Brunner and A. H. Meltzer (eds), *The Phillips Curve and Labour Markets*, North-Holland, Amsterdam.

KLEIN, L. R. (1974) 'Supply Constraints in Demand Oriented Systems: An Interpretation of the Oil Crisis', *Zeitschrift für Nationalokonomie*, vol. 34, pp. 45–56.

PHILLIPS, A. W. (1954) 'Stabilization Policy in a Closed Economy', *Economic Journal*, vol. 64, pp. 290–323.

PHILLIPS, A. W. (1957) 'Stabilization Policy and the Time-Forms of Lagged Responses', *Economic Journal*, vol. 67, pp. 265–77.

PRESTON, R. S. (1975) 'The Wharton Long Term Model: Input–Output Within the Context of a Macro Forecasting Model', *International Economic Review*, vol. 16, pp. 3–19.

11 POLICY EVALUATION

11.1 Types of policy evaluation

In the two previous chapters we have dealt with what are probably the oldest and most important applications of KK systems – forecasting and counter-factual analysis. In this chapter we turn to a third application – one which has developed rapidly in the last ten years and which seems to have great potential for further development. We refer to policy evaluation.

The procedures used in KK policy evaluation are quite varied. In one way or another, however, they all aim to provide 'a replay of history'. Thus in essence they are the same as the procedures used in causal analysis. Indeed KK policy evaluation can be regarded as a branch of causal analysis which has become sufficiently prominent to be accorded the status of a distinct application.

Policy-evaluation studies based on KK systems fall into two broad groups. The first group comprises studies in which a KK system is used to assess the effectiveness of the policy actually followed in a specific country in a specific historical period, e.g. the policies pursued by the US authorities in the period 1972–5. In the second group are studies in which a KK system is used to assess the effectiveness of a specific policy rule, e.g. a rule which requires the authority to maintain a specified constant rate of increase in the money supply.

In turn, each of these two broad groups can be divided into distinct sub-groups. The first group can be subdivided according to the assessment procedure used, while the second group can be broken up both according to the type of assessment procedure used and the type of policy rule examined.

The rest of this chapter falls into two parts. The first, comprising the next two sections, deals with policy-evaluation studies of the 'historical' kind, while the second, the subject of section 11.4, is concerned with evaluation studies of the 'rule' kind. The precise nature of the sub-groups mentioned in the previous paragraph will become clear as the discussion proceeds.

11.2 Evaluation of historical policies: search

The most primitive way of using a KK system to assess the effectiveness of a specific historical policy is what might be called the 'search' procedure.

The steps in this procedure are as follows: (i) use a KK system to perform a control run (deterministic or stochastic) for the relevant sequence of quarters (historical period), based on historical values of all exogenous variables, including the policy instruments; (ii) devise a set of alternative feasible time paths for the policy instruments for the relevant historical period; (iii) use the KK system to perform a series of shocked runs (deterministic or stochastic) for the relevant historical period, based on one of the alternative instrument time paths devised under (ii) and on historical values of all other exogenous variables; (iv) compare the solution values of selected target variables generated by each of the shocked runs over the relevant historical period with those generated by the control run; (v) use this comparison to determine whether the historical policy under examination could have been bettered, in the sense that an alternative feasible policy (perhaps more than one) would have led to a preferable time path over the relevant historical period for the target variables as a whole.

An example of the search procedure is to be found in Perry (1975). In this study Perry uses the search procedure, in conjunction with a quarterly KK system of the US economy, the MPS system, to evaluate the policy adopted by the US authorities in 1974.

As his relevant historical period Perry took the sequence of six quarters, 1973(IV) to 1975(I) inclusive. To devise his set of alternative feasible time paths for the policy instruments he took their historical time paths over the relevant historical period and modified them in the following six ways: (i) the historical time path for the money supply was replaced by a constant rate of growth time path (6 per cent per annum); (ii) the historical time path for the money supply was replaced by a constant rate of growth time path adjusted upwards in a specified way to cover the increases in world oil prices which occurred during the relevant historical period; (iii) the historical time path for the commercial paper rate was replaced by a constant-level time path (7 per cent); (iv) the historical time path for personal income taxes was replaced by one in which the figure was $20 billion less in each quarter than the historical figure; (v) the historical time path for the money supply was replaced by that detailed in (ii) and the historical time path for personal income taxes by that detailed in (iv); and (vi) the historical time path for the commercial paper rate was replaced by that detailed in (iii) and the historical time path for personal income taxes by that detailed in (iv).

To evaluate the policy adopted by the US authorities in 1974 Perry used the MPS system to perform a series of six shocked runs for the quarters 1974(IV) to 1975(I). These were based, respectively, on the alternative-instrument time paths, (i) – (iv) above, together with historical time paths for all non-instrumental exogenous variables.[1] He then compared the solution values for gross national product (both in current prices and in constant prices), for the inflation rate and for the unemployment rate, which were generated by each of the six runs for the relevant historical period with the historical values of those variables.[2] The conclusion that emerged from this comparison was that the policy actually followed by the US authorities in 1974 could certainly have been bettered. While some of the alternatives considered in the study would have been worse than the policy actually followed, one at least would have been better in terms of its consequences for GNP, the inflation rate and the unemployment rate. The alternative in question was the one corresponding to item (vi) of the previous paragraph.

11.3 Evaluation of historical policies: optimal control

It seems reasonable to require that a KK policy-evaluation procedure should have two essential features. First, it should incorporate a clear definition of 'best policy' and a definite way of measuring the extent to which a particular historical policy deviated from the best policy that could have been implemented in the circumstances of the time. Second, it should recognise that the effects of the policy which is implemented in any historical period will extend beyond that period and hence should not focus solely on the events of that period. The search procedure dealt with in the preceding section fails to meet either of these requirements and to this extent is deficient.

In the present section we deal with an alternative evaluation procedure which is more complicated than the search procedure but which does indeed possess the two desirable features just mentioned. The procedure in question will be referred to as the 'optimal control' procedure since it makes use of techniques for the optimal control of KK systems.

Before attempting to explain the optimal control procedure we propose to digress briefly to present a very brief summary of optimal control techniques as they are applied in the field of economics. We would emphasise that we are concentrating on a few basic points which are essential to a full understanding of the optimal control procedure and are making no attempt to be either balanced or comprehensive. The reader who wishes to pursue the subject in more depth should consult Chow (1981).

The basic concept in the field of optimal control is the concept of the *welfare loss function* or simply the *loss function*. The arguments of the loss function are the levels of the various target variables in quarter t ($t = 1, 2, \ldots, T$) expressed as deviations from the levels desired by the policy-maker and possibly the quarter t levels of the various instrument variables as well – again expressed as deviations from their desired levels. Quarter T is known as 'the planning horizon' and the sequence of quarters $1, \ldots, T$ as 'the planning interval'. As the name suggests, the loss function is a function giving the welfare loss which flows from specified values of its arguments, as the policy-maker sees it. It is natural to require that it be monotonically increasing in all its arguments, implying that the larger a specific target or instrument deviation, the greater the welfare loss, other deviations being given. A form of loss function which meets this requirement and which is frequently used in optimal control calculations is one which makes the welfare loss a weighted sum of squares of each argument. A loss function of this form is zero when all targets and instruments are at their desired levels throughout the planning interval and becomes increasingly positive as a specific target or instrument deviates more and more from its desired level, other deviations being given. The extent to which a particular target or instrument deviation contributes to a positive welfare loss depends on the weight which it carries in the loss function. The weight attached to a particular deviation is to be interpreted, therefore, as a number which reflects the concern which a unit value of that deviation causes the policy-maker, relative to the concern caused by a unit value of some other deviation.

A specific loss function of the form under discussion is the following:

$$L = \sum_{t=1971(\mathrm{I})}^{1975(\mathrm{I})} (\dot{p}_t - 7)^2 + 0.75(u_t - 4)^2 + (CB_t - 0)^2 + 0.1(G_t - G_0)^2 \tag{11.1}$$

where $\dot{p}$ denotes the inflation rate (per cent per annum), u the unemployment rate (per cent), CB the balance of payments on current account (billion dollars) and G government expenditure (billion dollars). In this case the planning horizon is 1975(I) and the planning interval the seventeen quarters beginning in 1971(I) and ending in 1975(I). The desired level of the inflation rate is 7 per cent per annum, the desired level of the unemployment rate 4 per cent, the desired level of the current-account balance zero, and the desired level of real government expenditure that of the quarter preceding the commencement of the planning interval (denoted in (11.1) by G_0). The weights in the function indicate that the policy-maker is equally concerned about a deviation from desired of 1 per cent per annum in the inflation rate and about a deviation from desired of \$1 billion in the balance of payments on current account. On the other hand, he is ten times as concerned about either as he is about a deviation from desired of \$1 billion in government expenditure.

The problem which the optimal control technique sets out to solve is the following – to find the time path which each of the policy instruments must follow over the planning interval, given that the expected value of the loss function is to be minimised under the following conditions: (i) the minimisation is to be subject to the constraint provided by some relevant KK system; (ii) the planning-interval time paths for the non-instrument current exogenous variables of this system are to be taken as given; and (iii) the estimated values for the parameters of the constraining system are taken to be identical with the true values. The problem which optimal control poses, then, is a constrained optimisation (minimisation) problem. The 'unknowns' are the time paths of the policy instruments over the sequence of quarters 1, 2, ..., T, the minimand is the expected value of the loss function, the constraint is a KK system relating to the economy under control and the data are the time paths for the exogenous variables of this system, other than the policy instruments, over the quarters 1, ..., T.

Three comments on this formulation of the optimal control problem are in order. The first relates to the specification of the minimand. The minimand is not the loss function itself but its *expected value*. In the (atypical) case where the constraining KK system is non-stochastic (not subject to random disturbance) the endogenous variables, and in particular the target variables, will be non-stochastic also. Hence the loss function will be a function of non-stochastic variables and so will itself be non-stochastic. This means, in turn, that in the non-stochastic case the loss function itself is the natural minimand. In the (typical) case of a stochastic-constraining KK system, on the other hand, the loss function is stochastic and its expected value is the natural minimand. We cover both cases, however, by specifying the expected value of the loss function as the minimand since when the loss function is non-stochastic the loss function and its expected value are one and the same thing.

The second comment concerns the formulation of the problem as a *constrained* optimisation problem. Such a formulation is essential because the arguments of the minimand include certain variables (the target variables) which must be regarded as endogenous and hence which must satisfy the relationships of any KK system in which they happen to appear. It follows that some such KK system must be introduced as a constraint on the minimisation process.

The third comment is that, as presented, the formulation yields a variety of special cases corresponding to particular forms for the loss function and for the constraining KK system. If we confine ourselves to the form of loss function considered earlier (quadratic), there are three cases of the optimal control problem which are of special interest in the present context. The first is the case of a constraining KK system which is linear and stochastic and whose parameter values change from quarter to quarter (are 'time-dependent'). The second is the case of a constraining KK system which is non-linear and non-stochastic and whose parameter values remain fixed from quarter to quarter (are 'time-independent'). And finally there is the case where the constraining KK system is non-linear and stochastic and has fixed parameter values. The last of these three cases is the only one which is of interest in its own right because it is the one invariably found in practice. The first two are of interest because in the process of solving them we learn something about the solution of the third. To the matter of solution we now turn.

Without entering into the details we begin by noting that a solution is available for the first of the three cases listed in the previous paragraph. We also note that a solution for the case of a linear KK system whose parameter values are time-dependent but which is *non*-stochastic follows from the aforementioned solution as the special case where all disturbances are zero. In turn, this solution provides a basis for solving the optimal control problem for the second case. One way of finding the solution for the second case is to proceed as follows:

(a) select a tentative path for each of the instrument variables for the planning interval;
(b) using these tentative paths, the given paths for the non-instrument, current exogenous variables and given initial values of the lagged variables, solve the non-linear constraining system for each of the quarters 1, ..., T;
(c) linearise the constraining system for each quarter around the values of the variables generated under (a) and (b) to produce a KK system which is linear and non-stochastic and whose parameter values are time-*dependent*;
(d) solve the optimal control problem in this new form – recall that a solution is available;
(e) repeat the above steps with the 'first-round solution' paths yielded by step (d) for the instrument variables taking the place of the 'tentative paths' selected in step (a);
(f) continue in this way to convergence.

It can be shown (again we omit all details) that the paths for the instrument variables yielded by the last iteration in the above procedure represent the solution for the second case of the optimal control problem.

Turning now to the third case, we note that no exact solution for this case is yet available. The iterative procedure described above works provided the solutions generated under step (b) satisfy the constraining system *exactly*. The solution meets this requirement when the system is non-stochastic, as in the second case. They fail to do so, however, when the system is stochastic, as in the third case, because here the solution procedure is unable to cope with the unknown (non-zero) random disturbances. When applied to the third case, therefore, the iterative procedure gives no more than an approximate solution to the optimal control problem.

To conclude this brief summary of optimal control techniques we present a key result for the first of the three cases distinguished earlier – a result which provides the rationale for the optimal control procedure. The result in question can be stated as follows.

Assume that each of the instrument variables follows its optimal path from quarter 2 up to quarter T. The minimand, L, can then be expressed as a function of the values assumed by the instrument variables in the *first* quarter. Denoting the vector of these first-quarter instrument values by $\mathbf{x_1}$ we thus have $L = \phi_1(\mathbf{x_1})$, provided that each instrument follows its optimal path from quarter 2 up to the end of the planning interval, quarter T. The function ϕ_1 involves the (given) values of the lagged predetermined variables for the quarter prior to quarter 1 and possibly for earlier quarters as well, the (given) values of the non-instrument exogenous variables for quarter 1 and the (time-dependent) matrices of the reduced form of the (linear) constraining KK system for quarters 1, ... T. The optimal values of the instrument variables for the first quarter ($\hat{\mathbf{x}}_1$) can be found by minimising $\phi_1(\mathbf{x_1})$ with respect to $\mathbf{x_1}$, giving $\phi_1(\hat{\mathbf{x}}_1)$ as the minimum value of the loss function – provided, once again, that each of the instrument variables follows its optimal path over the rest of the planning interval.

Assume now that each of the instrument variables follows its optimal path from quarter 3 to the end of the planning interval. Then the 'truncated' minimand (L, after the term for quarter 1 has been suppressed) can be expressed as a function of $\mathbf{x_2}$, the vector of values assumed by the instrument variables in quarter 2. Thus we have $L_2 = \phi_2(\mathbf{x_2})$. ($\phi_2$ is ϕ_1 with all time subscripts advanced one quarter. Thus ϕ_2 involves values of the lagged predetermined variables for quarter 1 and possibly for earlier quarters as well, values of the non-instrumental exogenous variables for quarter 2, and the (time-dependent) matrices of the reduced form for quarters 2, ..., T.) The optimal values of the instrument variables for the second quarter ($\hat{\mathbf{x}}_2$) can be found by minimising $\phi_2(\mathbf{x_2})$ with respect to $\mathbf{x_2}$, giving $\phi_2(\hat{\mathbf{x}}_2)$ as the minimum value of the truncated loss function. This is true whether or not policy was optimal in quarter 1.

Corresponding statements can be made about quarter 3, quarter 4, and so on.

As stated already, this result holds for the first case – where the constraining system is linear and stochastic with time-dependent parameter values. It also holds, as a special case, where the system is linear and non-stochastic with time-dependent parameter values. It holds, furthermore, for the second case since here, too, the constraining system is linear and non-stochastic with time-dependent parameter values at each and, in particular, at the final iteration. It does not hold exactly for the third case (the case of a non-linear, stochastic-constraining system with time-independent parameter values), but, like the 'solution' for this case, may be regarded as holding approximately.

We are now ready to consider the optimal control procedure for policy evaluation. Essentially this consists of comparing the value of the loss function associated with *actual* policy (the historical loss function) with the value of the loss function associated with *optimal* policy (the optimal or minimum loss function). The more closely the value of the historical loss function conforms to the value of the optimal loss function, the better is the performance of the policy authorities taken to be.

The comparison between the values of the historical and optimal loss functions can be made in various ways. One way proposed by Chow (1978) may be stated very briefly as follows. To evaluate the policy adopted in quarter 1 compute $\phi_1(\mathbf{x}_1) - \phi_1(\hat{\mathbf{x}}_1)$. To evaluate the policy adopted in the sequence of quarters 1, ..., N ($N < T$) compute $\sum_{t=1}^{N} [\phi_t(\mathbf{x}_t) - \phi_t(\hat{\mathbf{x}}_t)]$. The type of information needed to make these computations will be clear from earlier discussion. It consists of the appropriate historical values of the lagged predetermined variables, the appropriate historical values of the current non-policy exogenous variables and the time-dependent reduced-form matrices.

The rationale of Chow's proposal is provided by the result stated at the end of our discussion of optimal control. According to this result, if some *non*-optimal policy is chosen for the first quarter of the planning interval and the optimal policies for the remaining quarters, the value of the loss function will be $\phi_1(\mathbf{x}_1)$. On the other hand, if the optimal policy is chosen for quarter 1 also, the (minimum) value of the loss function will be $\phi_1(\hat{\mathbf{x}}_1)$. Hence $\phi_1(\mathbf{x}_1) - \phi_1(\hat{\mathbf{x}}_1)$ will represent the total loss associated with non-optimal policy in quarter 1. This provides a measure of the room for improvement in the policy chosen for quarter 1 and so provides a basis for evaluating that policy.

Similarly, $\phi_2(\mathbf{x}_2) - \phi_2(\hat{\mathbf{x}}_2)$ provides a measure of the room for improvement in the policy adopted in quarter 2, regardless of the policy adopted in quarter 1. Hence when added to $\phi_1(\mathbf{x}_1) - \phi_1(\hat{\mathbf{x}}_1)$ it provides a basis for evaluating the policy adopted in quarters 1 and 2 combined. The argument can be extended in an obvious way to quarters 1, 2, and 3, and so on.

It should be noted that the above approach to the comparison of the values of the historical and optimal loss functions is no more than an approximation when the constraining system is non-linear and stochastic, as is typically the case, since, as mentioned earlier, the result on which it relies does not hold exactly for that case.

An application of the measure $\phi_1(\mathbf{x}_1) - \phi_1(\hat{\mathbf{x}}_1)$ to US policy in the first quarter of 1971 can be found in Chow (1978). A loss function similar to the illustrative function presented in (11.1) is used and the constraining system is the Michigan quarterly econometric model (see Hymans and Shapiro, 1974). For the purposes of the exercise two of the current exogenous variables in this system are treated as instrument variables. They are *unborrowed reserves* (a monetary instrument) and *non-defense government purchases of goods and services* (both in current prices). (The first of these instrument variables, expressed in terms of deviations from a desired level, is one of the arguments in the loss function.)

The figure which Chow obtained from $\phi_1(\mathbf{x_1}) - \phi_1(\hat{\mathbf{x}}_1)$ for the first quarter of 1971 was 26.00, the two elements in the vector $\mathbf{x_1}$ being obtained by solving the appropriate optimal control problem with the seventeen quarters 1971(I) to 1975(I) as the planning interval. The significance of this figure can be gauged by comparing it with the figure of 248.03 for $\phi_1(\hat{\mathbf{x}}_1)$. Thus the extra loss attributable to the choice of a non-optimal policy in 1975(I) proves to be some 10 per cent of the minimum loss for the entire four years of the planning interval.

An alternative way of comparing the values of the historical and optimal loss functions has been proposed by Hirsch *et al.* (1978). This consists of the following steps:

1. Find the optimal values of the instrument variables for each quarter of the planning interval.
2. Solve the constraining system for the target variables for each quarter in the planning interval using the optimal values of the instrument variables and historical values of all other predetermined variables.
3. Repeat step (2) using historical values of the instrument variables.
4. Evaluate the loss function using the outputs of steps (2) and (3) to obtain the optimal and historical loss functions, respectively.
5. Compare the values of historical and optimal loss functions to evaluate policy over the entire planning interval.

The main difference between this approach to the comparison of the values of the historical and optimal loss functions and the approach adopted by Chow lies in the concept of the *historical loss function*. Chow's historical loss function is specific to a particular quarter and its value represents the loss associated with the choice of a *non*-optimal policy for that quarter and *optimal* policies for the rest of the planning interval. By contrast, the historical loss function of Hirsch *et al.* is not specific to a particular quarter (it relates to the planning interval as a whole) and does not assume the choice of optimal policies for any part of that interval.

The approach summarised in steps (1)–(5) above has been applied by Hirsch *et al.* (1978) to the evaluation of US policy in the period 1971(I) to

1975(I). Once again the loss function used is close to that given in (11.1) and there are three instrument variables – two fiscal and one monetary. In this case, however, the entire exercise is performed seven times with seven different constraining (non-linear) KK systems. The value of the historical loss function proved to be around 700, while the seven values of the optimal loss function ranged from a little over 250 to just under 485. Thus the extra loss attributable to the choice of non-optimal policies throughout the relevant historical period ranged from about 36 per cent to about 69 per cent of the minimum loss.

11.4 Evaluation of policy rules

So far we have been concerned with the use of KK systems in the evaluation of historical policies. We turn now to their use in the evaluation of policy rules. The rules which have attracted most interest and to which most of the evaluation work with KK systems has been directed are monetary rules – rules which prescribe a definite procedure for fixing the money supply – and we shall begin by considering some of the studies which have been undertaken in this field. One of the earliest of such studies, that of Cooper and Fischer (1972a), has been discussed already in Chapter 10 in another connection. We take this study as our starting-point.

The essential features of the Cooper–Fischer study may be summarised as follows. The focal point of the study was the much-discussed rule under which the monetary authorities are required to maintain a constant rate of growth in the money supply. Its main object was to compare the variability that would have been observed in the unemployment rate and the inflation rate in the USA over the sequence of fifty-two quarters beginning with 1956(I) and ending with 1968(IV) had this rule been followed with the variability that would have been observed if various alternative rules (of the 'proportional', 'derivative' and 'mixed' varieties) had been followed instead, with a view to determining whether the constant rate of growth rule could be improved upon from the standpoint of economic stability. The technique used was deterministic system simulation based on the MPS system. That is, MPS was solved for the unemployment rate and the inflation rate for each of the fifty-two quarters concerned with the money supply (treated as exogenous) following the constant rate of growth rule and then again with the money supply following each of the alternative rules. (Historical values were used for all other exogenous variables in all solutions.) Variability under the constant rate of growth rule was then measured by computing the standard deviation of the fifty-two solution values for the unemployment rate and the standard deviation of the fifty-two solution values for the inflation rate which corresponded to that rule. Variability under each of the alternative rules was measured in the same way. By comparing the standard deviations for the constant rate of growth rule with those for each of the alternative rules, Cooper and Fischer reached the conclusion that the degree of stability associated with rules in which a strong derivative element is present is likely to be significantly greater than that associated with the constant rate of growth rule.

In a second study Cooper and Fischer (1972b) have attacked the same problem but in a somewhat more refined way. The most notable differences in procedure are as follows. In the first place, whereas only one system (the MPS system) was used in the first study, two systems – one KK and one non-KK – were used in the second. The KK system used was the MPS system once again, while the non-KK system was the St Louis (monetarist) system.

Second, the basic technique used in the second study was *stochastic* system simulation, as opposed to the deterministic system simulation used in the first. Thus the first step in the second study was to generate a value for each MPS disturbance for each of the fifty-two quarters of the simulation period (the same simulation period was used in both studies), using the generating procedure outlined in Chapter 5, and similarly for each St Louis disturbance. This step was repeated for both systems – in the case of the MPS system twenty different sets of disturbance values were generated and in the case of the St Louis system ten sets. The next step was to solve the MPS system for the unemployment rate and the inflation rate for each of the fifty-two quarters concerned using one of the twenty sets of disturbances generated for that system and then to repeat the solution using, in turn, each of the other sets. These twenty distinct solutions were generated for the constant rate of growth and for each of the alternatives investigated. (Three alternatives, all of the mixed proportional–derivative variety and all suggested by the results of the earlier study, were investigated.) The same procedure was applied to the St Louis system also. Thus, in the case of the MPS system, twenty standard deviations were produced for the unemployment rate and twenty for the inflation rate – each corresponding to one of the twenty sets of disturbance values generated at the outset for this system – both for the constant rate of growth rule and for each of the three alternatives. Similarly in the case of the St Louis system ten standard deviations were produced for each variable for each rule. In the case of the second study, therefore, the quantity of relevant information produced was much more extensive than in the case of the first. Essentially this was due to the fact that stochastic rather than deterministic system simulation was the basic technique used in the second study.

The third main difference between the two studies was that formal statistical tests were applied to the standard deviations of the unemployment rate and the inflation rate in the case of the second study, whereas in the case of the first the methods of analysis used were essentially *ad hoc* in character.

Broadly speaking, the conclusion reached in the second Cooper–Fischer study was the same as the one reached in the first. Like the first study, the second suggested that rules embodying an appropriate combination of 'proportional' and 'derivative' components are likely to outperform the constant rate of growth rule judged from the standpoint of macroeconomic stability.

The problem of evaluating monetary rules has been approached from a rather different angle by Craine *et al.* (1978). In the two Cooper–Fischer studies the performance criterion used was macroeconomic stability – one rule is judged superior to another if the macro economy (represented by the unemployment rate and the inflation rate) is less variable under the former that it is under the latter. In the study of Craine *et al.*, on the other hand, performance was judged by means of a specific loss function – one rule is rated better than another if the value of the loss function concerned is smaller under the former than it is under the latter.

The loss function used by Craine *et al.*, has the same quadratic form as the illustrative loss function of (11.1). The arguments of the function are the level of the unemployment rate (in excess of 4.8 per cent), the level of the inflation rate (in excess of 2.5 per cent per annum), the change in the Treasury bill rate (in excess of 1.5 percentage points) and the level of the money supply (in excess of the level corresponding to a constant rate of growth of 5.1 per cent per annum), the first three being 'target' deviations and the fourth an 'instrument' deviation. A weighted sum of squares of these four arguments is summed over a sequence of quarters to give the loss function.

In the Craine *et al.* study, then, monetary rules were judged by reference to this loss function. In outline, the procedure used was as follows. First the money-supply series corresponding to each of the rules under investigation was generated for the sequence of eight quarters from 1973(III) to 1975(II). The MPS system was then solved for each of the three target variables appearing in the loss function, for each of these eight quarters and for each of the rules under investigation. Finally, the solution values for each rule were used to evaluate the loss function for that rule over the sequence of quarters concerned.

One of the rules considered was the constant rate of growth rule. To evaluate the loss function for this rule, the MPS system was solved for the unemployment rate, the inflation rate and the change in Treasury bill rate for each of the eight quarters 1973(III) to 1975(II). In performing this solution the series used for the money-supply variable (treated as exogenous) was the series generated at the outset for the constant rate of growth rule, while historical values were used for all other exogenous variables. The eight solution values for the three target variables in question were then substituted into the loss function together with the appropriate money-supply series to give the value of the loss function for the constant rate of growth rule.

As just mentioned, one of the rules examined in the Craine *et al.* study was the constant rate of growth rule. The other included a mixed porportional–derivative rule of the Cooper–Fischer type, and two rules (Bronfenbrenner's 'lag' rule and Poole's 'cautious re-entry' rule) of a somewhat more esoteric kind, into the details of which we shall not enter. One of the conclusions of the study, which is of particular interest in the light of the findings of the two Cooper–Fischer studies, was that, in terms of loss function values, the constant rate of growth rule performed rather better over the eight quarters considered than the mixed proportional–derivative rule of the Cooper–Fischer type.

So far we have been concerned with the use of KK systems in the evaluation of the alternative *monetary* rules. To complete the section and the chapter we now briefly consider their use in the evaluation of alternative *assignment* rules.

An assignment rule is a rule which assigns instrument variables to target variables via a specified set of reaction functions. Suppose, for example, that two target variables, the inflation rate p and the unemployment rate u, are considered and that two instrument variables, government expenditure G and the money supply M, are available. One possible assignment rule would be a rule which assigned G to u and M to p via the following pair of reaction functions:

$$\begin{aligned} G_t &= G_t^* + \alpha_1(u_{t-1} - u_{t-1}^*) \\ M_t &= M_t^* + \alpha_2(p_{t-1} - p_{t-1}^*) \end{aligned} \tag{11.2}$$

where * denotes 'desired' and α_1 and α_2 are specified numbers, α_1 being positive and α_2 negative. Thus under this assignment rule the fiscal authorities are required to increase government expenditure in quarter t (expressed in terms of deviations from its desired level) by some multiple of the unemployment rate in quarter $t - 1$ (again expressed in terms of deviations from its desired level). Similarly, the monetary authorities are required to reduce the money supply in quarter t by some multiple of the inflation rate in quarter $t - 1$, both in terms of deviations from desired levels.

One important study in which a KK system has been used to evaluate alternative assignment rules is the New Zealand study of Spencer and Grimes (1980). The Spencer–Grimes study is based on a small KK system of the New Zealand economy and has as its main object the evaluation of various assignment rules involving three target variables (output, the inflation rate and the balance of payments on current account) and three instrument variables (the level of government expenditure, the interest rate on long-term government securities and the exchange rate) and reaction functions of the form of (11.2).

The basic technique used is deterministic system simulation, which in this case proceeds as follows. First, a control run is performed. Next, a series of shocked runs is performed – one for each assignment rule under investigation. In every case the shock takes the form of a temporary increase (lasting four quarters) in import prices. Also in every case the appropriate variables are withdrawn from the exogenous category and endogenised via appropriate reaction functions. What the 'appropriate' exogenous variables are in any shocked run and which reaction functions are 'appropriate' for their endogenisation depend, of course, on the assignment rule to which the shocked run relates. Finally, the solution values of the three target variables in the control run and in the series of shocked runs are used to compute the following statistic for each target variable, y, for each assignment rule (shocked run):

$$\mathrm{RCSS}(y_t) = \sqrt{\sum_{j=1}^{t} (y_j - y_j^*)^2} \quad (t = 1, 2, \ldots, 20) \tag{11.3}$$

Here y_j is the solution value for the relevant target variable in the relevant shocked run and y_j^* the solution value in the control run. Thus the statistic defined in (11.3) is the square root of the cumulative sum of squares of the deviations from control in the target variable concerned up to the tth quarter of the simulation period. By plotting $\mathrm{RCSS}(y_t)$ against t for each target variable for each assignment rule (shocked run) Spencer and Grimes are able to determine which assignment rules are stabilising and which are not, and, in the case of the former, to compare the convergence properties of the various rules. Hence, in turn, they are able to evaluate the rules under investigation.

Notes

1. Since the money supply and the commercial paper rates are endogenous in the MPS model, Perry's shocked runs presumably involved some switching of variables between the endogenous and exogenous categories. See the discussion of the Cooper–Fischer (1972a) study in section 10.3.
2. In this respect Perry's procedure was faulty. His comparison should have been, not with historical values, but with the solution values generated in a control run. See the above outline of the search procedure and the discussion of section 7.2.

References and further reading

CHOW, G. C. (1978) 'Evaluation of Macroeconomic Policies by Stochastic Control Techniques', *International Economic Review*, vol. 19, pp. 311–19.

CHOW, G. C. (1981) *Econometric Analysis by Control Methods*, Wiley, New York.

COOPER, J. P. and FISCHER, S. (1972a) 'Simulation of Monetary Rules in the FRB–MIT–Penn Model', *Journal of Money, Credit and Banking*, vol. 4, pp. 384–96.

COOPER, J. P. and FISCHER, S. (1972b) 'Stochastic Simulation of Monetary Rules in Two Macroeconometric Models', *Journal of the American Statistical Association*, vol. 67, pp. 750–60.

CRAINE, R. A., HAVENNER, A. and BERRY, J. (1978) 'Fixed Rules vs Activism in the Conduct of Monetary Policy', *American Economic Review*, vol. 68, pp. 769–83.

HIRSCH, A., HYMANS, H. and SHAPIRO, H. T. (1978) 'Econometric Review of Alternative Fiscal and Monetary Policies, 1971–75', *Review of Economics and Statistics*, vol. 60, pp. 334–45.

HYMANS, S. H. and SHAPIRO, H. T. (1974) 'The Structure and Properties of the Michigan Quarterly Econometric Model of the US Economy', *International Economic Review*, vol. 15, pp. 632–53.

PERRY, G. L. (1975) 'Policy Alternatives for 1974', *Brookings Papers on Economic Activity*, no. 1, pp. 222–35.

SPENCER, G. H. and GRIMES, A. (1980) 'On the Stability of Alternative Policy Rules within a Model of the New Zealand Economy', in G. H. Spencer (ed.), *Experiments with a Core Model of the New Zealand Economy*, Research Paper No. 29, Reserve Bank of New Zealand, Wellington.

Part V Conclusion

12 THE FUTURE OF KK SYSTEMS

12.1 The evolution of KK systems

A modern KK system is a living thing in two distinct senses – one obvious and one not so obvious. It 'lives' in the obvious sense that it is never really finished. Respecification and re-estimation are continuous as is revalidation and the search for fresh applications. Moreover, this continuous maintainance and rebuilding is typically carried out within the framework of an established tradition – often largely oral. The membership of the research team changes from year to year but the broad thrust of the work and its methodological foundations remain relatively fixed.

The other, less obvious sense in which a modern KK system 'lives' is that it is a member of a class of economy-wide systems which, itself, is continually evolving. To appreciate the force of this remark one has merely to compare the prototype KK system presented in Chapter 1 with the latest product, from the point of view of specification, estimation, validation and range of application. Whether or not the latest product is better than the prototype, there can be no doubt that in all respects it is very different, and that over the first thirty years or so of their life KK systems have evolved at a rate which is truly remarkable.

There is no sign that this evolutionary process has faltered, let alone stopped, and to round off the book we propose to comment briefly on several developments which seem destined to play an important part in determining the shape of things to come, as far as KK systems are concerned.

12.2 Some developments in the field of KK systems

Linking of KK systems

One notable current development is in the area of linking. Linking is proceeding in two distinct directions.

On the one hand, we find a KK system for some economy being linked to a macroeconomic system of a different kind for the same economy. An example of this is WAM, the Wharton annual model of the US economy to which we referred in Chapter 10. The WAM KK system of the US economy is linked to a US input–output system. Others are the Brookings model, the DRI annual model, the LBS model and Candide, all of which are listed in Table 1.2. On the other hand, we find the KK systems of different economies being linked together to form a world KK system. The most ambitious project of this type is Project LINK (see Ball, 1973; Waelbroeck, 1976; Sawyer, 1979) which originated in 1968 and which is now well established with headquarters at the University of Pennsylvania. Project LINK produces regular forecasts of world trade and payments from the linked system and has also undertaken numerous simulation exercises relating to international economic problems in recent years. Another project for the linking of national KK systems is the World Econometric Model project of the Japanese government's Economic Planning Agency (see Amano, Kurihara and Samuelson, 1980; Amano, Sadahiro, Anai and Yoshizoe, 1980). The EPA project, like LINK, has as its objective the linkage of KK systems of a number of different economies to provide a world KK system. It differs from LINK in that the agency is itself undertaking the construction of all the individual-country systems rather than making use of existing working systems from the countries concerned.

Estimation of KK systems

It would appear that the most important current developments in the area of KK-system estimation relate more to the more efficient use of known estimators than to the invention of new ones. As a result some estimators which have hitherto been rarely used in the context of KK systems are likely to play a more active role in the future. One estimator of which a great deal more will probably be seen is the IV estimator. This applies in particular to its autocorrelation variants, which have recently become a good deal more attractive to the builders of KK systems because of improvements in the associated computer software.

At present there is relatively little experience with the FP estimators, especially those applicable to non-linear systems. To date the only example of the estimation of a working KK system by means of an FP estimator is the study of Salmon and Eaton (1975), in which an FP is applied to the LBS model, a medium-size KK system of the UK economy. Nevertheless, the FP estimators show great promise and are likely to become more popular with KK system-builders. Before this can occur, however, further development is required on at least two fronts. The first relates to computer software; no serious development of the software needed for the application of FP to large KK systems has yet occurred. The other relates to the handling of autocorrelation.

Another judgement which can be made with some confidence is that OLS and its variants (like NLLS, CO and Almon) are unlikely to lose their supremacy as preliminary estimators. Some system-builders have already recognised the usefulness of IV in this context and an increase in its popularity is therefore likely. Nevertheless, it is hard to see IV overtaking OLS as the estimator most frequently used at the specification stage.

Finally, one must expect to see greater use being made of the wide range of tests for the detection of mis-specification and for model selection which have been developed in the last few years (for further details see Breusch and Pagan, 1980; Sawa, 1978; White, 1980). These tests are both powerful and simple and their neglect by the builders of KK systems is therefore unlikely to last.

Stochastic simulation

There is general agreement that stochastic system simulation is superior to the deterministic variety, for several reasons. The main reason is that since the disturbances of a KK system are an essential part of the specification, there is no more justification for arbitrarily putting them to zero for simulation purposes than there is for putting the exogenous variables of the system at their historical mean values. Second, the complete (stochastic) system and its deterministic counterpart can, and frequently do, behave very differently in response to some exogenous shock. For example, it is well known that the introduction of random shocks into a stable system can induce cyclical behaviour. Finally, formal statistical tests can be applied to the output of repeated applications of a stochastic simulation. By contrast, the output of system simulation of the deterministic variety can be handled only by procedures of an *ad hoc* kind.

Studies in which the technique of system simulation has been applied to a KK system in its stochastic rather than its deterministic form certainly exist (see, for example, Cooper and Fischer, 1972; Hickman, 1972; Calzolari, 1979; Muench *et al.*, 1974). Nevertheless, they are comparatively rare; doubtless the main reason is that system simulation in stochastic form is much more demanding computationally and hence is a great deal more expensive than in its deterministic form. Be that as it may, one of the likely developments in the field of KK systems in the foreseeable future is the gradual elimination of deterministic system simulation and its replacement by well-designed and replicated simulation of the stochastic kind.

Optimal control

In Chapter 11 we drew attention to the possibility of applying optimal control techniques to KK systems for the purpose of evaluating historical policies. This, however, is by no means the only use to which these techniques can be put in the KK field and, as optimal control is a fast-growing discipline, one can reasonably expect to see it being applied much more widely in KK policy studies than has hitherto been the case.

One way in which optimal control techniques are likely to be more widely used in the KK field is for the purpose of policy formulation. When

KK systems have been used for this purpose in the past the technique applied has usually been the conditional-forecasting brand of counter-factual analysis discussed in section 10.2. That is, the KK system concerned has been used to make a series of forecasts for the main target variables each based on a set of alternative feasible, but otherwise purely hypothetical, time paths for the instrument variables. Then the alternative which appeared most attractive in terms of the associated time path for the target variables would be taken as the starting-point for policy formulation in the period concerned. In one of the earliest KK policy studies Klein (1947) considered post-war US policy along these lines, using a forerunner of the KK system presented in section 1.3 as his forecasting tool.

Compared with the procedure just described, the application of optimal control techniques has the advantage that it gives the policy-maker a time path for the instrument variables which is the 'best' that can be found, given the preferences which are expressed in the coefficients of the loss function. Of course, since by hypothesis the planning interval for the optimal control problem will, in this case, be in the *future*, its solution will require forecasts for the non-instrument exogenous variables for each quarter of the planning interval. However, this will be true whatever the procedure used to set policy. In particular it will be true when conditional forecasting is the technique employed.

One can also expect to see optimal control techniques applied more widely to policy evaluation than has so far been the case. As we have seen in Chapter 11, a use has been found for them already in the evaluation of historical policies. They provide an equally attractive approach, however, to the evaluation of policy rules. To evaluate a monetary rule, for example, one could begin by solving a KK system for some historical period on the assumption that the (exogenous) money supply obeyed the rule under investigation. One could then solve the system for the same period on the assumption that all the instrument variables had been set optimally. Using the two sets of solution values and, if necessary, the appropriate time paths for the instrument variables, one could then evaluate the loss function for both alternatives. Comparing the value of the loss function associated with the rule under investigation with its minimum value, the value associated with the 'optimal' alternative, one could then form some judgement about the value of the rule. Morever, one could easily rank a group of competing monetary and/or other rules in this way.

One can confidently expect that uses of this and similar types will be found for optimal control techniques in the KK field as they become more familiar and their potential becomes more widely recognised.

Multi-system studies

As will be clear from Table 1.2, the USA now has several working KK systems, each of which has special features reflecting the intellectual habits of its creators and the specific purposes for which it was built. For the USA, therefore, studies in which not one but a whole battery of KK systems is put to work on some policy problem are now definitely feasible and are likely to become increasingly common. No other country is quite as well endowed as the USA but several now have much more than one KK system and multi-system studies relating to the economies of these countries may also soon make their appearance.

Of course, no two KK systems will yield precisely the same answer to any question that might be posed. On the other hand, one can reasonably expect that the answers given to the same question by a group of, say, seven American KK systems will have a great deal in common – that there will be a consensus. And since the consensus is likely to carry much more weight than the answer given by any single KK system, it is worth finding if it exists. This is the case for multi-system as opposed to single-system studies; it is particularly strong when, as at present in the USA, there is no one KK system which is universally respected and whose pronouncements are widely accepted as authoritative.

Two recent US examples of multi-system studies of the type now under discussion have been mentioned in Chapter 11: Cooper and Fischer (1972) and the Hirsch *et al.* (1978). The latter is particularly noteworthy in that the answers given by the seven KK systems employed contained a fairly definite and clear consensus. As pointed out in Chapter 11, all seven systems suggested that a substantial welfare loss flowed from the choice of non-optimal policies in the relevant period. Furthermore, there was general agreement as to the ways in which the historical policy was deficient compared with the best that could have been adopted. As regards fiscal policy, the consensus was that policy was about right in the middle of the relevant period but was insufficiently expansionary up to the middle of 1972 and after the middle of 1973. As regards monetary policy, all systems agreed that policy was about right in 1971–2 but was insufficiently expansionary by far in 1974–5.

The above are but a few of the important developments which are either already in the pipeline or on which KK systems seem certain to embark in the next few years. Along with others which cannot yet be clearly discerned, these developments will ensure that both the KK systems of the year 2000 and the uses to which they will be put will be very different from what has been presented in this book.

References and further reading

AMANO, A., KURIHARA, E. and SAMUELSON, L (1980) *Trade Linkage Sub-Model in the EPA World Econometric Model,* Economic Bulletin No. 19, Economic Research Institute, Economic Planning Agency, Tokyo.

AMANO, A., SADAHIRO, A., ANAI, F. and YOSHIZOE, Y. (1980) *The United States of America*, EPA World Econometric Model, Discussion Paper No. 2, Economic Research Institute, Economic Planning Agency, Tokyo.

BALL, R. J. (1973) *The International Linkage of National Economic Models*, North-Holland, Amsterdam.

BREUSCH, T. S. and PAGAN, A. R. (1980) 'The Lagrange Multiplier Test and its Applications to Model Specification in Econometrics', *Review of Economic Studies*, vol. 47, pp. 239–53.

CALZOLARI, G. (1979) 'Antithetic Variables to Estimate the Simulation Bias in Nonlinear Models', *Economics Letters*, vol. 3, pp. 323–8.

COOPER, J. P. and FISCHER, S. (1972) 'Stochastic Simulation of Monetary Rules in Two Macroeconometric Models', *Journal of the American Statistical Association*, vol. 67, pp. 750–60.

HICKMAN, B. G. (ed.)(1972) *Econometric Models of Cyclical Behavior*, Columbia University Press, New York.

HIRSCH, A., HYMANS, H. and SHAPIRO, H. T. (1978) 'Econometric Review of Alternative Fiscal and Monetary Policies, 1971–75', *Review of Economics and Statistics*, vol. 60, pp. 334–45.

KLEIN, L. R. (1947) 'The Use of Econometric Models as a Guide to Economic Policy', *Econometrica*, vol. 15, pp. 111–51.

MUENCH, T., ROLNICK, A., WALLACE, N. and WEILER, W. (1974) 'Tests for Structural Change and Prediction Intervals for the Reduced Forms of Two Structural Models of the US: The FRB–MIT and Michigan Quarterly Models', *Annals of Economic and Social Measurement*, vol. 3, pp. 491–520.

SALMON, M. H. and EATON, J. R. (1975) 'Estimation Problems in Large Econometric Models: An Application of Various Estimation Techniques to the London Business School Model', in G. A. Renton (ed.), *Modelling the Economy*, Heinemann, London.

SAWA, T. (1978) 'Information Criteria for Discriminating Among Alternative Regression Models', *Econometrica*, vol. 46, pp. 1273–91.

SAWYER, J. A. (1979) *Modelling the International Transmission Mechanism*, North-Holland, Amsterdam.

WAELBROECK, J. L. (1976) *The Models of Project LINK*, North-Holland, Amsterdam.

WHITE, H. (1980) 'Maximum Likelihood Estimation of Misspecified Models: I and II', mimeo, University of Rochester.

INDEX

ACF 162
across-equations covariance 77–8
ad hoc modification 53–5
adaptive mechanism 63
adjustment relationship 12
Aitken estimator 85, 94
algorithm 108
Allen, R. G. D. 2, 22
Almon estimator 83, 223
  see also PDL
Amano, A. 223, 226
Amemiya, T. 126, 127, 137
Anai, F. 223, 226
analysis of alternative regimes 158, 194–5, 201–3
Ando, A. 11, 22
Arai, K. 139
arithmetical forecasting 178–84
  see also forecasting
ARMAX estimator 83–4, 85, 119, 126, 132–3, 136
Artis, M. J. 23
asset portfolio 58
assignment rule 217–18
asymptotic results 70
Australian Bureau of Statistics 11, 50
Australian economy, models of 11, 12
Australian Treasury *see* Department of the Treasury
autocorrelation 53–4, 77, 78, 82–3, 117, 118–19, 132–3, 161–2
autocorrelation function (ACF) 162
autoregressive moving average exogenous estimator 83–4, 85
  see also ARMAX
autoregressive process 132

Bailey, R. E. 137
Ball, R. J. 11, 22, 173, 175, 223, 227
Bank of Canada 11, 22, 58, 63, 68
Bank of England 11, 58, 64, 68
Bank of England system 11, 58, 137
Basmann, R. L. 88, 102, 105, 106, 122
Basmann's conjecture 105, 116
behavioural relationship 26
Belsley, D. A. 126, 137
Bergstrom, A. R. 2, 12, 22
Berry, J. 219
bias 114, 116
Boatwright, B. D. 11, 22
Boot, J. C. G. 159, 160
Box, G. E. P. 162, 167, 175
Box–Jenkins method 167, 182
Brainard, W. C. 58, 68
Breusch, T. S. 224, 227
Bronfenbrenner's lag rule 217
Brookings Institution 11
Brookings system 10, 11, 222
Brown, B. W. 137
Brown, M. 182, 192
Brown, R. L. 164, 175
Brown–Durbin–Evans procedure 164
Brundy, J. M. 91, 102
Brunner, K. 24, 69, 204
budget deficit 58
Burns, T. 11, 22, 173, 175

χ^2 test 162
CA *see* constant-term adjustment
Calzolari, G. 224, 227
Canadian economy, models of 11
Candide system 11, 223
capital 67
capital flows 61
Carlson, J. A. 64, 68
Caton, C. N. 201, 204
causal analysis 194, 199–201
  criticisms 203–4
Challen, D. W. 3, 23, 136, 137
channels of dynamic response 174
  see also response dissection analysis
characteristic root 131, 146–7, 151
characteristic vector 131
Charatsis, G. 43
chi-square test 162
Chiu, J. S. 120, 124
Chow, G. 164, 175, 207, 212, 213, 219
Christ, C. F. 106, 122, 173, 175
classical assumptions 82, 162
CO estimator 83, 85, 119, 132–3, 136, 223
Cobb–Douglas production function 19
Cochrane–Orcutt estimator 83, 85
  see also CO estimator
coefficient of multiple determination
    see $\bar{R}^2$
competing imports 196–7

computational cost 134–5
computer algorithm 108
con-adjustment *see* constant-term adjustment
conditional forecasting 194, 195–8
see also counter-factual analysis
consistent estimator 82, 116–17
constant-price variable 55–6
constant-term adjustment 185–90
control run 152, 153–4, 195
see also shocked run, system simulation
convergence 34
Cooley, T. F. 164, 176, 204
Cooper, J. 199–201, 204, 214, 215, 219, 224, 226, 227
counter-factual analysis 194–204
covariance matrix
at a single sample point 80, 97, 99, 107, 132
estimation of 82, 92
of estimator 81, 87, 89, 99
of system 74–80, 91, 96
Cragg, J. G. 117, 118, 119, 120, 122, 123
Cooley–Prescott procedure 164
correlogram 162
Craine, R. A. 216–17, 219
cumulative-interim multiplier *see* intermediate-run multiplier
current-price variables 55–6

Data Resources Inc. 11, 23, 137, 138
De Bever, L. 173, 176
deduction 104, 106
definitional relationship 5, 26
degrees of freedom 128
degrees of freedom problem *see* undersized sample problem
delay multiplier 144–5, 150
demographic variables 182
Department of the Treasury (Australia) 11, 23, 50, 58, 59, 65, 68, 137, 138
derivative rule 200, 215–17
see also proportional rule
deterministic equation 71
deterministic simulation 153
see also system simulation
deterministic system 66
deviation from control 155
Dhrymes, P. J. 82, 90, 91, 100, 101, 102, 163, 176
discrete time 3
distributed lag 63, 82, 83–4
Dixon, P. B. 20, 23
Draper, N. R. 85, 102
DRI system 10, 11, 137, 223
Duesenberry, J. S. 123
Duggal, V. G. 11, 23
dummy variable 28, 54, 65, 181
Durbin, J. 164, 175
Durbin–Watson statistic *see* D–W statistic
Durbin's *h* statistic see *h* statistic
Dutta, M. 91, 101, 102
D–W statistic 53–4, 161–2
dynamic 4
dynamic error 170
dynamic multiplier *see* intermediate-run multiplier
dynamic simulation 55, 152, 169–70
see also system simulation
dynamic stability *see* stability
dynamic system 4, 133
stability 147, 151

Eaton, J. R. 91, 103, 130, 137, 139, 223, 227
Eckstein, O. 11, 23
Economic Council of Canada 11
economic system 2
see also KK system, macroanalytical system, macroeconometric system
economic theory 50–2, 56
efficient estimator 82
eigenvalue *see* characteristic root
eigenvector *see* characteristic vector
elasticity 157
endogenous variable 4, 16, 25, 49, 55–6
EPA model 137, 223
error decomposition 168–71
estimate 9, 71, 163, 164
plausibility of 163
see also estimator, parameter, prior information
estimation 46, 70–1
estimation procedures 5
see also estimation
estimation residual *see* residual
estimator 71
asymptotic properties 104
choice of 125–36
computational cost 134–5
finite-sample properties 104–21
performance criteria 114
types 80–1
undersized sample problem 128–32
see also FISE, LISE, SIE
evaluation procedures
dynamic properties 172–5
individual equation 161–4
tracking performance 164–72
whole system 164–75
Evans, H. P. 11, 24, 173, 176
Evans, J. M. 164, 175
Evans, M. K. 131, 138, 190, 191, 192
ex ante forecasting 175
see also forecasting

ex post forecasting 171
 see also tracking performance (outside sample)
ex post prediction *see* prediction
exact sampling studies 105
exchange rate 60–1
exogenous variable 4, 16, 49, 55–6
 forecast of 181–3
 see also endogenous variable, predetermined variable
expectational variable 48, 52, 61–5
 modelling of 62–5
exports 60–1
extrapolative mechanism 63

F-test 163, 164
Fair, R. C. 138, 190, 192
Federal Reserve Board 11, 199
FIIV 92, 99–100, 129
 properties 100
FIML 92, 95–9, 125–6
 properties 99, 117, 119
final form 143, 150
final-form multiplier *see* long-run multiplier
finite-sample properties
 analytical results 104–6, 130
 experimental results 117–21
 Monte Carlo method 106–17
 see also estimator
FISE 81, 91–100, 117–21, 125, 126, 129, 132, 133, 134, 135–6
Fisher, F. M. 133, 138
finite-sample results 70
 see also finite-sample properties
Fischer, S. 199–201, 204, 214, 215, 219, 224, 226, 227
FitzGerald, V. W. 173, 176
fixed-point estimator *see* FP estimator
flow-of-funds identities 58
forecast error 172
forecasting 178–92
 accuracy 190–2
 ad hoc methods 182
 arithmetical 178–84
 conditional 194, 195–8
 constant-term adjustment 185–90
 judgemental 184–92
 of exogenous variables 181–3
 of lagged endogenous variables 179–81
foreign exchange transaction 58
formation-table identity 57, 58
FP estimator 90–1, 99, 117, 121, 126, 129, 131, 223
Friedman, M. 199
Fromm, G. 11, 23, 123
full information estimator *see* FISE
full information iterated instrumental variables *see* FIIV
full information maximum likelihood *see* FIML

Gandolfo, G. 2, 23
Garbade, K. 164, 176
Gauss–Seidel method 33–7, 42–3, 179
 see also system solution
general-equilibrium system 18–19, 20
generalised least squares 85
Giles, D. E. A. 11, 23, 90, 91, 102, 127, 130, 133, 137, 138, 163, 176
Goldberger, A. S. 101, 102, 126
Goldfeld, S. M. 118, 119, 123, 127, 133, 138
goodness of fit 162–3
 see also tracking performance
government budget deficit 58
government expenditure 55–7
Green, E. W. 11, 23
Grimes, A. 217, 219

h statistic 53–4, 161
Hagger, A. J. 3, 23, 136, 137
Haitovsky, Y. 191, 192
Hall, B. H. 112, 123
Hall, R. E. 112, 123
Hall, V. E. 137
Harrison, R. W. 118, 123
Havenner, A. 219
Helliwell, J. F. 173, 176
Hendry, D. F. 118, 121, 123, 132, 133, 138
Hickman, B. G. 224, 227
Higgins, C. I. 173, 176
Hillier, G. H. 105, 123
Hirsch, A. 213, 226, 227
HM Treasury 11, 23, 58, 63, 68
homoskedasticity 77, 78
Howrey, E. P. 191, 192
Hughes-Hallett, A. J. 43
hybrid system 196
Hymans, S. H. 213, 219, 227

identification 88, 95, 101, 105
impact multiplier 144, 150, 156
 see also multiplier
IMPACT project 20
imports 60–1, 196–7
impulse change 157
 see also shock type
impulse-change multiplier 158–9
 see also multiplier
IMSL 121, 123
in-sample tracking performance *see* tracking performance (within-sample)
induction 106
information matrix 99

input–output system 20–2, 195–8
  see also WL system
institutional framework 26
instrumental variables estimator *see* IV
interim multiplier *see* delay multiplier
intermediate-run multiplier 145, 151, 156
  see also multiplier
International Mathematical and Statistical Libraries (IMSL) 121, 123
international trade 60–1
international transactions 60
intertemporal stability 164
Intriligator, M. D. 82, 86, 96, 101, 102, 105, 116, 117, 120, 122, 123, 136, 138, 163, 176
intrinsic non-linearity 84
iterative instrumental variables 90
iterative method 33–43, 83, 84, 111
  see also Gauss–Seidel method, Newton–Raphson method
IV 53, 86, 88–90, 223
  properties 89, 105

Jacobian matrix 38–9, 99
Jenkins, G. M. 167, 175
Johansen, L. 2, 19, 20, 23
Johnston, J. 85, 88, 101, 102, 117, 118, 123, 130, 132, 138, 162, 176
Jonson, P. D. 12, 23, 137, 138
Jorgenson, D. W. 91, 102, 126, 138
judgemental forecasting 184–92

Kadane, J. B. 105–23
Kato, H. 139
k-class estimator 88, 105
Kelejian, H. H. 119, 123, 127, 138
Kendrick, D. A. 102, 122
Keynes, J. M. 2, 23, 46, 66, 68
Keynes–Klein system *see* KK system
Kinal, T. W. 105, 123
KK system
  available estimators 80–101
  choice of estimator 135–6
  concept 2–3
  counter-factual analysis 192–204
  defined 3, 25
  dynamic character 4
  dynamic properties 172–5
  estimated system 70
  estimator types 80–1
  estimators in 5, 125–36, 223–4
  evaluation 161–75
  evolution of 222
  features 3–5, 7–9
  flows in 4
  general representation 28, 33, 37, 38, 72
  illustrative simulation 153–9
  information content 71–80
  linking 222–3
  multiplier analysis 142–59
  non-linearity of 4–5, 125–8
  ordinary least squares in 82
  prototype 5–9, 10, 66–8
  simulation 152–9
  size 10, 128
  solution of 32–43
  specification 46–68, 133
  stability 147, 151, 158
  structural form 72, 73
  true system 9, 70, 71
  undersized sample problem 128–32
  validation 133, 142–75
  variables of 4
Klein, L. R. 2, 5, 11, 23, 101, 102, 123, 130, 131, 136, 138, 190, 191, 192, 195–6, 204, 225, 227
Klein system 5–9
  features 7–8
  relationships 6–7
  variables of 6
Kloeck, T. 130, 137, 138
Kmenta, J. 24, 82, 83, 84, 85, 88, 95, 99, 101, 102, 106, 108, 118, 123, 126, 132, 137, 138, 192
Knight, M. D. 12, 23, 137, 139
Koutsoyiannis, A. 101, 102
Kuh, E. 123
Kurihara, E. 223, 226

labour supply 67
Ladd, G. W. 120, 123
Laffont, J. 126, 138
lagged dependent variable 132
lagged endogenous variable 4, 72, 73, 106, 133
  defined 4
  experimental evidence 118
  forecast of 179–81
Lakin, A 121
large system 128, 135
Latter, A. R. 11, 23, 137, 139
LBS system 11, 61, 223
least squares *see* OLS, NLLS
Leontief, W. W. 2, 23
level of significance 117
LIIV 90–1
likelihood function 95–6, 97
limited information estimator *see* IV, LISE
limited information iterated instrumental variables *see* LIIV
limited information maximum likelihood *see* LIML
LIML 86, 88–9, 128, 129

linear system
  matrix representation 25–8, 72, 147
  multiplier analysis 142–51
  reduced form 29, 86–7, 131, 143, 147
  restricted form 29, 32
  solution of 25–32
  stability 147, 151
  structural form 29–30, 32
  unrestricted form 29, 32
LINK *see* Project LINK
linked systems 222–3
  see also hybrid system
LISE 81, 85–91, 92, 100–1, 117–21, 125, 129, 130, 131, 132, 133, 134, 135–6
Lobban, P. W. M. 11, 22
logarithmic differentiation 19
London Graduate School of Business Studies 11, 68
long-term multiplier *see* long-run multiplier
long run 15–16, 67–8
long-run multiplier 145–6, 151
  see also multiplier
loss function 207–8
Lucas, R. E. 203–4
Lyttkens, E. 91, 102

McCarthy, M. D. 11, 23, 127, 130, 133, 139, 191, 192
McNees, S. K. 191, 192
macro system 2
macroanalytical system 2, 46–7, 66–8
macroeconometric system
  concept 2–3
  types of 2–3
  see also KK system
Madansky, G. S. 106
Maddala, G. S. 91, 102, 106, 130, 139
MAE 114
maintained change 157
  see also shock type
Malinvaud, E. 85, 102, 115, 123
Mariano, R. S. 88, 102, 105, 106, 123
Massachusetts Institute of Technology 11, 199
Masumoto, H. 139
matrix representation *see* linear system
maximum likelihood estimator 99, 101
  see also FIML, LIML
Maxwell, T. 11, 23, 137, 139
mean absolute error 114
mean square error 114, 115
measurement error 118, 120
Meltzer, A. H. 24, 69, 204
Mennes, L. B. M. 130, 137, 138
Michigan quarterly model 213
micro system 2
Mikhail, W. M. 105, 124
Miller, G. W. 11, 22, 173, 175
Minford, A. P. 17, 24, 62, 69
mis-specification 117, 132, 133–5, 162, 224
  see also model selection, specification error
Mizon, G. E. 132, 138
model design 107–8
model selection 224
model size 121
modified system 174
  see also response dissection analysis
Modigliani, F. 173, 176
moments, of estimator 105
  existence 105–6, 114–15
money formation 57–8
monetary sector relationships 57–9
money supply 57–9
Monte Carlo method 106–21
  illustrative experiment 107–16
  performance criteria 114
  studies 117–21
Moore, G. H. 191, 192
Morgan, A. 163, 176
Morgan, G. H. T. 11, 23, 127, 133, 138
Mosbaek, E. 117, 118, 120, 121, 123
Moses, E. R. 137, 138
MPS system 10, 11, 199–201, 206, 214–16
MS system 17–18, 62
MSE 114, 115
Muench, T. 224, 227
multi-system studies 225–6
multicollinearity 117, 120, 131
multiplier 142–51
  see also delay multiplier, impact multiplier, intermediate-run multiplier, long-run multiplier
multiplier analysis
  defined 142
  linear systems 142–51
  non-linear systems 151–9
Muth, J. F. 3, 24
Muth–Sargent system *see* MS system

Nagar, A. L. 105, 123, 124
Nagar, T. H. 108
naive models 166–7
Naylor, T. H. 108, 122, 124
Nehlawi, J. E. 127, 139
Nelson, C. R. 162, 167, 176
New Zealand economy, models of 11, 12
Newton–Raphson method 33, 37–43, 84–5, 99
NIF system 10, 11, 50–3, 58, 65, 137, 202
NLLS estimator 84–5, 99, 126, 136, 223
NL2SLS 119, 126–8
NL3SLS 126–8
Nobay, A. R. 23
non-competing imports 196–7
non-linear 4–5, 19, 119, 125
non-linear least squares *see* NLLS estimator

non-linear system
error decomposition 168–71
estimation of 119, 125–8
general representation 33, 37, 38
matrix representation 38
multiplier analysis 151–9
simulation of 152—9
solution of 32–43
stability 158
non-linear three-stage least squares *see* NL3SLS
non-linear two-stage least squares *see* NL2SLS
non-stochastic regressor 82, 85
normal equations 95, 96
null hypothesis 117

observed expectations data 62, 64
OLS 53, 81–2, 125, 129, 136, 223
finite-sample bias 82, 130
properties 82, 105, 116, 117, 120, 121
omitted-variables error 5
open-economy relationship 60–1
optimal control 207–14, 224–5
ORANI system 20
ordering 42
ordinary least squares estimator *see* OLS
Ormerod, P. 22, 23

Pagan, A. R. 84, 102, 224, 227
parameter 5, 9, 16, 163
restrictions on 15
see also estimate, prior information
Parkin, J. M. 58, 64, 68, 69
Parmenter, P. B. 23
partial-adjustment process 12–14, 52
participation rate 67
PB system 2, 12–16, 137
PDL 83, 85
performance criteria 114
Perry, G. L. 206, 219
Phillips, A. W. 2, 24, 59–60, 69, 200, 204
Phillips, P. C. B. 99, 103, 105, 124, 137
Phillips–Bergstrom system *see* PB system
Phillips relationship 59–60
Pierce, D. A. 162, 175
planning horizon 207
planning interval 207
plausibility of parameter estimate 163
policy evaluation 205–18
policy instrument 66–7, 181
policy-reaction function 14
policy rule 199–200, 214–18
polynomial distributed lag 83, 85
Poole's cautious re-entry rule 217
portfolio model 58
Powell, A. A. 3, 24
power 117
predetermined variable 4, 25, 49
forecast of 179–83
types of 4, 49
prediction
ex post 54, 55
outside-sample 54
within-sample 55
predictive success 54, 55
Prescott, E. C. 164, 176, 204
Preston, R. S. 195, 204
primary liquidity 58
principal components 130–1
prior information 73–4, 163, 164
Project LINK 10, 137, 223
proportional rule 200, 215–17
see also derivative rule
pseudo-random numbers 108
public-sector borrowing requirement 58
public-sector deficit 58

Quandt, R. E. 118, 119, 120, 123, 124, 127, 133, 138
quasi-rational expectations 62

$\bar{R}^2$ 53–4, 162–3
Ramsey, J. B. 24, 192
random disturbance 5, 9, 66, 162
in Monte Carlo experiment 108–10
random number generator 108, 122
rank condition 128, 131, 137
rational expectations 17–18, 62
RBII model 137
RBA79 system 12, 14–16
RBNZ system 11, 12, 14, 16, 133
RCSS 218
RDX2 system 10, 11, 58, 61, 63–4, 137
reaction function 16, 217
recursive 120
reduced form 29, 86–7, 131, 143, 147, 179
restricted 90, 111, 112, 131
unrestricted 86–7, 129, 131
reduced-form coefficients 29, 129, 131
reduced-form residuals 29
regressor 81–2
relationship
deterministic 66
numerical 6
stochastic 5
types of 66
see also behavioural relationship, definitional relationship, institutional framework
Renton, G. A. 22, 24, 103, 139, 176
replication 107, 110, 113
Reserve Bank of New Zealand 11
reserve deposit requirement 58
residual 9, 53, 87, 162, 170
of reduced form 29
of structural form 29

residuals correlogram 162
residuals run 168–9
response dissection analysis 173–4
restricted form 29–30, 32
restricted reduced form *see* reduced form
restricted reduced-form two-stage least squares 90
Richardson, D. H. 105, 106, 122, 124
Riley, C. J. 11, 24, 173, 176
RMSE 165–6
RMSPE 165–6
Rohr, R. J. 106, 122
Rolnick, A. 277
root cumulative sum of squares 218
root mean squared error *see* RMSE
root mean squared percentage error *see* RMSPE
Ryland, G. J. 23

Sadahiro, A. 223, 226
St Louis system 215
Saito, M. 190, 192
Sakuma, T. 139
Salmon, M. H. 91, 103, 130, 137, 139, 223, 227
sample point 71, 128
sample size 121
Samuelson, L. 223, 226
Sargan, J. D. 105, 124, 139
Sargent, T. J. 3, 17, 24
Sasser, W. E. 120, 124
Sawa, T. 88, 102, 105, 123, 224, 227
Sawyer, J. A. 223, 227
Schink, G. R. 138
Schink, W. A. 121, 124
search procedure 205–7
seasonal dummy variable 54
seed number 108
seemingly unrelated regressions 101, 120
sensitivity analysis 158
serial correlation *see* autocorrelation
Shapiro, H. T. 213, 219, 227
Shepherd, J. R. 11, 24
shock size 156
  see also shock type
shock type 157
  see also shock size
shocked run 152, 154–6, 195
  see also control run; deviation from control, system simulation
short run 15–16
SIE 81–5, 118–21, 125, 126, 132, 133, 135, 136
Simister, L. T. 118, 123
Sims, C. A. 191, 192
simulation 55
  see also dynamic simulation
simulation error 165
  decomposition 168–71
simulation experiment 152, 153–9
  see also system simulation
simulation model 154, 155
simulation period 152, 153, 195
simultaneity error 170
Sinai, A. 11, 23
single-equation information estimator *see* SIE
Smith, H. 85, 102
Smith, V. K. 106, 117, 121, 124
Social Science Research Council 11
solution *see* system solution
solution expressions 29, 179
solution value 36
Sowey, E. R. 117, 124, 153, 160
sparseness 120, 135
specification 46
  individual equation 50–5
  see also model selection, specification error
specification error 118, 119, 133–5
  see also mis-specification
Spencer, G. H. 11, 12, 24, 173, 176, 217, 219
spherical disturbance 82, 83
stability 147, 151, 158
  see also intertemporal stability
stacked matrix 94, 100
stacking 147–50
standard deviation 201, 214
standard normal random deviate 108
starting values 34
static simulation 152, 169–70
  see also system simulation
Stekler, H. O. 182, 190, 193
stochastic 5, 66
stochastic regressor 82, 85
stochastic simulation 153, 215, 224
  see also system simulation
stochastic variable 5
structural disturbance 9, 71, 72, 99, 117
  see also random disturbance
structural form 26, 29, 71
subsidiary hypotheses 62, 63–4
Summers, R. 108, 117, 120, 124
supply of capital services *see* capital
supply of labour *see* labour supply
supply side 67, 198
Sutton, J. 23
synthetic variable 65
system *see* dynamic system, economic system, KK system, large system, macro system, macroanalytical system, macroeconometric system, micro system, MS system, PB system, system solution, WJ system, WL system
SYSTEM I 26–7, 30–2

SYSTEM II 33–42, 153–9
SYSTEM III 71–80, 86–7, 96–8, 107–16
system simulation 152–9, 195
  deterministic 153
  dynamic 152, 169–70
  illustration 153–9
  mode 154, 155
  residuals run 168–9
  shock size 156
  shock type 157
  static 152, 169–70
  stochastic 153, 224
  time paths 153
system solution 25–43, 195
  concept 25
  final form 143
  Gauss–Seidel method 33–7, 42–3
  linear systems 25–32, 142–3
  Newton–Raphson method 33, 37–43
  non-linear systems 32–43
system stability *see* linear system, non-linear system, stability

2SLS 86–8, 89–90, 91, 92, 119, 132, 134
  properties 87–8, 89, 105, 116–17, 121, 128, 129
2SPS 130, 132, 136
3SLS 92–5, 129
  properties 95, 106, 117
t-ratio 53–4, 118, 163
target variable 66–7
Taubman, P. 182, 192
tax indexation 202–3
Theil, H. 87, 88, 95, 99, 101, 103, 159, 160
three-stage least squares *see* 3SLS
Tobin, J. 58, 68, 69
tolerance level 34, 37
total multiplier *see* long-run multiplier
tracking performance
  outside-sample 187
  summary measures 165–6
  turning-points analysis 167
  use of naive models 166–7
  whole-system 164–72
  within-sample 162–3
trade *see* international trade
Treasury (UK) *see* HM Treasury
Treasury system 11, 58, 63
Trevor, R. G. 12, 23
Treyz, G. 191, 192
true system 9
truncated-2SLS 130, 132
TSP 112
turning-points analysis 167
Turnovsky, S. J. 2, 24
two-stage least squares *see* 2SLS

UK economy, models of 11
Ullah, A. 105, 124
unbiased estimator 82
undersized sample problem 128–32
uniform distribution 108
University of Pennsylvania 11, 199, 223
unrestricted form 29, 32, 86
unrestricted reduced form *see* reduced form
US economy, models of 5–9, 11, 136–7

validation 142–75
  see also evaluation procedures
Vandaele, W. 163, 176
variable 5
  classification of 16, 20, 49
  types of 4
  see also endogenous variable, exogenous variable, predetermined variable, stochastic variable
variance 114
vector autoregressive process 132
Vincent. D P. 23

Waelbroeck, J. L. 10, 24, 137, 139, 223, 227
wage relationship 59–60
Wallace, N. 227
Wallis, K. F. 162, 176
Wallis statistic 53–4, 161
Walras, L. 2, 24
Walras–Johansen system *see* WJ system
Walras–Leontief system *see* WL system
Warburton, P. J. 11, 22
Waslander, H. E. L. 11, 24
Weiler, W. 227
welfare loss function *see* loss function
Wharton Annual Model 195–8
Wharton School of Finance and Commerce 11
Wharton system 10, 11, 131, 133, 222
White, H. 224, 227
Wickens, M. R. 99, 103
within-equation covariance 77
within-equation variance 77
within-sample tracking performance *see* tracking performance
WJ system 18–20
WL system 20–2
Wold, H. O. 117, 118, 120, 121, 123
Wonnacott, R. J. 101, 103
Wonnacott, T. H. 101, 103
working system 9–10, 11
Wymer, C. R. 12, 23, 125, 137, 138, 139

Yoshitomi, M. 137, 139
Yoshizoe, Y. 223, 226
Young, R. H. 192

zero restrictions 74